Pagan Roots

*Reclaiming Concepts
of the Sacred*

Also by Yvonne Aburrow

All Acts of Love and Pleasure: Inclusive Wicca (second edition),
Avalonia, 2025.

Changing Paths, 1000Volt Press, 2023.

Secret Night Song, poetry collection, Birdberry Books, 2023.

The Night Journey: Witchcraft as Transformation,
Doreen Valiente Foundation in association with the Centre for
Pagan Studies, 2020.

Dark Mirror: The Inner Work of Witchcraft,
Doreen Valiente Foundation in association with the Centre for
Pagan Studies, 2020.

Pagan Consent Culture: Building Communities of Empathy & Autonomy
(edited with Christine Hoff-Kraemer), Asphodel Press, 2016

All Acts of Love and Pleasure: Inclusive Wicca (first edition),
Avalonia, 2014

The Endless Knot, poetry collection, Birdberry Books, 2012

Many Names, poetry collection, Birdberry Books, 2012

The Magical Lore of Animals, Capall Bann Publishing, 2000.

A Little Book of Serpents, Birdberry Books, 2012.

Auguries and Omens: The Magical Lore of Birds,
Capall Bann Publishing, 1994.

The Sacred Grove: Mysteries of the Forest,
Capall Bann Publishing, 1994.

The Enchanted Forest: The Magical Lore of Trees,
Capall Bann Publishing, 1993.

Pagan Roots

Reclaiming Concepts
of the Sacred

Yvonne Aburrow

First Printing, 2025

Book design by keifel a. agostini

Cover artwork by Lydia Knox, design by keifel a. agostini

ISBN: 979-8-9921834-0-5

Although the publisher and the author have made every effort to ensure that the information in this book was correct at press time, and while this publication is designed to provide helpful information in regard to the subject matter covered, the publisher and the author assume no responsibility for errors, inaccuracies, omissions, or any other inconsistencies herein and hereby disclaim any liability to any party for any loss, damage, or disruption caused by errors or omissions, whether such errors or omissions result from negligence, accident, or any other cause.

1000voltpress.com

I am located on the traditional territory of the Anishinaabe and the Hodínöhšö:ni:h. This land is part of the Dish with One Spoon Treaty between the Hodínöhšö:ni:h and Anishinaabe peoples, who have taken care of the land for millennia.

This book is dedicated to

Lydia Knox,
Andrew Knox,
Heather Duke,

and in memory of
John Duke.

All that is gold does not glitter,
Not all those who wander are lost;
The old that is strong does not wither,
Deep roots are not reached by the frost.

J. R. R. Tolkien

The *Pagan Roots* Playlist

https://open.spotify.com/playlist/1utzxiIyRU4o8RJoCo31cA

Prélude à l'après-midi d'un faune
Claude Debussy

Hymn To her
KT Tunstall

Revecy venir du Printans
Claude Le Jeune

The Fabled Hare
Maddy Prior

The Lark Ascending
Ralph Vaughan Williams

Hal-an-Tow
Oysterband

Robin (The Hooded Man)
Clannad

Nature Boy
Ella Fitzgerald, Joe Pass

Herne
Clannad

The Rigs O' Barley
Nina Åkerblom Nielsen

John Barleycorn
Traffic

Lyke-Wake Dirge
Pentangle

Gower Wassail
Nowell Sing We Clear

The Mummers' Dance
Loreena McKennit

Pagan Roots

All of Nature is our kin
Fur and feather, frond and fin
And all the gods that dwell within:
Many genders, many faces
Found within the sacred places.
We love the stars, the Moon, the night
As much as Sun and warmth and light.
All genders are equal, all bodies are valid,
The myriad forms of love are sacred.
Pleasures of the mind and body
All are wondrous, good, and holy.
We love the stories of the land,
Passed down by mouth, written by hand.
The ancestors guide our winding ways,
Kin of spirit, of blood, and of place,
As we seek the true self that's hidden
Beneath the faces we wear as bidden.
Born and reborn from age to age
We follow the path of the Pagan mage.
Magic is a right by birth,
For all who dwell on Mother Earth.

Yvonne Aburrow
10:46 a.m., October 2, 2023

Praise for *Pagan Roots*

"Words have real power, and in Pagan Roots, Yvonne Aburrow invites readers to explore and reclaim the transformative energy behind key spiritual terms. Whether you're just starting out or have been practicing for years, this book is accessible yet rich with insight. Aburrow dives into the language of spirituality and the divine, offering practical exercises, journal prompts, and ritual ideas to help you integrate these powerful words into your own Pagan practice."

—Dodie Graham McKay, author of *Earth Magic* and *A Witch's Ally*

"Yvonne Aburrow guides you through the first steps of acquiring and developing the language essential to exploring and refining your Pagan spirituality and understanding the unique ways modern Pagan traditions express a connection with the numinous. That process culminates in an examination of certain words that are commonly used in Christian contexts, seeking to reclaim and restore an understanding of them that is more appropriate within a Pagan context. This book is a must-read whether you're seeking to deepen your Pagan faith or want to understand loved ones who follow such a tradition."

—Jarred the Wyrd-Worker,
musings.northerngrove.com

"Yvonne Aburrow's latest book, Pagan Roots: Reclaiming Concepts of the Sacred, is a fascinating read for anyone either involved with, or interested in, contemporary Paganism. It is divided into three parts. Part One provides a detailed overview of where contemporary Paganism has come from, together with an explanation of its main precepts. The second part, Pagan Concepts, gives the distinctly Pagan meanings for many words (e.g., "darkness" and "polarity," which are "foundational to the worldview of many contemporary Pagans." The third part, Reclaimed Concepts, examines many words used by other religions and faith traditions (e.g., "grace" and "holy"), and explains how they might be "reclaimed" and applied in a Pagan context. It includes an extensive bibliography, for following up some of the fascinating ideas they present"

—Rev. Sue Woolley, Unitarian minister
forloveofwords.com

Note: Throughout this book, I have used a capital initial letter for contemporary Pagans and Heathens, because we identify as such, and a lowercase initial letter for ancient pagans and heathens, who did not identify as such. I have also capitalized the term Indigenous Peoples.

Contents

Introduction

The stone that the builders rejected became a
cornerstone.

—Tehillim (Psalms), 118:22

The fact that astronomies change while the stars
abide is a true analogy of every realm of human
life and thought, religion not least of all. No
existent theology can be a final formulation of
spiritual truth.

—Harry Emerson Fosdick (1956),
The Living of These Days

For many Pagans, the spiritual journey is a unique path to
discovering the authentic self and connecting with Nature. Many
Pagans want to jettison spiritual and religious concepts that do
not fit with a Pagan path, but how do you evaluate whether or not
they fit, and can any of them be reclaimed from the discard pile?
Have Pagans included concepts in our lexicon that do not serve
us, or rejected ideas that might be useful? We need to discuss these
rejected concepts—otherwise we may be discarding something that
might be useful.

Many previous attempts at recovering Pagan ideas from
folk traditions and Christian holy days have simply removed
any mention of Jesus or attempted to turn him into a stand-in
for a Pagan deity, such as Jupiter. However, Paganism is not
Christianity with the serial numbers filed off, nor is it Christianity
with the Goddess added on top. It has its own distinct cosmology,
symbolism, mythology, and a unique spiritual journey. When
ancient pagan religions were largely destroyed by Christianity,

Christianity absorbed many of their spiritual practices and concepts, and gave them new meanings, but there were many concepts that it could not assimilate, such as polytheism, the celebration of the body that was part of ancient Greek paganism, and the veneration of gods of the wilderness and of sexuality. It has been argued that the veneration of saints was a continuation of polytheism, and in some ways that is true. Saint Nicholas seems to have taken over the patronage of Poseidon; the Virgin Mary was crowned Queen of Heaven (previously that title was given to Juno or Hera); Saint Clement became the patron saint of smiths; and so on. There are even saints who are clearly thinly-disguised Pagan deities. In Italy, there is a place called San Gemini not far from a Roman temple of Castor and Pollux, the divine twins who appear in the constellation of Gemini. But the characteristics of saints are very different to those of gods, because Christian virtues are different from Pagan virtues.

Contemporary Paganism has sought to recover some concepts that were lost or rejected in past centuries, but it has ignored or rejected others that were absorbed into Christian discourse. Can we reclaim some of these terms and recover their original meanings?

It has often been claimed that Christianity is a distorted version of first century CE Judaism that was syncretized with themes from the forms of paganism that were around at the time. It is hard to disentangle all the strands that went into the making of Christianity, but it certainly drew on the mystery cults of the time for some of its themes and rituals, as well as the philosophy of Plato and Aristotle for some of its ideas about God. In his speech to the crowds in the agora (marketplace) of Athens, Paul of Tarsus, formerly known as Saul, quoted from two Pagan poets,

Epimenides and Aratus, to get across his ideas about the Christian god:

> For in Him we live and move and have our
> being, as even some of your own poets have said,
> "For we are also His offspring."
>> (Acts 17:28, KJV, NKJV, ASV, ERV)

> But thou art not dead: thou livest and abidest forever,
> For in thee we live and move and have our being.
>> — Epimenides, "Cretica"

> Let us begin with Zeus, whom we mortals never leave unspoken.
> For every street, every market-place is full of Zeus.
> Even the sea and the harbor are full of this deity.
> Everywhere everyone is indebted to Zeus.
> For we are indeed his offspring...
>> — Aratus, "Phaenomena", 1–5

So there are certainly many Pagan ideas in Christianity, but (as with the Jewish ideas that were imported into Christianity) how they are interpreted within the Christian framework is rather different. So if we want to recover the Pagan meanings of some of these ideas, a bit of detective work will be needed.

Our culture's contemporary understanding of religion is of a separate activity, set apart from everyday life. Ancient pagan traditions, however, were interwoven with everyday life and regarded as integral to the success of all endeavors.

Many people think of religions as totalizing systems that claim to be self-sufficient and sole possessors of the truth, that regard all other religions as wrong or only having a partial view of the truth. This is not actually the case, although it tends to be a characteristic of some of the major religions. In polytheistic and pluralist religions, it is possible to honor the gods of other religions alongside our own, and to learn from the spiritual practices and concepts of others in a respectful manner. Unfortunately, due to the commodification of spirituality by capitalism, and the oppressive systems of colonialism, the opportunities for sharing on a level playing field are greatly diminished, and you need to be mindful that if you are living in a colonized country, you cannot lift concepts and practices from Indigenous spiritual traditions; you should seek to recover the concepts and practices of the ancient pagan religions that are the wellsprings of contemporary Pagan culture. For most Europeans, these would include the ancient Greeks and Romans as well as the Celtic, Norse, Slavic, Baltic, Tartessian, and other pre-Christian cultures.

Some people assume that all religions have concepts of salvation or enlightenment or whatever the main concept of their religious tradition is. But in reality, each religion was born out of a unique cultural context and set of circumstances, so they are neither mutually interchangeable nor mutually exclusive. When Christianity was getting started, there were numerous mystery cults and messianic and millennial proto-religions, and there was considerable interchange of ideas among the cultures around the Mediterranean, such as the Greeks, Romans, and Jews. So it is reasonably certain that Christianity assimilated many of their ideas.

I

n later centuries, Christianity (especially at the fringes of its territory) frequently came into contact with other religions. Usually it sought to convert their adherents—often by force, sometimes by persuasion, and often, as Thomas King has written in *The Inconvenient Indian* (2012), it was "the gateway drug to supply-side capitalism." But European culture and religion was nonetheless influenced by these encounters, especially on the few occasions when genuine interfaith dialogue took place.

If, like me, you are fascinated by the etymology of words and the history of ideas, this book is for you. It is for people who want to disentangle Pagan spirituality from ideas that do not serve our needs, and to reclaim concepts that have been rejected. Have you ever been told that "prayer is not a Pagan practice" or that it is "just passive magic" and found that these claims did not sit right with you? Or that you ought to "kill the ego" because that is supposedly part of every spiritual quest, but that did not feel right to you? Have you ever been presented with a spiritual practice or concept and wondered if it was compatible with your Pagan ideals and values? Have you ever asked yourself why there are certain words you just can't say in Pagan circles? Or have you had a conversation with an adherent of another religion, and found it difficult to communicate because they did not understand where you were coming from?

Just as there are people who assume that religion does not change over the centuries, there are people who assume that the meaning of words does not change. However, an academic paper that I read once identified seventy-one different ways of using the word "paradigm," and Christianity has at least seventeen different versions of the doctrine of atonement. The form, meaning, and pronunciation of many words has changed over the centuries.

5

One of my favorite examples is the alleged reaction of Charles Stuart (Charles II) on seeing Christopher Wren's new Saint Paul's Cathedral in London. He said it was "very artificial, proper, and useful" in a royal warrant. In our lexicon that means it was not organic; but he meant that it was full of craftsmanship. It is also said that the design was selected by the dean and chapter of the cathedral because it was the "most awful." The contemporary meaning of awful is "bad," but they meant that it was awesome or awe-inspiring.[1]

I was prompted to start talking and writing about these rejected concepts when someone objected to me referring to the list of virtues in Doreen Valiente's "The Charge of the Goddess" as "the Eight Wiccan Virtues" (analogous to the Nine Noble Virtues of Heathenry). I was somewhat surprised, as they are clearly virtues, there are eight of them, and they appear in a major piece of Wiccan liturgy. If they were objecting to the list of virtues being seen as normative virtues for Wicca, that is a reasonable criticism; but many people object to the word virtue because they associate it with Christianity—even though virtue ethics were first propounded by ancient pagan authors in the West, and Confucianist authors in the East.[2] Similarly, when I started talking about Pagan theology, many people objected that theology is a Christian construct, which is odd as the word was coined by Cicero, a pagan writer. I quickly identified other rejected concepts like prayer and worship, along with concepts that are often misrepresented within Pagan discourse, such as fertility, polarity, and tradition.

I have studied and researched these ideas in the course of writing my previous books and while studying for a master's degree in Contemporary Religions and Spiritualities. I am also

---

1 Garson O'Toole (2012), 'St Paul's Cathedral Is Amusing, Awful, and Artificial.' Quote Investigator.
2 Rosalind Hursthouse, Glen Pettigrove (2022), 'Virtue Ethics.' Stanford Encyclopedia of Philosophy.

fascinated by the evolution of ideas and how they are used in various discourses, sometimes to include and sometimes to exclude.

The first part of the book deals with the Pagan spiritual journey, and discusses various ideas about the goals of Pagan spirituality. Is it discovering the authentic self? Is it about connecting with Nature? Is it creating a beloved community? Or is it all of these? What does it mean to "get back to nature?" Does it mean returning to a natural state, connecting with all of Nature, or living a natural life? What does a "natural life" look like?

Is it possible to identify spiritual practices or concepts that are not part of Paganism (because they are not in line with the goal of the Pagan quest), but which have been imported to Pagan discourse and traditions out of a misunderstanding of what ancient paganism was, or what contemporary Paganism could be?

I believe that the Pagan quest is unique and distinct, because it is not a pouring out of self in order to become filled with the divine, but the removal of accretions to uncover the authentic self, get closer to nature, and become divine ourselves.

The book explores how to identify your personal spiritual goals, evaluate whether a concept fits with your path, and offer ways of engaging creatively with these reclaimed concepts as part of a Pagan path. It seeks to identify how the Pagan quest is unique and distinct, because everyone's authentic self is different.

The second part of the book will examine the history and roots of both theological concepts and spiritual practices. It will explore the Pagan roots of words like religion, theology, belief, faith, heresy, tradition, polarity, fertility, myth, virtue, god, perichoresis, worship, holy, prayer, grace, charity, sacraments, apotheosis (as distinct from theosis), and pilgrimage, and it will seek to recover their original Pagan meanings and contexts so that we can build them back into our collective quest for meaning. People have frequently encountered or learned these words in oppressive fundamentalist contexts, and so the practices or concepts with which these concepts are associated have become tangled up in people's minds with the oppressive atmosphere in which they learned the word. Many religions, including ancient pagan traditions, have used these concepts and practices, so I think it is time to dust them off and look at them in a fresh light.

Some of the concepts (such as fertility, polarity, and tradition) have been used within contemporary Paganism, but in peculiar and oppressive ways, so I want to expand these concepts to be more inclusive and less heterocentric.

Hopefully this book will also give you the tools to evaluate concepts for yourself and decide whether you want to include them in your personal spiritual journey. Everyone's journey is unique to them, so only you can decide whether these concepts are valuable for you.

The Pagan Journey

> Only one heart had to find its true position
> and travel on from there and all the rest would
> follow, for no matter how isolated the one felt
> itself to be, in the deeps of all life all were united
> and no one could move accurately without all
> ultimately moving with it.
>   —Laurens van der Post, *A Far-Off Place* (1974)

The Pagan quest has much in common with the spiritual paths of other religions. This is because we are all human and we all have a body, consciousness, and a subconscious. Different psychologists have offered different models of the psyche, but it is noticeable when studying the stories of mystics of various religions, that they all have similar experiences, and these experiences are mirrored in the initiatory journeys of Wicca and of OBOD Druidry (the Order of Bards, Ovates, and Druids). One of the most striking commonalities is the experience of the long dark night of the soul, but also that of the sacred inner marriage (sometimes visualized as a marriage between two aspects of the psyche, or as a marriage of the soul with the divine beloved).

The Inner Garden

The spiritual journey is very much like the discovery of a new garden. The first degree initiation in traditional initiatory Wicca, and the bardic grade of OBOD Druidry, both encourage exploration and creativity. In your first year in a new garden, you simply enjoy the sights and smells and sounds of the new garden. You wait to see what will grow as the seasons unfold, and you watch where the birds will nest. You tend the flowerbeds and the grassy area (which could be a meadow instead of a lawn). You don't bring in very many new plants (in case you displace existing ones). You work with the garden as it is. You are just enjoying the flowers and the new experience. This is very much like the first phase of exploring a new spiritual path.

The second year in a garden is like the second degree of traditional initiatory Wicca or the ovate grade of OBOD Druidry; things get a bit more challenging but you are also more familiar with the new environment. You are able to share gardening tips with the other people who work on the garden. Once you know where everything is, you can experiment more: moving plants around, introducing new plants, maybe opening up a new path. Maybe things get difficult when you start digging more.

Many mystics have recorded their experiences with the "long dark night of the soul." This is an experience of separation, loss, grief, and spiritual infertility. In gardening terms, everything in the garden is blighted and you find yourself in the middle of a wasteland. The wasteland in the Grail stories is reminiscent of this experience. The Fisher King lies wounded in the Grail Castle, and the knight must ask the right question if fertility is to be restored to the land. This is a profound metaphor for the experience of feeling disconnected, confused, and alienated. But within the dark night of the soul there lies a possibility for healing, because you can meet the Divine in the depths of your own soul—if only you ask the right questions.

The dark night of the soul is an initiation, a transformation, a descent into the depths of the psyche. It can be an experience of hitting rock bottom and discovering that you have survived the experience (and the only possible direction of travel from rock bottom is upward).

> A dark night of the soul is a kind of initiation,
> taking you from one phase of life into another.
> You may have several dark nights in the course
> of your life because you are always becoming
> more of a person and entering life more fully. At
> least, that is the hope.
>
> —Thomas Moore[3]

After the problem of the wasteland is resolved, the Grail is found, the wasteland is transformed into fertile land once more, and the wounds of the King are healed, everything is in balance. To return to the metaphor of the garden, you have now got the hang of your new garden: what will grow there, and what will not. Now you start to achieve a new level of comfort and confidence with your garden. Maybe you are ready to show other people some gardening tricks, and perhaps extend your gardening wisdom to other areas of life. A new synthesis has been achieved. A sacred marriage, one might say. In folk tales, this is the "happy ever after." The quest has been achieved, the lost treasure recovered, the harmony of the lands restored. This phase is mirrored in the druid grade of OBOD Druidry, and the third degree of traditional initiatory Wicca.

Of course, real life has a habit of getting in the way, and even when you think you have achieved your happiness, quite often something comes along to break it up: death, illness, divorce, old age, grief, the passage of time. Sometimes these events take us right back to the dark night of the soul; but now you have the experience of the inner marriage to sustain you.

In the novel *What's Bred in the Bone* by Robertson Davies, the protagonist, Francis Cornish, has an oddly structured life and is

---

3   Thomas Moore (2015), 'A Dark Night of the Soul and the Discovery of Meaning.' Kosmos Journal.

not particularly pursuing a spiritual quest, but nonetheless succeeds in "making up his soul" (an expression that Davies uses to represent a completion or culmination of the inner work).[4] He is an artist who has learned to paint in the medieval style, and he paints an exquisite triptych entitled *The Marriage at Cana* which includes all the people who have formed him. Saraceni, his mentor in the novel, describes the process of painting this masterpiece as "making up his soul." Ironically, Cornish can never claim the painting as his own work because it is in an anachronistic style and would be dismissed by critics if it was ever discovered that it was not medieval. This could be a metaphor for the idea that the culmination of the inner work and the achievement of the mystic inner marriage may well be invisible to other people.

There are also phases in life where you reach a resolution or a place of balance and then discover that there is a new level of experience. This is aptly described by the concept of the periodicity of planets. When you were born, the planets occupied a specific position on your astrological chart. Each planet travels around the Sun, taking a number of years to complete a full revolution. The planet Saturn takes 29.4 years to travel around the Sun, and therefore returns to the same zodiac sign that it occupied when you were born. It stays in that zodiac sign for just under two and a half years. Astrologers say that the Saturn return (when Saturn returns to its position on your natal chart) is especially significant. During my first Saturn return, I realized that there is no need to do things (such as pursuing a career) because other people say you ought to do them; you should do them because you want to do them, provided it does no harm to others, of course. In some ways, it represents the moment when you realize that you are not immortal, time is fleeting, and you had better find your life's work and do it.

---

4   Lihua Gui (1998), 'Robertson Davies' Innovative Use of the Trilogy Form in his Fiction.' PhD Thesis. Page 263.

The second Saturn return is an even more profound shift, where you move into the role of a mentor. Chani Nicholas says that the first Saturn return[5] is your initiation into adulthood, the second Saturn return is "when you turn toward those entering their first Saturn return and offer the wisdom you have gathered since then as a guidepost," and the third Saturn return is when you "gather the wisdom of your life and distill it into seeds to be left for future generations." The second Saturn return occurs in your late fifties, and the third occurs when you are in your late eighties.

Other planets also have periods of revolution around the Sun, and their returns to their positions on our natal chart are also meaningful. Chani Nicholas says that the Jupiter return allows us to discover new wisdom, growth, and abundance.[6] Jupiter takes twelve years to orbit the Sun, so Jupiter returns happen once every twelve years. The first Jupiter return, when you are twelve years old, is a massive change. As Nicholas explains:

> Because Jupiter is the planet of expansion and wisdom, most of us go through a fairly significant awakening at that age. Our worldview changes. We become more interested in spirituality, or at least the bigger questions and quests of life. We outgrow our childhood selves. Not all at once. But by the time our Jupiter return has ended, we're no longer comfortable at the kids' table.

An astrological chart is based on a geocentric model of the solar system, so it tracks the apparent path of the planets through the heavens from the perspective of the Earth, not their actual path around the Sun. That is why there is also a solar return, when the

5   Chani Nicholas (undated), 'How to Explore Your Saturn Return.' Chani.
6   Chani Nicholas (2022), 'What is your Jupiter Return, and how can you work with it?' Chani.

Sun occupies the same position that it did on your natal chart. A solar return is more commonly known as a birthday, of course. People often use their birthdays to take stock of their lives and make changes. Because the Sun represents your true self, your vitality, and your will, making an astrological chart for your solar return can give you insight into career, relationships, your values, the direction you want to take, and other core aspects of your life.[7]

One of the key things about the Pagan worldview is that it emphasizes cyclicity. Life is a series of interlocking cycles. Day and night come and go as the Earth rotates on its axis. The seasons change because of axial tilt as the Earth moves around the Sun. When the North Pole is tilted toward the Sun, it is summer in the Northern Hemisphere and winter in the Southern Hemisphere. When the South Pole is tilted toward the Sun, it is winter in the Northern Hemisphere and summer in the Southern Hemisphere.

I find the concept of cyclicity immensely comforting. The cycle of the seasons is like the cycle of birth, life, death, and rebirth. Suffering is also part of the process of growth; just as a tree is shaped by the wind, so people are shaped by their experiences. All beings suffer, but when they accept that suffering as part of life, and not a consequence of some cosmic catastrophe, then they can acquire sufficient depth to know the fullness of joy. It is then that the full light of consciousness dawns and mystical communion with the divine may be achieved.

But what if consciousness never emerged into the light? What if we continued to suffer? This would only be the case if time were linear and not cyclical. In the Wiccan worldview, people go through cycles of birth, death, and rebirth, but not in an endlessly repeating manner—instead, there is change and growth. The

---

7   Maressa Brown (2021), 'What Your Solar Return Means—and How to Make the Most of It.' Shape.

pattern is an ascending spiral, not a treadmill. It's not like the movie Groundhog Day, where the protagonist has to live the same day over and over again. The cycle passes through light (spring and summer) and descends into darkness (autumn and winter). But just as the seasons are not the same each time, nor are the greater cycles. Everything dies in the winter, dropping seeds and shrinking back into the earth, as the days get colder and colder and eventually everything is covered in snow. The winter solstice is a moment of the death of the old year and the birth of the new. Traditional stories tell us that the Sun is reborn at the solstice.

Springtime represents childhood, youth, vitality, freshness, and innocence.

In Canada, the snow arrives just after Yule and stays until the end of March or April. The trees start budding toward the end of February, and the occasional brave bird returns from the south, but things do not really get started until the spring thaw at the end of April, and then everything seems to come up at once in a great green shout.

In England, the winter is short and frosty, and the first flowers—snowdrops—appear at the end of January, just in time for Candlemas. Then celandines and daffodils and primroses come up for Spring Equinox. Everything comes into bloom gradually; first the blackthorn blossom, then the cherry blossom, and eventually the hawthorn blossom,[8] which is a traditional seasonal marker for May Day. The wild rose and the St John's Wort come out for Midsummer.

Midsummer, when the Sun is at its highest point in the sky, represents the prime of life, middle age, and midday. Everything is growing and burgeoning, and the days are at their longest. But

---

8   Snowdrop (Galanthus nivalis); Lesser Celandine (Ficaria verna); Daffodil (Narcissus pseudonarcissus); Primrose (Primula vulgaris); Blackthorn (Prunus spinosa); Bird Cherry (Prunus padus); Common Hawthorn (Crataegus monogyna).

if everything continued to grow and expand, there would be no room for new life, and so old age and death are a necessary part of the cycle. As Unitarian Universalist folk musician Ric Masten wrote in his song, "Let It Be a Dance":

> A child is born, the old must die;
> a time for joy, a time to cry.[9]

Autumn, twilight, old age, decay, and death are necessary parts of the cycle. A friend of mine had a wonderful tile on her bathroom wall, painted with the words, "Everything is always changing, transforming into something else; nothing is ever lost." After the cold and darkness of winter comes the growing light and warmth of spring; after death comes rebirth. Awareness of the cycles of the seasons, and celebrating them year after year, can provide comfort because of the inevitability of it all. Yes there is suffering and death, but there is also joy and rebirth. The darkness, cold, and winter are necessary for rest, growth, and regeneration. Death is not evil, but a necessary adjunct to life. If there was no death and dissolution, there could be no change or growth. The cycle of birth, life, death, and rebirth is part of the interaction of the polarities of light and darkness, expansion and contraction, growth and decay. Because I see the cycles of the Moon waxing and waning, and the Sun rising and setting, and the coming and going of the seasons, I see that Nature is profoundly cyclical, and it helps me to trust that after death comes rebirth. Even if that "rebirth" is the atoms of the body continuing to exist in some form, just as they existed before you were born, you are still part of the great cycles of Nature, as A E Housman's poem "From Far, From Eve" suggests:

---

9   Kimberley Debus (2017), 'STLT#311, Let It Be a Dance.' NOTES FROM THE FAR FRINGE: Hymns, Sermons, and Other Reflections.

From far, from eve and morning
And yon twelve-winded sky,
The stuff of life to knit me
Blew hither: here am I. [10]

Coming to terms with death is part of the Pagan journey—indeed, it is part of the human journey, but the Pagan worldview gives us more resources to cope with death and even embrace our mortality. Humans are embodied beings, with a finite and local perception of the world and time in which we exist. Because of our finitude and our physical existence in spacetime, we are necessarily mortal. If humans were immortal, we would be unchanging (rather like the Elves in Tolkien's legendarium, who do not die—instead, they fade).

Because Pagan traditions see the cycle of life, death, and rebirth reflected in all of Nature, and much of our mythology and symbolism illustrates that cycle, Pagans seem to be generally more relaxed about it than religions that see it as a linear journey, or as a consequence of some external interference in Nature (such as the concept of the Fall in Christianity).

The Pagan worldview and philosophy are reflected in many other traditional and Indigenous religions around the world that also believe in reincarnation and living close to Nature. The fact that so many different religions have broad areas of agreement on how the world works is comforting.

---

10   A E Housman (1896), A Shropshire Lad: XXXII.

Meditation: The Cycles of Nature

Find a spot where you are unlikely to be disturbed, such as under a tree in the woods. Make yourself comfortable, close your eyes, and take a few deep breaths. If you are sitting outside, listen to the wind moving through the leaves, the birds singing, and the sound of running water. Feel the temperature around you; immerse yourself in the sounds and scents of Nature. Now try to visualize the place where you are sitting as it moves through the seasons. It is still the same place, with its own unique shape, but it changes through the seasons. Similarly, you change throughout your life—and when you are reincarnated—but you are still the same being.

Exercises and Journal Prompts

- **Keep a diary of your local seasonal markers.** Note when particular flowers come out, when a species of bird returns from its annual migration, when the trees come into leaf. This can be as simple as taking pictures and posting them on social media with a few notes, or as elaborate as keeping a diary. I took photos of the maple tree outside my window at different times of year for a couple of years, and I feel very connected to that tree.

- **Get your astrological chart done** (there are websites that will provide you with a free astrological chart, and many will provide an analysis as well). Have a look at what houses and signs the planets are in on your natal chart. Work out when your Saturn returns and Jupiter returns will happen, or have happened in the past, and see if you can correlate them to significant events in your life.

- **Reflect on times of transition in your life.** These could be initiation ceremonies, rites of passage, or significant life events: birth, changing schools, the first time you rode a bike, learning to swim, moving house, going to university, graduation, your first job, initiation, coming out, gender transition, receiving gender affirming care, marriage, divorce, the death of a loved one or close family member (including companion animals), and many others. What helped you to get through these changes?

- **What do you find comforting?** Make a list of all the things you find comforting, such as cuddles, hot baths, comforting foods, cooking, reading, or going for a walk.

- **What is your life's motto?** It can be a motto that you have created, or one that you read somewhere, but what concept sums up your values and your life's work? (Mine is "only connect" from E.M. Forster's novel Howards End.)
- **What are your core values?** What do you hold to be sacred? Make a list of these, with an explanation of why they are important to you.

Ritual: The Tree

Roles: Narrator, spirit of the oak tree.

Setup: Create your ritual space as you normally would. If you do not have a usual method of setting up your ritual space, you can start the ritual with soft drumming. The ritual should take place at the best time of year for planting seeds in your bioregion.

Place a small table with one pot of earth labeled for each participant in the middle of the circle, and a smaller bowl of acorns. Make sure there are three acorns for every person. This prevents disappointment if one of the acorns doesn't come up.

> **Narrator** *(facing North)*: We stand at the moment of death and rebirth, midnight and midwinter. All is cold and still. Seeds sleep in the earth.
>
> **Narrator** *(facing East)*: We face the dawn, the time of youth, the springtime of the year, the moment when the seed bursts open and pushes forth a green shoot, and the buds burst open on the boughs.
>
> **Narrator** *(facing South)*: We stand at the zenith, the culmination, midday and midsummer. Everything is growing and flowering and the acorns begin to ripen.
>
> **Narrator** *(facing West)*: We face the dusk, the time of old age, the autumn of the year. The tide ebbs away, the twilight descends, the leaves fall, the ripe acorns drop to the ground.

Oak spirit: Three hundred years the oak tree grows,

Three hundred years it grows,

Three hundred years decays.

Each of you has your life's work, your dreams, your hopes and fears, the winds of fortune pushing you hither and thither.

But now I invite you to plant an oak tree.

This tree will represent your life's work.

Just as your life's work will continue beyond your lifetime,

So this oak will continue to grow,

offering a home to birds and insects and small animals.

All plant their acorns in the pot with their name on it, reflecting on their life's work as they do so. Each person waters their acorns and carries them around the circle to each quarter in turn, asking the blessing of the four winds on the tree.

Oak spirit *(facing North)*: North wind, winter wind, blow softly over these acorns as they rest in the earth.

Oak spirit *(facing East)*: East wind, wind of springtime, awaken these seeds and let them put forth green shoots to greet the rising Sun.

Oak spirit *(facing South)*: South wind, bringer of Summer rains, look kindly on these young trees as they grow and branch and bud.

Oak spirit *(facing West)*: West wind, restless wind of autumn, carry the messages of the ancestors to these trees that they may grow strong and tall.

All: Liege of the wildwood,

Door of the ancients,

Sheltering branches,

Steadfast roots,

A mighty oak

From a tiny acorn.

The Quest for the Authentic Self

> I am Pagan. I am a part of the whole of Nature
> . . . I have my own special part to play and I
> seek to discover and play that part to the best of
> my ability. I seek to live in harmony with others
> in the family of Nature, treating others with
> respect.
>
> — Selena Fox, "I Am Pagan"

Many Pagans are on a quest for the authentic Self. This is often visualized as something we already possess; we just have to clear away the accretions caused by so-called civilization. In this model, the true Self can be found by getting in touch with Nature.

Some religions take the view that the ego must be slain in order to progress spiritually. In some forms of Christian mysticism, this takes the form of *kenosis* (pouring out of self) and *theosis* (being filled with God). The slaying of the ego is a violent assault on the "natural self," the inner child, the playful and joyful aspect of ourselves. Some Christians (especially fundamentalist and evangelical ones) are taught that self-esteem and valuing oneself is "sinful." This view gets carried over as unexamined baggage into other post-Christian and non-Christian forms of spirituality.

The Slaying of the Primordial Being

If you go back to some of the earliest mythological stories, a primordial being is killed and dismembered, and the world is created from their body parts. In ancient Mesopotamia, the world was said to have been created from the slaying of the primordial dragon goddess Tiamat, who represented the waters of the sea. The gradual establishment of order from chaos, civilization from wilderness, happened as the younger gods killed the elder gods and built the world from their remains. A similar story comes from ancient Norse mythology, where the giant Ymir was licked out of the ice by the primordial cow Auðumla. Later, Ymir was killed by three brothers, Odin, Vili, and Vé, who fashioned the earth from his bones.

These myths can be seen as a metaphor for the emergence of consciousness from the unconscious, or they can be interpreted as a model for how you should act in relation to the ego. I believe that the ego is a necessary part of consciousness, and therefore that these myths are about how consciousness arises from unconsciousness.

In her book *Wicca: The Old Religion in the New Age* (1989), Vivianne Crowley writes that the ego doesn't need to be slain, but rather its position in relation to the rest of the psyche needs to be adjusted. She uses the image of a large flat stone covering a well. The stone is the ego, and the well is the unconscious. The stone has to be moved aside in order to access the water in the well.

The Uncarved Block

In the Tao Te Ching, a foundational text of Taoism, Lao Tsu writes about the Uncarved Block (Pu or unworked wood) or the self that has not been molded and shaped by society. The Uncarved Block exists as a non-dual state of potentiality, before experience has arisen. A Taoist practitioner seeks to recover the state of unworked wood.

> Be the valley of the universe!
> Being the valley of the universe,
> Ever true and resourceful,
> Return to the state of the uncarved block.

When the block is carved, it becomes useful.
When the sage uses it, he becomes the ruler.
Thus, 'A great tailor cuts little.' [11]

The Uncarved Block is a state of innocence, but it is a state that the Taoist must return to through the practice of Taoist arts (such as T'ai Chi), and which must be maintained. Some people may never leave their primordial state of innocence, but most people do, and have to recover it through practice.

The Taoist Farmer

The equanimity of the Uncarved Block is illustrated by the story of the Taoist farmer, who had one son and a horse. One day his horse escaped, and everyone in the village exclaimed about what a terrible misfortune this was. The farmer shrugged and said, "Maybe, maybe not." A few days later, the horse came back with a few wild horses, and they all stayed in the farmer's field. Everyone in the village commented on how lucky this was. The farmer shrugged and said, "Maybe, maybe not." Then the farmer's son broke his leg while trying to tame the wild horses. The villagers commented on how unlucky this was. The farmer shrugged and said, "Maybe, maybe not." A few weeks later, the army came to the village and conscripted all the young men for a distant war, except for the farmer's son, because he had broken his leg. Everyone in the village commented on the farmer's good fortune. The farmer shrugged and said, "Maybe, maybe not." It is said that this train of events is still going on.

---

[11]   Lao Tsu, Tao Te Ching, stanza 28. (Translation by Gia-fu Feng and Jane English)

The Lady of the Lake

There's a similar story in the Welsh tradition, known as *The Three Causeless Blows* or *The Lady of the Lake*. There was once a young farmer who lived near Llyn Y Fan Fach in Wales. One day he was walking along its banks when he saw a beautiful lady in the water. He fell in love with her and offered her bread and cheese, which she refused. He returned there the next day with unbaked dough, but she still did not accept. Finally on the third day she agreed to marry him but said that she would leave him when he struck her for the third time without cause. He protested that he would never do such a thing. Then she went to fetch her father, who presented him with a test to see if he could tell the difference between the lady and her identical sister. He succeeded only because earlier he had noticed her unusual sandal thong, and she thrust her foot forward. She came out of the lake with her faery cattle and sheep, and they were married. They were happy together for seven years, and had three sons. One day they were going to a wedding and she said she did not want to go because she was tired. The farmer said he would saddle a horse for her, and she also asked him to fetch her gloves. When he returned from doing that, she had not stirred from where she was sitting, so he playfully struck her with the gloves. "That is the first causeless blow," she said. Many years later, they were at a christening, and all the guests were rejoicing, but the lady wept. Her husband tapped her on the shoulder and asked why she was crying. She explained that the child's life would be full of suffering and pointed out that he had struck her the second causeless blow. Finally the child died in agony, and the lady laughed merrily at the funeral. Her husband was shocked and tapped her, saying that she should be quiet. She said: "The last blow has been struck. Farewell." She went home and gathered all of her faery cattle and sheep (including a calf that had been killed but came to life again) and disappeared back into the lake. Her husband was heartbroken and threw himself into the lake. Her three sons were also deeply distressed and almost did the same, but their mother appeared to them. She told them that their destiny was to be healers, and she showed them healing herbs and taught them the healing arts. They became the Physicians of Myddfai and their descendants were famed as healers throughout Wales.

In this story, the lady, who has foreknowledge of events, weeps when ordinary mortals would be merry and laughs when ordinary mortals would cry. Like the Taoist farmer, she may represent the natural, original self. (The story can also be read as a proto-feminist morality tale about domestic violence, of course.)

The Seal Wife

Another story of a wife who comes from the realm of water is the story of the seal wife. There are many variants of this story, but the most widely known one is the version where there is a lonely fisherman who lives by the shore, and one day he wanders down to the beach at full moon and sees the selkies come up out of the sea. Selkies are magical beings who are part seal, part human. Every full moon, they come to shore and dance on the beach in the moonlight. When they do this, they temporarily shed their seal-skin.

As the selkies are returning to the sea, one stays on the shore for a little longer, and while she is standing there, the man steals her seal-skin and hides it among the rocks. She is forced to go home with him, and she marries him and bears his children. One day, many years later, her children are playing on the beach, and find her seal-skin hidden among the rocks. They show it to her, and she slips it on and returns to the sea. Occasionally they see her playing in the waves, but she never comes to shore any more, in case her seal-skin gets stolen again.

There are many different interpretations of this story. One is that people often let our true nature be stolen from us, especially when we have to perform a role for other people. Clarissa Pinkola Estes calls this story *Sealskin, Soulskin*.[12] Her title very effectively conveys the essence of the story.

Wilderness and Civilization

Much of European literature is about the distinction between wilderness and civilization. The wilderness is characterized as "pagan" and civilization as "Christian." (There's a reason why fourteen popes took the name Urban.) Naturally the Pagan Revival ran with this distinction and inverted the value system associated with it to mean "wilderness is good, civilization is bad."

Pagans want to return to a state of wildness, where instinct, sensation, emotion, and intellect are balanced. This state of wildness occupies a similar place in Pagan thought to the Uncarved Block in Taoist thought.

However, if you look back at ancient pagan and polytheistic societies, they had deities of architecture, mathematics, agriculture, medicine, art, music, drama, and other activities that are part of civilization. The idea that civilization is inherently Christian is incorrect. Indigenous Peoples of both North and South America had cities (for instance, there was a large Indigenous city in Illinois called Cahokia). Ancient pagan and polytheistic societies had cities. They also practiced scientific inquiry and extolled virtues such as piety, kindness, and truthfulness.

---

12   Clarissa Pinkola Estés (1992), Women Who Run with the Wolves: Myths and Stories of the Wild Woman Archetype. Ballantine Books.

The first phase of the Pagan Revival was part of the Enlightenment in the eighteenth century. Many people realized how the creationist beliefs that most Christians held were markedly at odds with the scientific truths they were beginning to discover, such as the great age of the Earth that was apparent from studying geology and fossils. As a result, they looked back to earlier religions to see if they could find the purest and most ancient form of religion, which was then regarded as some variation upon deism (the belief that the laws of Nature had been set in motion by the Creator but after that, the universe operated according to the laws of nature, without divine intervention).

In the early nineteenth century there was a revival of popular Christianity, and the Romantic movement, despite being about "getting back to Nature" in many ways, was largely Christian in its approach. It was not until the turn of the twentieth century that people began to talk more about Paganism, as there was a fascination with Pan in literary circles. As more and more people began living in cities, many of them sought to recover their connection with Nature and wildness. Books such as *The Wind in The Willows* (1908)[13], *Puck of Pook's Hill* (1906), *Rewards and Fairies* (1910)[14], and *The Open Road* (1906)[15] helped to popularize these ideas. At the same time as these ideas were coming to the fore, there was a surge of interest all over Europe in folk tales, folk songs, folklore, folk dances, and other forms of folk culture (they were also accompanied by nationalist movements that ultimately became fascist, racist, and völkisch[16]). All of these strands set the stage for the Pagan Revival.

---

13   Grahame also wrote a collection of essays called Pagan Papers, published in 1893.
14   Puck of Pook's Hill (1906) and Rewards and Fairies (1910) were written by Rudyard Kipling (1865-1936), who spent much of his life in India, but moved to Sussex in 1902.
15   The Open Road is little known now, but it had run to 30 editions by 1920, and is mentioned by one of the characters in Howard's End by E.M. Forster. The full text is available online.
16   Ethan Doyle White (2017). "Northern Gods for Northern Folk: Racial Identity and Right-wing Ideology among Britain's Folkish Heathens". Journal of Religion in Europe. 10 (3): 241–273. The term völkisch refers to the notion that ethnic groups have biological characteristics that make them superior or inferior, and that their mythology arises from some inherent relationship between the people and the land, which excludes others from participating in that relationship.

The Authentic Self and Nature

When you are seeking your authentic self and trying to recover your relationship with Nature, the Earth, or the land, you need to consider what it is that you mean by these terms. If you live on colonized land (North or South America, Australia, Aotearoa New Zealand), who holds political power? How do you relate to land that was stolen from Indigenous Peoples? If you live in Europe, where immigrants are not colonizers because they do not hold political power, forming a relationship with the land you live on is less politically fraught, but if your relationship with it excludes hospitality to refugees and displaced people, then you are violating the ancient pagan ethic of hospitality which was sacred to every pagan culture from the Greeks to the Vikings.

If you look at the ancient tales that have come down to us—mythology and folk tales—they extol the virtues of hospitality, kindness, and giving people the benefit of the doubt.

Clarissa Pinkola Estes (not a Pagan but a Jungian psychotherapist), in her classic work *Women Who Run with the Wolves*, explores fairy tales from the perspective of recovering wildness, with the wolf as the ultimate symbol of wildness. But her image of the wolf is not that of the "lone wolf" but that of a member of the pack, with cunning, intuition, co-operation, and other qualities that lead to survival.

When you have recovered your wild, authentic self, and are living your "one wild and precious life,"[17] you are balanced, in touch with Nature, and in harmony with all beings. You can access all the modes of experience: instinct, sensation, emotion, and intellect. You are letting "the soft animal of the body love what it loves."[18]

---

17 Mary Oliver, "The Summer Day".
18 Mary Oliver, "Wild Geese".

When people are born, we possess all these modes, but experience leads us to rely on one of them. As we differentiate ourselves from our surroundings, we develop a shadow and a bright self. The work of discovery is to reintegrate the shadow aspects of the self to create a new synthesis.

This process of recovering the authentic self can take a lifetime. Why bother to find the authentic self? Because if you don't recover your shadow side, it will continually come back to bite you, as is illustrated in the traditional Tarot card of the Fool, which depicts a little dog biting the Fool from behind and tearing his breeches. If people don't get their warring impulses harnessed for good, they end up lashing out at other people—and destroying their own lives in the process. Hence the need to set out on the spiritual journey, the Quest.

The interesting thing, though, is that you cannot fully return to the primordial state of innocence (in the sense of inexperience). The lady of Llyn Y Fan Fach returns to the lake, but she is presumably changed by her experiences in the human world, and the human world is changed by her. Notice also that the times when her husband strikes her are when she is failing to conform to expected norms—all of us are subjected to such blows as we move through life. It is these attempts to force us to conform to some external norm that we must re-examine to find the authentic self.

The Taoist farmer shrugs off both fortune and misfortune with equanimity, but he must have been affected by these events. You can remove accretions that do not sit right with your intrinsic nature, but you will have been changed by your experiences in the world. That is, of course, a good thing, because people learn by experience, and many spiritual traditions take the view that this is the reason why we are incarnate in the physical world.

So what does it mean to return to the authentic self? It does not mean ignoring the suffering of others and retreating into a fantasy world of our own devising. I think it means being in touch with the wellsprings of joy, the fresh perspective of the child, as well as the wisdom that comes from experience.

Meditation: The Inner Child

Find a spot where you are unlikely to be disturbed. Make yourself comfortable, close your eyes, and take a few deep breaths. Think back to your favorite place when you were a child, preferably somewhere that you were able to play and use your imagination. Take a few moments to build up an image of that place, or if you cannot see with your mind's eye, try to remember your emotional response to it. Try to experience it from the perspective of a child, which is typically several inches lower than that of an adult.

Now think back to a favorite activity that you enjoyed in that place. Visualize yourself doing that activity, in the uninhibited way that you would have done it as a child.

You can repeat this visualization for different places and activities, such as swimming, building sandcastles, climbing trees, swinging on swings, or whatever other things you did as a child. If you were deprived of these activities as a child, try to think of some activity that made you happy.

Exercises and Journal Prompts

- **Sort through your unexamined baggage.** Consider your beliefs, habits, thought patterns, and values. Which of these are an intrinsic part of who you are, and which of them were imposed on you by circumstances or by other people?

- **Make time for creativity in your life.** What activities have you always enjoyed but do not have time for as an adult? What activities have you always wanted to do but not yet had a chance to do? Make time to do those activities.

- **Nourish your inner child.** What foods did you enjoy as a child? What sensuous experiences did you enjoy? Seek out those foods and experiences. If the food is something you can prepare with your own hands, do that. What books did you enjoy as a child? Rereading the books you enjoyed as a child is a lovely way to reconnect.

- **Reflect on your journey so far.** Are you the main character of your own story? If yours was an adventure tale, what sort of tale would it be, and what sort of character are you? Can you write your life story as if it was a folk tale, with archetypal characters representing the circumstances you have encountered in your life?

- **Make an altar or shrine for your inmost self.** It can include pictures of people you admire, objects representing activities you love, your favorite flowers, favorite deities, a pebble from your favorite place— whatever you need.

Ritual: Finding the Self

When performing this ritual, the protagonist should be a person who wishes to recover their authentic self. I have used the story of The Seal Wife as the basis for this ritual, but you can choose a different story as long as it has a similar structure.

Roles: a narrator, the Seal Wife, the fisherman, their children. If there are more people, they can be villagers or selkies.

Setup: Create your ritual space as you normally would. If you do not have a usual method of setting up your ritual space, you can start the ritual with soft drumming. If you have a pebble drum or a rain stick, use that to evoke the sound of the sea.

Place a small table with conch shells on it in the middle of the circle.

The villagers all stand in a circle and hold hands, swaying gently from side to side as if being rocked by gentle waves. The selkies are in the center of the circle, facing outward.

> **Selkie 1:** Feel the rhythm of the sea, the primordial mother. We come from the great sea, and we return to the great sea.

> **Selkie 2:** Feel the movement of the sea in your blood. The great salt tides of the sea echo in the pumping of the blood in your body.

> **Selkie 3:** Take up the conch shell and place it next to your ear. Hear the roar of the ocean in your blood.

> **Selkie 4:** Close your eyes and see the Moon rising above the sea, her light reflected in the waters.

Begin to dance slowly in towards the center of the circle and out again.

Selkie 1: We are drawn to the shore by the yearning of our bones for the land. Feel the solidity of your bones upholding you.

Selkie 2: We are drawn by the light of the Moon to dance upon the shore.
We shed our seal-skins and dance on the strand, wild and free.

Selkie 3: We feel the sand beneath our feet, the meeting place of earth and sea.

Selkie 4: We see the rocky shore standing proud against the starry sky. We are one with land and sea; we are the ocean and the land.

Villager 1: We gather round the hearth fire, we feel the warmth of it in our bodies. Not for us the cold depths of the sea.

Villager 2: We burn the driftwood from the sea in our hearth fires and watch the flames dancing in colors on the hearth.

Villager 3: The fire of the sun makes our crops grow tall. Our children dance in the sunlight—yours dance in the moonlight.

Villager 4: The fire of the oven bakes our bread. The warmth of the hearth fire keeps us snug in bed.

Villager 1: We breathe the air in and out, in the rhythm of our lives.

Villager 2: We speak our poetry and our stories into the night, and they are conveyed by the wind to all corners of the world.

Villager 3: The wind blows across the land, spreading new ideas and inventions into every nook and cranny.

Villager 4: Our dreams are filled by the rocking waves, but our waking hours are filled with the blowing of the wind across the hills.

Fisherman: The moon is full, the tide is high. I will go down to the shore and see which way the wind is blowing.
I hear the waves pounding on the rocks.

Seal Wife: I will go with my siblings to the shore to dance in the moonlight.
I feel the pull of the Moon towards the shore.
I feel in my bones that it is time to seek out the land.

The selkies dance their sinuous dance.

Fisherman: How beautiful they are in the moonlight.
Oh! They are returning to the sea.
One of them is lingering on the shore.

The fisherman hides her seal-skin when she is looking the other way.

Seal Wife: Oh, I cannot find my seal skin. What shall I do?

Fisherman: You can stay with me if you like.

Seal Wife: Oh, I suppose I will have to. Thank you.

Narrator: The seal woman stayed with the fisherman, unaware that he had hidden her seal skin on purpose. She fell in love with him and they had children, but always she yearned and pined for the open sea. One day her children were playing on the beach, when they found a curious thing: a seal skin.

Child 1: I wonder what this is? It's so soft and smooth.

Child 2: Let's show it to Mother.

Narrator: The children took the seal skin and showed it to their mother.

Seal Wife: Oh children, my beloved children! You have found my seal skin, my soul skin. I must return to the sea, but look for me always at full moon. I shall not come to shore any more, but you will see me among the waves.

Narrator: She hugged her children goodbye, and returned to the sea. She had always suspected that her husband had a hand in the loss of her seal skin, so she did not wait for him to return from his fishing trip but went back to the sea straight away. The other selkies welcomed their lost sister, and they never danced on that beach again. But the children saw their mother among the waves at every full moon, as they stood upon the headland and looked out to sea.

Solo version of the ritual

Face West and say:

I feel the rhythm of the sea, the primordial mother.

We come from the great sea, and we return to the great sea.

I feel the movement of the sea in my blood. The great salt tides of the sea echo in the pumping of the blood in my body.

Take up the conch shell and place it next to your ear.

I hear the roar of the ocean in my blood.

I see the Moon rising above the sea, her light reflected in the waters.

Facing North:

I am drawn to the shore by the yearning of my bones for the land. I feel the solidity of my bones upholding me.

I am drawn by the light of the Moon to dance upon the shore.

I shed my seal skin and dance on the strand, wild and free.

I feel the sand beneath my feet, the meeting place of earth and sea.

I see the rocky shore standing proud against the starry sky.

I am one with land and sea; I am the ocean and the land.

Facing East:

I breathe the air in and out in the rhythm of my life.

I speak my poetry and stories into the night,
and they are conveyed by the wind to all corners
of the world.

The wind blows across the land, spreading new
ideas and inventions into every nook and cranny.

My dreams are filled by the rocking waves, but
my waking hours are filled with the blowing of
the wind across the hills.

Facing South:

I feel the warmth of the hearth fire in my body.

Not for me the cold depths of the sea.

I burn the driftwood from the sea in my hearth
fire

and watch the flames dancing in colors on the
hearth.

The fire of the sun makes the crops grow tall.

The fire of the oven bakes our bread.

The warmth of the hearth fire keeps me snug in
bed.

As the Fisherman:

The moon is full, the tide is high.

I will go down to the shore and see which way
the wind is blowing.

I hear the waves pounding on the rocks.

As the Seal Wife:

I will go with my siblings to the shore to dance in
the moonlight.

I feel the pull of the Moon toward the shore.
I feel in my bones that it is time to seek out the land.

Dance the sinuous dance of the selkies.

As the Fisherman:
How beautiful they are in the moonlight.
Oh! They are returning to the sea.
One of them is lingering on the shore.
The fisherman hides her seal skin when she is looking the other way.

Seal Wife: Oh, I cannot find my seal skin. What shall I do?
Fisherman: You can stay with me if you like.

Seal Wife: Oh, I suppose I will have to. Thank you.

Narrator: The seal woman stayed with the fisherman, unaware that he had hidden her seal skin on purpose. She fell in love with him and they had children, but always she yearned and pined for the open sea. One day her children were playing on the beach, when they found a curious thing: a seal skin. They wondered what it was, this thing that felt so soft and sensuous, so beautiful. They decided to show the seal skin to their mother.

Seal Wife: Oh children, my beloved children!
You have found my seal skin, my soul skin.
I must return to the sea, but look for me always
at full moon. I shall not come to shore any more,
but you will see me among the waves.

Narrator: She hugged her children goodbye and
returned to the sea. She had always suspected
that her husband had a hand in the loss of her
seal skin, so she did not wait for him to return
from his fishing trip, but went back to the sea
straight away. The other selkies welcomed their
lost sister, and they never danced on that beach
again. But the children saw their mother among
the waves at every full moon, as they stood upon
the headland and looked out to sea.

The interesting thing about doing this as a solo ritual is that
you are both the selkie yearning for the freedom of the open
sea and the fisherman who has stolen her seal skin. A lot of the
time, people steal their own seal skin from themselves, depriving
themselves of the freedom of the open sea.

The Pagan Psyche

There is a thinking in primordial images, in
symbols which are older than the historical man,
which are inborn in him from the earliest times,
eternally living, outlasting all generations, still
make up the groundwork of the human psyche.
It is only possible to live the fullest life when we
are in harmony with these symbols; wisdom is a
return to them.

—Carl Gustav Jung,
The structure and dynamics of the psyche (1960)

I believe that the purposes of the individual Pagan quest are
to uncover the authentic self, to reconnect with Nature, and
to promote human flourishing and happiness—also known as
eudaimonia.

To that end, it is a good idea to adopt a hermeneutics of
suspicion toward spiritual practices or concepts that are not part of
Paganism (because they might not get us nearer to the goal of the
Pagan quest), but which have been imported to Pagan discourse
and traditions out of a misunderstanding of what ancient paganism
was, or what contemporary Paganism could be.

The first step is to identify what your personal goal is, and then
evaluate your practices against that goal. Will they get you nearer
to your goal, or further away from it?

What makes you feel happy and fulfilled? If you are not sure,
try several different activities. These can include things that are
classified as spiritual, such as meditation, visualization, and forest-

bathing, and things that are usually classified as creative, such as writing, painting, creating art, making music, and things that are generally classified as physical, such as hiking and wandering in Nature.

What makes you feel more aligned with your chosen spiritual path or tradition? If it also makes you feel happy and fulfilled, that is even better. Many Pagans and witches like to collect rocks, twigs, books, and houseplants. Many of us also like to do magic and ritual. Some people advocate for daily magical or spiritual practice, but if you find yourself feeling guilty because you have failed at this, then re-examine if you need it and refocus your efforts on maintaining a frame of mind that is aligned with your path or tradition.

If the goal of your path includes feeling more connected with Nature, which practices and activities help with that goal? Some people like to learn about the flora and fauna of where they live, or the geology, or the ecosystems. Others like to commune with the landscape through art or meditation.

If you agree that one of the goals of Pagan spirituality is to uncover the authentic self, which practices align with that goal? Clearly practices from traditions whose goals include the annihilation of the self or of the ego are not compatible with this goal.

If your Pagan tradition or path wants you to suppress an aspect of yourself, such as your lived experience of gender or your sexual orientation, repressing such an essential part of yourself will not contribute to your personal happiness and flourishing. I would advise you to find a path or tradition that is inclusive and affirming of gender and sexual diversity.

If a concept or practice comes from a tradition with a very different set of goals to the ones that Pagans generally embrace, look at it carefully. Can it be adapted to fit within the Pagan worldview, or is it too different?

Throughout this book, I look at concepts that have been rejected as part of Pagan discourse because their original meanings have been distorted—sometimes by other spiritual traditions and sometimes by other Pagans. There are ways of engaging creatively with these reclaimed concepts as part of a Pagan path, but it may mean that you need to embrace the reclaimed meaning and develop your own version of the practice.

Once you have established the goal of your path and evaluated your practices, you have cleared the ground so that you can embark on the inner work. This will very likely include shadow work.

As children, certain aspects of our personalities are rewarded and encouraged by being called good, while others are rejected as bad. People quickly learn to repress the aspects labeled as bad, and pretend that they are not part of the core self.

Rather than trying to eradicate these aspects of ourselves, the goal of shadow work is to befriend them and integrate their energy into our conscious self. There are several methods for doing this.[19]

Author Scott Jeffrey, who has studied Carl Jung extensively, recommends starting with a centering exercise. My favorite centering exercise is to visualize yourself as a tree, with roots extending down into the earth, branches extending up into the sky, and a line of energy running along your spine, connecting you to earth and sky. Start by focusing on your breath, and as

---

19   Scott Jeffrey (undated), A Definitive Guide to Jungian Shadow Work: How to Get to Know and Integrate Your Dark Side.

you breathe in and out, extend roots down from your feet into the earth. Draw up the earth's energy into your spine, allowing it to rise naturally toward your head. From there, let it extend up into branches. Then as you breathe in and out, draw the energy of the sky and the stars down into your branches. Let the energies of earth and sky meet and mingle in your belly, then spread out to warm and energize your whole body.

The next exercise that Scott Jeffrey recommends is self-compassion. It is hard to accept the less lovely parts of your psyche if you do not have compassion for yourself. He suggests focusing on the heart and accepting your own humanness.

After that comes self-awareness—allowing yourself to observe and reflect on your reactions to the situations you're in, without criticism or judgment. The process of seeing and acknowledging the repressed parts of the self is easier if people are honest with themselves. He also recommends journaling about our reactions to situations and other people.

At the end of each day, practice reflection: Make a note of all the times when you have felt angry or irritated. It is likely that the aspects of other people that pushed your buttons are actually aspects of yourself that you have suppressed.

An excellent way to identify shadow traits is to think of a specific person who irritates you, and make a list of the aspects of them that you find annoying. Now draw a box around your list, and add a heading: "My Shadow Self." However, rather than looking at how their negative quality manifests, look at the underlying impulse that drives it. For example, if they are always negative toward a specific group of people, it may be because of a fear of difference and a desire for the comfort of the familiar; it is not, however, that you are necessarily harboring negative feelings towards the same group. It might be more that you prefer the comfort of the familiar.

Another way to discover your shadow side is to look at opposites: Make a list of your positive qualities and then write their opposite qualities next to them. These are probably aspects that you have repressed. Make friends with the repressed aspect; it is probably draining a lot of energy from you.

Another way to engage with these repressed aspects is called "naming the parts" or inner dialogue. You can give the repressed parts of yourself names, and have conversations with them. Ask them what they want and why they are hurting you.

A lesser-known aspect of the psyche is the golden shadow. These are qualities that people have repressed—not because these qualities are "bad," but because people believe they are unattainable. You can usually discover what these qualities are by thinking of a person you admire and making a list of their admirable qualities. Now draw a box around the list, and write "my golden shadow" at the top. You have made a list of qualities that you possess or are developing.

Another part of the psyche identified by Jung is the anima and animus. The anima is the "feminine self." It is not inherently feminine, but rather it consists of all the qualities and attitudes that our culture associates with "the feminine." Conversely, the animus is the "masculine self." It is not inherently masculine; instead it consists of all the qualities and attitudes that our culture associates with 'the masculine.' One of the interesting things about being nonbinary is that you get to pick from the menus of both "masculine" and "feminine" traits. In reality, most people possess traits from both sets; there are nurturing men and assertive women, and so on.

49

In Western patriarchal culture, men are encouraged, even mandated, to repress personality traits associated with the feminine, or to display them only in very intimate settings. To a lesser extent, women are encouraged to repress "masculine" personality traits, and discouraged from being assertive or aggressive, as these are seen as "masculine." Consider the traditional sayings that police the boundaries of gender roles, such as "boys don't cry" and "a woman's place is in the home" and "the angel in the house."

When people fall in love, they tend to project on the beloved all the qualities of their ideal beloved (the anima or animus, or the complex of gendered qualities that they choose not to embody). This is the phase of being "in love." After a while, they settle down and start to perceive the real human being underneath their projected image. If the projection was a good fit, they will then proceed to the phase of conjugal love. If it was a bad fit, they will very likely break up with the person. If it was a very bad fit, there will probably be bitter mutual recriminations.

Jung believed that the goal of the individuation process[20] (becoming an individual) is to integrate the shadow side of the personality, uncover the true inner self, and expand the self into the Self: the archetype of fully realized humanity. This wiser, deeper Self, he believed, is present as the archetype of the wise old person, guiding us on the journey of the inner work.

Archetypes are constructs or primary types that represent the range of basic human motivations[21], a shorthand for describing different personality types. Before becoming individuated, people identify with an archetype; then, as they integrate more of their

---

20   Scott Jeffrey (undated), A Closer Look at Carl Jung's Individuation Process: A Map for Psychic Wholeness.
21   Conor Neill (2018), Understanding Personality: The 12 Jungian Archetypes.

shadow side, they become aware of their uniqueness and of what they have in common with other people. There are twelve main archetypes, and many sub-archetypes representing the negative sides of the archetype, both active and passive. Traditional stories and folktales make extensive use of these archetypes and illustrate encounters between them.

During the ascendancy of patriarchal religions, darkness, wildness, and the feminine have been rejected and reviled. Pagan and Indigenous religions and spiritualities are reclaiming them and celebrating them, but it will take some time before they are restored to their rightful places in the collective consciousness of humanity.

The themes of darkness and Nature are also found in expressions of queer and LGBT spiritualities. Darkness and Nature are seen as refuges from homophobic society. In *De Profundis* (1905), Oscar Wilde speaks of the nurturing and nonjudgmental qualities of Nature:

> Society, as we have constituted it, will have no place for me, has none to offer; but Nature, whose sweet rains fall on just and unjust alike, will have clefts in the rock where I may hide, and secret valleys in whose silence I may weep undisturbed. She will hang the night with stars so that I may walk abroad in the darkness without stumbling, and send the wind over my footprints so that none may track me to my hurt: she will cleanse me in great waters, and with bitter herbs make me whole.

Edward Carpenter was an enthusiastic advocate of Nature as a place of freedom, and following him, his friend E.M. Forster made the hero of his novel Maurice feel "at one with the forests and the night" as soon as he had made the decision to adopt an actively gay lifestyle.[22] Harry Hay, founder of the Radical Faeries, who was a Carpenter enthusiast, also stressed the importance of communing with Nature.[23]

Nathan Foster, a gay Anglican priest, writing more recently, draws parallels between the darkness of the church at Advent, the darkness of the night, where it is safe for same-sex relationships to flourish, and the vulnerability of being penetrated:

> In the light two men cannot come together, they
> need the dark for protection. Two men cannot
> embrace and still be thought to be real men.
> You can only hope to become a man if you are
> separate, not if you are connected to each other,
> certainly not if you are coupled or copulating.
> Nothing must go into a man's body in the
> light because then we would all see that we all
> have holes. That there are holes in the bodies
> of boys and men, that we can receive and be
> vulnerable.[24]

Robin Hawley-Gorsline suggests that darkness is generally seen as a negative cultural meme—dark sexuality, dark continents, dark people—and that Christian spirituality is focused on the light.[25] This negative view of darkness increases its power as a meme; darkness is equated with exotica, and especially sexual difference. Blacks and blackness are associated with sexuality and sensuality; and "deviant" sexuality is kept hidden, in the dark. A

22   Hutton, R. (1999) The Triumph of the Moon: a history of modern Pagan witchcraft. Oxford: Oxford University Press. Page 27, 50.
23   Conner, R.P., Sparks, D.H., and Sparks, M. (1997) Cassell's Encyclopedia of Queer Myth, Symbol and Spirit. London and New York: Cassell, p 173.
24   Foster, N. (undated) A Prayer in the Dark. Lesbian and Gay Christian Movement.
25   Robin Hawley-Gorsline, (2003), 'James Baldwin and Audre Lorde as Theological Resources for the Celebration of Darkness.' Theology and Sexuality 10(1), pp. 58–72.

Black transgender activist, Miss Lorrainne Sade Baskerville, said to Saadaya:

> Why is black the color of evil? Why is the color
> black bad and impure and why does white
> represent light, wisdom and purity? ... Black
> is [a] mysterious color, a beautiful color! It
> represents mystery! [26]

The celebration of darkness, which is widely regarded as the realm of evil, allows us to transcend boundaries:

> Darkness requires performance and each of us
> is called upon to perform, to play across the
> boundaries of those worlds we have been told are
> dark and therefore evil or bad or alien.[27]

It also allows us to escape the hierarchical view of the cosmos which is associated with the exclusive honoring of the light:

> Baldwin and Lorde, each in their distinctive
> ways, show us that turning to the dark,
> celebrating darkness, and turning away from
> dichotomous thinking in which light and dark
> are opposed—with light as a positive force for
> conquering the negative dark—offer hope for
> saving humanity from destructive hierarchies
> based on supremacies of race, sex and gender. [28]

The integration of the psyche is achieved by the marriage of light and darkness, not the slaying of the dark shadow. There is no need to "kill the ego," but rather make it aware of its place in the

---

26   Saadaya (undated) Coming Out as a Rite of Passage.
27   Robin Hawley-Gorsline, (2003), 'James Baldwin and Audre Lorde as Theological Resources for the Celebration of Darkness.' Theology and Sexuality 10(1), pp. 58–72.
28   Hawley-Gorsline, R. (2003), 'James Baldwin and Audre Lorde as Theological Resources for the Celebration of Darkness.' Theology and Sexuality 10(1) pp 58-72.

grander scheme of things, part of the dance of elements that exist within the integrated Self.

Meditation: The Cave

It is twilight. You are standing in a sacred grove, trees all around you. Look at the trees and touch their bark. Feel the earth beneath your feet, the cool grasses brushing against you. Smell the breeze and listen to the wind rustling the leaves of the trees in your grove.

Now look beyond the grove to the landscape beyond. Ahead of you is a small hill. As you walk toward it, you see an opening in the side of the hill, with a low stone doorway—two uprights and a huge lintel.

You stoop down to enter the doorway and find yourself in a tunnel which goes upward into the hill. It is not too dark; there seems to be a light source up ahead.

Eventually you emerge into a big open space, and as you stand blinking, your eyes adjusting to the light, you see that there are two people in the cave: an old person and a child. They are sitting by a fire, which reflects its warmth and light onto their faces.

Look at the old person: How are they dressed? Take their hand: How does it feel? Look into their eyes, listen to them, talk to them, give them a gift. Perhaps they will give you a gift.

Now the child: How are they dressed? What will they tell you? Talk with them, look into their eyes. Maybe you exchange gifts with them.

And now, look into the fire, and notice how its dancing flames form shadows on the walls of the cave: hairy arms, hands, tongues, and beast shapes rise up and flicker on the walls of the cave. They are scary but you have the comforting presence of the old person and the child to reassure you.

You look again into the flames and see an image of your ideal beloved forming in the fire, beautiful and golden. They rise out of the fire, the embodiment of your dreams. They smile at you. Gaze into their eyes, let your gaze caress them, but do not touch them.

In turn, the light from the ideal beloved illuminates a deep pool at the back of the cave. Its dark waters are smooth and peaceful, rippling gently toward the shore, as the pool is fed by a spring.

You see that the moon has risen and is shining through a small opening in the roof of the cave, and it is reflected in the dark water. You can stoop down and drink the water if you wish. Feel the silver moonlight filling you.

Now it is time to go, and when you turn around, you see that the flames have died down to embers, the beloved has disappeared, and the old person and the child are two stalagmites in the cave.

You turn and walk back down the passage, stoop low to go out of the entrance, and are back on the green slope of the hill. Ahead of you is your sacred grove. Walk back to the grove, greet the trees, and sit down once more on the earth. As you sit, close your eyes, and feel yourself gradually returning to this place and this time and this room.

Exercises and Journal Prompts

- **Ground and center.** Do the tree visualization described earlier in this chapter, where you align yourself with earth and sky.

- **Practice self-compassion.** Focus on the heart.

- **Keep a gratitude journal.** List the beautiful and joyful things that you have seen throughout the day.

- **Practice self-awareness.** Be aware of what pushes your buttons, and that moments of anger and irritability are likely triggered by the contents of your shadow side.

- **Perform the shadow exercise.** Make a list of the traits of a person who irritates you, and label it "my shadow."

- **Then do the golden shadow exercise.** Make a list of the traits of a person whom you admire, and label it "my golden shadow."

- **Meditate on Tarot cards.** The Major Arcana of the Tarot is a set of archetypes. Reflect on their meanings and symbolism. Which ones do you identify with, and why? Which ones do you dislike, and why?

- **Notice archetypes** in books, folktales, movies, and TV shows. Which ones do you identify with, and why? Which ones do you dislike, and why?

- **Gather images** of archetypes you identify with. Paste them in a scrapbook or on a mood board and label them with names.

Ritual: The Naming of the Parts

Roles: This is a ritual for one person.

Setup: Create your ritual space as you normally would. If you do not have a usual method of setting up your ritual space, you can start the ritual with soft drumming. Adapt the quarter calls for your tradition's elemental attributions if you like.

> **Self** *(facing North)*: The North is the place of breath, the breath that sustains me.

> **Self** *(facing East)*: The East is the place of fire, the energy that runs through my body, keeping me warm.

> **Self** *(facing South)*: The South is the place of earth, the element that makes my bones, which support me and give me strength.

> **Self** *(facing West)*: The West is the place of water, the water that fills my body, giving me fluidity and motion.

> **Self:** I am a being of many aspects, many intersections of identity. I am my own person, yet I exist in a community of others. I have different roles and responsibilities in different communities, and I embody different archetypes. I have come to name and acknowledge each of these parts, and greet them with love.

If you have gathered images or objects to represent the parts of yourself (both archetypes that you embody and roles that you play), these should be placed around the circle. You could also use Tarot or oracle cards to represent the parts.

Name each of the parts, archetypes, and roles, and describe how it empowers you. If it restricts you in some way, you could add that you wish to be free of the restrictions it imposes, and cut a cord to symbolize being released from that restriction.

The parts might include witch, poet, lover, parent, spouse, activist, sibling, child, or different archetypes such as femme fatale, mystic, hermit, and so on.

Finally, gather all the images together and bind them together with a ribbon, or put them in a box, to symbolize that they are all part of you.

> **Self:** These are the aspects of my being,
> Woven together in my one wild and precious life.[29]
> All these I am, and they are seen in me.[30]
> I have named them so that they are seen and acknowledged,
> valued and cherished, woven into my tapestry.
> They are strands of rainbow light blended into a single ray.

29   Mary Oliver, "The Summer Day".
30   Dion Fortune (1938), The Sea Priestess. Weiser Books.

Connecting with Nature

The earth is a living, conscious being. In
company with cultures of many different times
and places, we name these things as sacred: air,
fire, water, and earth. Whether we see them
as the breath, energy, blood, and body of the
Mother, or as the blessed gifts of a Creator,
or as symbols of the interconnected systems
that sustain life, we know that nothing can
live without them. To call these things sacred
is to say that they have a value beyond their
usefulness for human ends, that they themselves
become the standards by which our acts, our
economics, our laws, and our purposes must
be judged. . . To honor the sacred is to create
conditions in which nourishment, sustenance,
habitat, knowledge, freedom, and beauty can
thrive. To honor the sacred is to make love
possible. To this we dedicate our curiosity, our
will, our courage, our silences, and our voices.
To this we dedicate our lives.

—Starhawk, *The Fifth Sacred Thing* (1993)

What does it mean to "get back to Nature?" Does it mean
returning to a natural state, connecting with all of Nature, or living
a natural life? Does it mean that we want to connect with all of
Nature—the whole universe? Or perhaps with the Earth, the only
known habitable planet, and our sacred home? Or maybe with
your local ecosystem, the patch of land you call home.

American historian and author Chas Clifton divides "Nature" into three categories: Cosmic Nature, Gaian Nature, and Embodied Nature.[31] He defines Cosmic Nature as the system of magical correspondences that are held to be the key to the hidden workings of the universe. I would also define it as the wonders of the cosmos: planets, stars, galaxies, and nebulae. Gaian Nature, by contrast, is Nature as Goddess, to be venerated in her own right as a conscious entity and/or self-regulating system. Finally, he describes Embodied Nature as an erotic theology of the body, where the body and its desires are seen as sacred, natural, good, and a way of linking to wild Nature.

Cosmic Nature

You can connect with Cosmic Nature in a variety of ways. One is by looking up at the stars. There is an amazing smartphone app (SkyView Lite) that overlays the constellations and their names on the quadrant of sky you are looking at. You can also get reasonably good portable telescopes these days. I have always enjoyed looking at NASA's Astronomy Picture of the Day, which features a high-resolution photograph of an astronomical phenomenon such as a distant galaxy or nebula every day. You could also take up astrology, which gives an appreciation of the hidden workings of the universe. There are numerous other forms of divination available that work on the basis of hidden synchronicities and patterns, such as the I Ching, lithomancy, geomancy, and many more.

Visiting stone circles and burial mounds is also an excellent way to get in touch with Cosmic Nature; many people believe that the purpose of stone circles and some burial mounds was to track sunrises and sunsets, moon phases and stellar alignments.

---

31   Chas Clifton (2006), Her Hidden Children: The Rise of Wicca and Paganism in America. Altamira Press. Page 43 ff.

Even if this was not their main purpose, they are often aligned on astronomical events. One especially famous example of this is the main chamber at Newgrange in Ireland, where there is an opening aligned so that the winter solstice sunrise shines through it and illuminates the whole chamber.

Gaian Nature

Awareness of Gaian Nature involves becoming aware of Planet Earth and her ecosystems as a self-regulating entity. Connecting with Gaian Nature involves remembering that humanity is part of this giant ecosystem. People have always been connected to Nature, but they forget that connection because they get distracted by technology and cities.

Many people feel disconnected from Nature because they live in a city, do not have a garden, buy all their food from supermarkets, and perhaps cannot get out into natural spaces. However, even cities are not completely devoid of Nature; there are parks, and street trees, and plants pushing up through the cracks, and wildlife, and birds. People tend to think of ecosystems and the environment as being outside of cities, but cities are also ecosystems—sometimes damaged or broken ecosystems because of pollution, but still ecosystems.

There are many ways to reconnect with Nature. You can take up gardening—even if you do not have a backyard, you can grow plants in pots on your window ledge—or get involved with a local urban farm. I enjoy gardening because I love planting things and watching them grow, and then keep coming back year after year. If I have planted food plants, I get to eat the produce from them as well. This is very satisfying. It also makes you aware of which plants will grow in your local climate. In North America, there are maps of climate bands, showing which plants will survive at different latitudes.

It is a great idea to plant flowers that feed bees and other pollinators such as hummingbirds. These vary by region, so research the best bee-friendly flowers in your region, and get ones that support a variety of wild bees and other pollinators.

You can go for walks in wild places, such as by the seashore or lakeshore, along a river, through woodland, or in a public park or conservation area. Brian Mertins makes a distinction between hiking and wandering.[32] Hiking is when you are focused on walking the trail within a set amount of time, hardly glancing at the trees and rocks and views along the way. I experienced this once when I hiked up to the top of a hill with a friend. Having got to the top, I wanted to look at the view, but he did not seem interested in the view, only the exercise. Wandering, on the other hand, is when you stop to look at the flowers, trees, rocks, views, and critters that you meet along the way. It is also more relaxing than the hiking approach just described. You can approach the landscape from different directions and perspectives, and there is no pressure to get to the top of the nearest mountain.

As you walk, be mindful of the dictum, "Take only photographs and memories, leave only footprints." Lately there has been a fashion for leaving clooties (pieces of cloth) tied to trees. These are harmful to trees and wildlife, and the build-up of thousands of these "offerings" has become a huge issue in some places. If you feel the urge to leave an offering at a sacred site, do a litter cleanup (including the removal of clooties) or volunteer with a conservation group.

Some people make pretty patterns with biodegradable materials found at the site (such as twigs, pebbles, leaves, and nut casings). This is okay, but if hundreds of people started doing this, it would become almost as big a problem as the clooties.

---

32   Brian Mertins (undated), 'How To Connect With Nature.' Nature Mentor.

If there is already a sacred structure at a site (such as a petroglyph, burial mound, or stone circle), do not interfere with it, add to it, or leave little piles of rocks. This is disrespectful. If you encounter wildlife, keep a safe distance—for your sake and that of the animals.

A really great way of experiencing yourself as part of Nature is to incorporate the sit spot into your practice. The sit spot is a place in Nature where you can sit comfortably for fifteen minutes. While there, you slow your breathing, quiet your mind, and listen to the sounds around you: the rustling of the wind in the leaves, water flowing or falling, bird song. You return to the same spot on a regular basis to become attuned to that particular place and its sounds, energies, spirits, seasons, and moods.

Another way to deepen your engagement with Nature is to learn about birds and their calls, flowers, trees, animals and their tracks, mushrooms, and grasses. It is also fascinating to learn about geology, which explains the shape of the hills, and soil chemistry, which explains what crops will grow where, and the history of farming, which explains types of land use in different regions. The geology and farming style can affect the shape and size of the fields, the style of hedges or walls, and the number of mature trees left standing.

In his wonderful book *Landmarks* (2015), Robert Macfarlane talks about how a deep engagement with the smells, textures, sights, and sounds of your local landscape, flora, and fauna, can enable you to connect with Nature as a whole. He shares lists of local dialect words for specific types of landscape features and discusses writers who have deeply connected with a specific landscape.

Learning about flora and fauna will enable you to really see individual flowers and trees and learn their characteristics, when they come into flower or fruit, and when their leaves fall. Find out the local names for them in your area. When do they come into flower or leaf? When do their fruits ripen? What animals and birds like to eat them? If you forage for wild edible plants, never take more than 10 percent of what is growing in any one place. Leave plenty for wildlife, for the plants to regenerate, and for other foragers. Foraging is a wonderful way to deepen your relationship with the land you live on, but be aware that some plants and mushrooms are poisonous. Take care to identify the foods you have gathered, and prepare them correctly.

If you live in Turtle Island (North America), find out the name for the flora and fauna you are studying in the local Indigenous languages, and search for stories that Indigenous people have shared about them. Be sure to learn from Indigenous sources and not fake ones. Never take money or claim credit for these stories; it is best if they are shared by Indigenous people in an Indigenous cultural context. Many Indigenous stories are meant to be told only by specific elders at a specific time of year. Attend your local powwow (a powwow is a traditional gathering to celebrate Indigenous arts and culture[33]), visit Indigenous-owned art stores and bookstores, and follow Indigenous artists on social media. Learn about the history of Indigenous Peoples' relationship with the land, and support the Land Back movement.

If you live in England or Wales, learn about the Enclosures (how the rich enclosed the land and rolled back the people's rights to common land), the resistance to Enclosures, the Kinder Scout Mass Trespass (when protesters won the right to walk on the hills and moors), and the Right to Roam movement. If you live in Scotland,

---

[33]   Michael John Simpson, Michelle Filice (2016), 'History of Powwows.' Canadian Encyclopedia.

learn about the Highland Clearances (when peasants were moved off the land and replaced with sheep). If you live in Ireland, learn about the Famine. These events caused mass emigration from Scotland and Ireland, and, as many of the displaced people moved to North America, they displaced its Indigenous Peoples.

Many people think that Nature would be better off without humans, and although industrialized societies and intensive agriculture have caused a lot of harm to Nature, Indigenous Peoples have usually lived in harmony with the land, only taking as much as they need and being mindful of the need to ensure that the plants and animals they rely on for food will reproduce. Indigenous Peoples generally stay in small areas and live sustainably; it is agricultural and industrialized societies that have destroyed entire ecosystems and spread beyond their original locales. Indigenous land use is beneficial to the land, because Indigenous Peoples have spent thousands of years developing a relationship with the specific area of land on which they hunt and gather. In fact, 80 percent of the world's biodiversity is in areas managed by Indigenous Peoples.[34] So, in order to support Nature and biodiversity, people need to support land rights for Indigenous Peoples.

The United Nations identifies Indigenous Peoples as ethnic groups who maintain their ancestral connection to and knowledge of the land in which they live, and who are marginalized by settler colonialism.[35]

As the effects of the climate emergency become more and more apparent, the need for humanity to get back into harmony with Nature becomes ever more apparent.

---

34 Eugenia Recio, Dina Hestad (2022), 'Indigenous Peoples: Defending an Environment for All.' The International Institute for Sustainable Development (IISD).
35 United Nations Permanent Forum on Indigenous Issues (undated), 'Who are indigenous peoples?'

Although ancient polytheistic religions were not specifically focused on being attuned to Nature, they did treat it with respect. Ancient cultures had deities associated with the wilderness, the sky, the ocean, hunting, and farming, as well as deities of the arts, writing, mathematics, architecture, and cities.

Because the Pagan Revival was started in response to the Industrial Revolution and increasing urbanization, it has included a strong emphasis on reconnecting with Nature. This tendency has been very strong in North America, with its traditions of regarding the wilderness as a cure for the ills of civilization.[36]

Embodied Nature

Embodied Nature is feeling at home in our bodies and regarding all bodies and erotic desires as sacred and natural. The emphasis on ritual nudity in much of initiatory Wicca is based on the sacralization of the body. As the well-loved poem "Wild Geese" by Mary Oliver puts it, "You only have to let the soft animal of your body love what it loves." The body and its desires are sacred in Wicca because Nature is sacred, and our bodies are part of Nature. The erotic impulse is sacred because pleasure is a good thing. As Doreen Valiente wrote in "The Charge of the Goddess", "All acts of love and pleasure are My rituals." And as I have pointed out in my earlier books, that means all acts of love and pleasure, including same-sex love, queer love, trans love, and nonsexual or platonic love and pleasure. The sensual pleasures of eating, swimming, sleeping, and cuddling are also acts of love and pleasure.

Consent is important, of course, because if a thing is pleasurable to one person but not to another, then the person for whom it is not pleasurable has a right to refuse it.

---

[36] Chas Clifton (2006), Her Hidden Children: The Rise of Wicca and Paganism in America. Altamira Press, p. 42 ff.

The body has its own natural rhythms, called Circadian rhythms.[37] These are regulated by biological clocks in your cells, which are synchronized by a cluster of cells in the brain called the master clock. Circadian rhythms govern when you feel wakeful and when you feel sleepy, and they can be disrupted by flying to a different time zone. They also regulate eating patterns, hormonal cycles, and body temperature. It is a good idea to work with your Circadian rhythms by going to sleep and waking up at around the same time each day. It is also true that teenagers naturally wake up later than adults. The amount of sleep different people need varies according to their time of life and general health.

Another way of becoming attuned to your body is listening to its wants, whether those are for food, sleep, or other sensual pleasures. It can also mean being aware of pain in your body and tending to it. Pain is a natural signal that something is wrong and needs fixing. Rather than ignoring it, be compassionate to yourself, and value yourself enough to address the issues that the pain is raising. For instance, if you have a cramp in your leg, it may mean that you need to move it more, or drink more water, or take some magnesium supplements. If you are exhausted or overwhelmed, get some sleep or take a bath. You are worthy of love and care, and so is your body (which is a part of you, after all).

The patriarchal/kyriarchal/hegemonic culture seeks to regulate and control the body—especially queer bodies, female bodies, and Black queer and/or female bodies—because these marginalized people are constructed as the Other, the site of resistance to the kyriarchy. Because our existence provokes fear of the Other, fear of wildness, fear of sexuality, fear of letting go—our bodies and our hair (traditionally hair is a source of magical power) must be controlled, groomed, reduced, covered, suppressed. If women

---

37   National Institute of General Medical Sciences (undated), Circadian Rhythms.

cover too much, they are censured for prudery; if they don't cover enough, there is slut-shaming. If women's bodies are too hairy, they must be shaved; if they are too generously proportioned, they must be reduced in size.

But the body manifests in many different shapes and sizes and colors. There are female bodies, male bodies, intersex bodies, modified bodies, disabled bodies, different-colored bodies, tattooed bodies, scarred bodies, hairy bodies, smooth bodies, short bodies, tall bodies. There are bony bottoms, and bottoms that spread like the sheltering boughs of a chestnut tree. There are small breasts and large breasts, perky breasts and pendulous breasts, six-packs and beer barrels. The body reflects our embodied histories as people. Gravity and age conspire to make breasts head south, but it doesn't make them any less beautiful.

The body is not a commodity for positioning ourselves in some marketplace of attractiveness. The body is not a "vehicle" or an "overcoat" for the soul. Perhaps, in some mysterious way, it is the soul made manifest.

Bodies, whatever size and shape and color they are, are beautiful. Especially when lit by candlelight or firelight. But most of all, a body is a person—it's not just an appendage attached to a head, it is part of the person and worthy of respect.

Throw away your preconceived ideas about slimness and muscle tone, and learn to appreciate bodies as people. Throw away the pre-packaged concepts of beauty imposed by the kyriarchy, and learn to look at bodies the way an artist would: as compositions of line and tone and form, of light and shadow.

Look at the *Venus of Willendorf*—really look at her. Look how the sculptor loved the generosity of her curves, the abundance of food that her body fat represented. Look at the sculpture of the *Sleeping Lady* of Hal Saflieni—another large woman celebrated by an ancient culture. Look at the sculpture of the laughing Buddha. If deities can be fat, then people can be fat, and vice versa. There are also sculptures of thin deities. If deities can be thin, then people can be thin, and vice versa. Deities come in all shapes and sizes, and so do people.

Celebrate the curves of the land, and the hills and valleys, and see them reflected in the bodies of your cuddly friends. Look at the slender trees, and see them reflected in the bodies of your lithe friends. Celebrate the beauty and diversity of the human body.

All of Nature

The molecules and atoms that make up your body were forged in the heart of ancient stars—you are literally made of star-stuff. You eat the food that is grown in the land where you live, and it forms your flesh and bones—you are literally made of the earth on which you live. Your body is intimately connected with the land and with the stars. The human body is made of 80 percent water, so you are also connected to the sea. You are part of Nature and you always have been—you just need to remember your connection to all the beings and ecosystems with whom you share this planet.

Meditation: An Intentional Nature Walk

Go somewhere where you will be able to walk about in Nature looking at things without attracting unwanted attention. This could be your back garden, a public park, or a piece of local woodland. Look around you and choose something to focus on, such as a flower or tree or rock. Really look at it, noting every detail (veins on the leaves, details of the flower, patterns on the rock). When you have finished, stand up, look around, and find a new thing to focus on. Walk toward it and examine it closely. Repeat this process for five or ten minutes (depending on how many things there are to look at in the space). Afterwards you could write a poem or a journal entry about the process.[38]

---

[38] I learned this technique from British Unitarian minister, John Harley.

Exercises and Journal Prompts

The sit spot. Practice sitting quietly in the same spot for at least fifteen minutes on a regular basis, observing the sounds, smells, and sights all around you. Feel the wind and the sun on your face, and perhaps the bark of a tree at your back. Be aware of bird songs, animal sounds, and the rustling of leaves in the wind. As thoughts arise, let them go, not following the thought but staying present in Nature.

Get to know your local flora and fauna. Note down at least five birds, flowers, animals, insects, trees, mushrooms, mosses, and grasses that are in your local area. Write down any medicinal uses, folk names or Indigenous language names, folklore, or symbolism associated with them.

Know the land. Learn about the geology, soil chemistry, and history of farming in your bioregion.

Keep Nature notes. Write about your walks, listing the temperature, cloud conditions, smells, sounds, textures, what was in flower or leaf, and any wildlife you spotted.

Gather traditional recipes. Ask your family and people from your local area for them, especially the type of recipes that are intended to make use of seasonal fruits and vegetables.

Learn traditional crafts. Investigate hedging, spinning, weaving, natural dyeing, basketmaking, bowl turning, and so on.

Ritual: From the Wild to the Table

This ritual will work with one or more participants.

Preparation: Gather wild apples, berries, edible mushrooms, herbs, or nuts (be sure to take less than 10 percent of the available produce). You can either find a recipe that uses them, or pile them on a plate. If you bake with the food, light some incense in the kitchen while you bake, consecrate your kitchen tools, and stir good wishes into the mixture as you prepare it.

Roles: Gatherer(s).

Setup: Create your ritual space as you normally would. If you do not have a usual method of setting up your ritual space, you can start the ritual with soft drumming.

> **Gatherer 1** *(facing North)*: We thank the powers of the North for the gift of the air, bringing carbon dioxide and nitrogen to nourish the plants.
>
> **Gatherer 2** *(facing East)*: We thank the powers of the East for bringing us the warmth and light of the Sun, which encourages the plants to grow.
>
> **Gatherer 3** *(facing South)*: We thank the powers of the South for the gift of the rich earth in which our food grows.
>
> **Gatherer 4** *(facing West)*: We thank the powers of the West for the gift of rain and flowing streams, which provides the plants with water.
>
> **Gatherer 1:** We set aside some of the food we have gathered for the birds that visit the garden

(place them in a separate bowl so that they can be scattered outside later).

> **Gatherer 2:** We offer some of the food we have gathered to the powers of the land, in gratitude for their bounty

(place some of the food in the fire or pass it through a candle flame).

> **Gatherer 3:** We set aside some of the food we have gathered for the animals that visit the garden.

> *(Place them in a separate bowl so that they can be scattered outside later.)*

> **Gatherer 4:** We offer some of the food we have gathered to the waters.

(Set aside some of the food for offering to a local lake or river—but make sure it will not harm the fish or amphibians.)

> **Gatherer 1:** And now we eat the food with gratitude and mindfulness for the bounty of the Earth, and the Sun, and the winds, and the waters; the bees that pollinate the flowers to make the fruit; the birds and animals that carry seeds from one place to another in their bellies; the spirits of plants, and the wights of the places where they grow.

> **Gatherers 2, 3, 4 *(in unison)*:** We eat with gratitude!

All eat mindfully.

The Old Gods

Once every people in the world believed that
trees were divine, and could take a human or
grotesque shape and dance among the shadows;
and that deer, and ravens and foxes, and wolves
and bears, and clouds and pools, almost all
things under the sun and moon, and the sun
and moon, were not less divine and changeable.
They saw in the rainbow the still bent bow of a
god thrown down in his negligence; they heard
in the thunder the sound of his beaten water-jar,
or the tumult of his chariot wheels; and when a
sudden flight of wild duck, or of crows, passed
over their heads, they thought they were gazing
at the dead hastening to their rest; while they
dreamed of so great a mystery in little things
that they believed the waving of a hand, or of a
sacred bough, enough to trouble far-off hearts,
or hood the moon with darkness.

—W.B. Yeats, *Ideas of Good and Evil* (1903)

The thought of the ancient Pagan deities has always filled me
with excitement. I remember my parents telling me that in ancient
times, at the winter solstice, people would go to hilltops and light
fires to implore the sun to return. I was excited by the concept
of magic having a direct effect on the world, and the vision of
darkness and fire and Nature that this story conjured up struck a
deep chord in the center of my being.

The Pagan gods can be the consciousness of natural phenomena
and cosmic forces, deified heroes, spirits of place, personifications

of cities, and patrons of the arts and sciences. They are not infinitely powerful or omnipresent, and that is part of their appeal; they have distinct personalities and you can connect with them.

Not all Pagans worship or honor deities, but the majority do. Pagans' theological perspectives vary widely. They can be atheists, pantheists, panentheists, deists, monists, duotheists, polymorphists, polytheists, and sometimes people say that they embrace all of the above at different times and in varying circumstances. This diversity also occurs within Pagan traditions such as Wicca and Druidry.

Even those who do worship or honor deities do not necessarily place them at front and center of their practice. Some regard them as allies and partners, others regard them as patrons who are beyond us in glory and power.

I am a relational polytheist. While the gods are important, because they are the consciousnesses of specific places and natural phenomena, they are not more important than the ecosystem, Nature, the Earth, and the species who share the planet with us. As a relational polytheist, I feel that it is necessary to focus on right relationships with other beings, starting with other animals, including humans, and with the ecosystem in which you live, of which the deities are the conscious emanations.

I do not believe that the gods are merely archetypes. I believe the gods are real and have agency. I am not sure if the gods are made of energy or consciousness or both, but I am sure that they are distinct identities.

In his ode, "Nemea," the classical poet Pindar wrote:

> There is one race of men, one race of gods;
> both have breath of life from a single mother.
> But sundered power
> holds us divided, so that the one is nothing, while
> for the other
> the brazen sky is established their sure citadel
> forever.
> Yet we have some likeness in great intelligence,
> or strength,
> to the immortals,
> though we know not what the day will bring,
> what course after nightfall
> destiny has written that we must run to the
> end.[39]

So, according to Pindar, humans and gods are related, and we have the "breath of life from a single mother." This passage is part of the basis of my relational polytheism. The gods have different powers, being immortal—they are nonlocal and do not have a physical form. So they need our temporally focussed and physically located consciousness in order to be able to affect events in the physical world; and humans need their eternal and non-local perspective in order to access the divine realms.[40]

An Ethic of Hospitality

In ritual, you express your deepest yearnings toward what you hold to be of greatest worth. Some rituals can be shared with people who see the world differently; other rituals can't be shared. That's okay. In Wicca, it's possible for a polytheist, an atheist, a

---

39 Pindar, The Odes.
40 This explanation of the mutual dependence of gods and humans came from Scottish Pagan, John Macintyre.

duotheist, and an animist to circle together, if the participants share the same values and a similar practice. I wouldn't circle with someone who was a racist or a homophobe or a transphobe—but I am fine with people with different theological perspectives, as long as they respect my theological perspective. The group might even refine their working hypotheses of how it all works by engaging in dialogue. But one of the guidelines of interfaith dialogue is deep listening and being open to the other person's perspective. As long as you can respect my relational mystical polytheist Wicca, I will respect whatever your view is. This is the sacred ethic of hospitality: If I invite you into my space, I have certain obligations as the host, and you have obligations as a guest. The ethic of hospitality is one of mutually respectful behavior.

Learning from Different Perspectives

The reason I welcome different perspectives on deities, and reality in general, is that I think our perspective is limited by our finite and localized nature in space-time. If you have an encounter with a deity, they are often kind enough to appear in a form that you can recognize, such as a vision of a humanoid form (I say humanoid so as not to exclude Ganesh, Pan, and other theriomorphic deities). However, I do not think for a moment that this humanoid form is necessarily their only form. Someone once described deities as "possibly anthropomorphic interfaces of vast cosmic forces"—a description that sums it up pretty well for me.

This is why I think practitioners need to approach the gods with a certain humility—and with an awareness that their nature is a mystery.

While deities are not merely archetypes, they do include archetypal qualities (as do we all).

People's beliefs and hypotheses wax and wane; after all, we live in a highly rationalist and materialist culture—it is hard to maintain a faith in conscious cosmic forces in the face of all that. There is room for honest doubt, apophatic theology, and mystical approaches—and archetypalists, too.

To me, polytheism means belief in many gods, and in its most basic form, it does not include anything about defining what gods are or how you relate to them. Devotional polytheism means serving or being devoted to them and believing they have agency and are entities. Relational polytheism is forming relationships with them and believing they have agency and are entities. If people want to define a specific tradition within polytheism as having even more requirements, good for them. But I don't think you can define simple polytheism beyond the concept of belief in many gods.

What Is Real?

The nature of reality can be viewed from many perspectives: On the quantum level, everything is quarks and leptons and bosons and strangeness and charm. At the level of chemistry, it's all about the chemical interactions. On the cellular biology level, cells join and divide and exchange chemical signals. On a psychological level, no one would deny that love and hate and other emotions are real, and only the most reductionist person would insist that they are merely biochemical signals. Then there are interpersonal relationships, social movements, discourses, historical trends, and other macro-level processes, all the way up to the movement of galaxies and the expansion of the universe. From the perspective of the universe, our little lives are pretty insignificant; from my personal perspective, my life is very significant to me.

I would say that something is "real" if it has a real effect on existence. In this view, ideas are real because they affect people's lives. However, ideas are not things, and they are not people. That's why the "gods have agency" part of contemporary polytheism is important, because gods are not just ideas or archetypes, but beings with will and agency. There are plenty of people who experience the gods as beings with will and agency, but on the whole, that is a matter of faith.

Most Pagans view the deities as immanent in the world, rather than existing only on some other plane of reality. If they are immanent and many, then they could very well be the consciousnesses of natural phenomena.

I have always thought that the deities of Nature are the emergent consciousness of complex phenomena, such as sacred places, mountains, trees, storms, forests, and so on. If this is the case, then any anthropomorphic appearance they choose to adopt is only one aspect or facet of their vast and complex nature. From our finite perspective, humans cannot say with any certainty that we know them fully or that we know exactly what they are. We can only say that we do experience them as distinct beings with agency, and that when we experience the presence of a deity, we know that we are blessed by their presence.

When I feel the presence of a deity, I feel their unique personality and energy. Some are reassuring and comforting, others feel more remote and challenging, but all are beings of majesty and power.

When I visit a sacred place, I can often feel the presence of the numinous, the spirit of place. If I am visiting a stone circle or a burial mound, I wait at the perimeter of the *temenos* (sacred area) and ask permission of the spirit of the place to enter the sacred precincts. I get a feeling of slight pressure or resistance while waiting for permission to enter, and then a lessening of that pressure when permission is granted.

Not all deities and spirits of place have a name; this is why the Romans made altars dedicated to unknown gods. Sometimes you can visit a place and become aware of its personality or vibe, which is perhaps the unnamed deity or spirit of the place impinging on your awareness.

Can Belief in Deities Be Compatible with Science?

Some have argued that any form of theism is incompatible with science. This seems odd when so many scientists are theistic in some way.

The bitterest argument between science and theism is between evolutionary biology and creationist monotheism, for obvious reasons. Physicists, on the other hand, because of quantum theory, tend to be a bit more mystical.

According to my research,[41] only about 50 percent of Pagans believe in a creator deity. Many would say that the universe was born, not made. And they would regard the Big Bang as the moment of birth.

"Compatible with science" means different things to different people. Many rationalists tend to conflate rationalism and empiricism, but these are two very different worldviews. Rationalism is the assumption that you can work out how the world works from *a priori* rational principles (such as "I think, therefore I am"). Empiricism denies the existence of any *a priori* principles and states that people have to work out how the world works from experience. These two schools of thought were

---

41   Yvonne Aburrow (2008), Do Pagans see their beliefs as compatible with science? MA Dissertation, Bath Spa University.

reconciled around 1900 in a new synthesis, but unless you're referencing that synthesis, beware of conflating them.

There are also conflicts within science between a belief that science can work out and describe the nature of reality, and a belief that all our theories will only ever be a model of reality.

The Pagan Revival has mostly had an ambivalent attitude to belief. It started at a time when religion generally was on the back foot because of the advance of scientific understanding of reality.

There have been two responses to the rise of scientific explanations of the origins of the universe. The response of liberal religions has been to say that religious accounts of creation are a metaphor. More conservative traditions have retreated into fundamentalism in a sort of knee-jerk reaction to the scientific revolution.

The Pagan Revival mostly started from the assumption that the scientific account is correct and proceeded to creatively work within it. Academic studies of Pagan beliefs suggest that most people have come to belief from significant disbelief and that they shift about on the belief spectrum.

Pagans do not generally believe in a separate spiritual or supernatural realm; rather, we believe that spirits are immanent in Nature. I think that "spirits" and "magic" are properties of nature in the same way as consciousness is. Pagans revere the divine in Nature. Sixty-five percent of my study sample agreed that deities and other spirits have developed out of our social and ritual interaction with place and space, and seventy-two percent agreed that the divine is (or deities are) immanent in the universe. Twenty percent were neutral on this issue. (The ones who didn't agree that the divine was immanent in Nature were also the ones who didn't believe in the divine.)

Instead, Pagans interact with the preternatural, as described by religious studies scholar Michael York:

> The supernatural as we know it is largely a
> Christian-derived expression from the idea that
> its "God" is over and "above" nature—material/
> empirical reality. It is this notion that is the
> target of secular and naturalistic animosity alike.
> Instead, rather than "supernatural," I turn
> instead to the "preternatural" that expresses
> the non-causal otherness of nature—one
> that comprehends the magical, miraculous,
> numinous, mysterious yet non-empirical quality
> of the sublime. Most important, however, the
> preternatural does not demand belief or faith
> but instead encounter and experience—whether
> through contemplation, metaphor, spontaneous
> insight, ecstasy, trance, synchronicity or ritual or
> any combination of these.[42]

American anthropologist Tanya Luhrmann identified four possible positions that magical practitioners take when justifying their views to skeptics.[43] The first is realism, the idea that "there is a knowable objective reality and that magic reveals more of it than science." The second position that she identifies is the "two worlds" view, that "the objective referent of magical claims is unknowable within the terms of an ordinary, scientific world." The third position is relativism, which "defines all truth as relative

42   Michael York (2009), 'A Pagan Defence of Theism.' Theologies of Immanence Wiki.
43   Tanya Luhrmann (1989/1991), Persuasions of the Witch's Craft: Ritual Magic in Contemporary England. Harvard University Press.

and contingent" (which Luhrmann found to be quite a common view). The final position is the metaphorical view, that magic is metaphorical and is probably objectively not true, but it is nevertheless a creative and enjoyable practice.

Consciousness as Emergent Complexity

When discussing the existence of gods, it would be more accurate to talk about the nature of gods. At a minimum, gods exist as an idea. Anyone can grasp the idea of, say, Aphrodite. If you have a concept of something, it exists as a concept. But is Aphrodite a meme, an archetype in the collective unconscious, a cosmic process with a personality, an actual non-incarnate mind floating about, a physical being in another plane who can somehow manifest in this plane?

What is known from the science of consciousness is that the consciousness that inhabits our brains is an emergent property of the complex biology of our brains.

I think it is possible, therefore, that gods and spirits are emergent properties of the complexity of the universe. They are not supernatural, i.e., not separate or distinct from nature, but preternatural, emergent identities. They are not necessarily persons or entities. Just as people shape each other's personalities by social interaction, it is possible to shape the "personality" of a place by interaction with it—hence the concept of the numinous and spirits of place.

Creative Uncertainty, Shared Values

Taking rigid positions on theology, whether our own theological stance or those of other people, is unrealistic. People who insist that all theists are irrational believers in supernatural entities are creating a caricature of theistic beliefs that most theists would not recognize as a description of their nuanced beliefs and hypotheses. People who insist that atheists cannot be Pagans are obviously wrong: There were atheist pagans in antiquity, and there are atheist Pagans now.

The nature of gods is unknown, but many people experience the world as having consciousness. It is my view, as a relational and mystical polytheist, that our relationship with the world around us (animals, birds, the ecosystem, and other human beings) is more important than our relationship with the gods. Humans can only ever guess what the gods want—if they can be said to want anything—so we should base our moral decisions on what we can see and know, and on the fact of our embodied existence in an ecosystem that humanity is close to destroying.

The urgency of climate change, habitat destruction, and extinction compels those of us who care about the planet to work together, regardless of belief (or lack of it) in gods. If different groups of people have shared values, they can still work together.

Meditation: Connecting with your Personal Deity

Just beneath your heart, visualize a shrine or altar. It can be simple or elaborate, depending on your personal taste. You can place sacred objects on your inner altar. Beside the altar, there is a tree, illuminated by the light, and bejeweled with sparkling gems of dew. Sit down next to your inner shrine, and contemplate a deity to whom you wish to become closer. Imagine a small space opening in your body (it can be anywhere you choose, but visualizing it near the heart was what worked for me). Allow the energy of your chosen deity to enter that space. You can expand the space as wide as it feels comfortable for you.

Exercises and Journal Prompts

- **Gather images.** Gather images of deities you are interested in and create a collage or mood board.

- **Create a shrine.** Set up a spot in your home dedicated to your personal deity or deities. If you do not yet have a personal deity, make an altar to them anyway, on the principle of "if you build it, they will come," and place items on it that are especially meaningful to you.

- **Research a deity.** Read all the stories and poetry you can find about your chosen deity.

- **Get creative!** Write poetry, write a ritual, draw a picture, sculpt a statue, compose music for your chosen deity.

Ritual: Devotion to the Gods

Note: Gods is used in this ritual in its original gender-neutral sense, to mean a deity of any gender. If you prefer, you can substitute the word "deities" where I have used "gods."

Roles: devotees, facilitator.

Setup: Create your ritual space as you normally would. If you do not have a usual method of setting up your ritual space, you can start the ritual with soft drumming.

> **Facilitator** *(facing North)*: Beneath the navel of
> heaven, the pole star, we honor the gods.
> Gods of the heavens, gods of the stars,
> Gods of the whole cosmos.
>
> **Facilitator** *(facing East)*: As the sun rises in the
> East, illuminating the world, so the light of the
> gods illuminates the realms of spirit.
>
> **Facilitator** *(facing South)*: Upon this sacred
> ground, The place of our meeting, we honor the
> gods. Gods of the land, gods of the earth,
> And spirits of place.
>
> **Facilitator** *(facing West)*: As the waters flow into
> the ocean
> We honor the gods of the sea,
> Primordial source of all life.

Each person steps forward and performs a devotion to a specific deity or spirit they feel connected to.

The act of devotion might include any of the following:

- **Lighting a candle or incense** for the deity.

- **Reading a poem.** This does not have to be specifically about the deity; it might be about a theme that the deity is associated with.

- **Talking about the deity.** What are their attributes? Perhaps tell a story about the deity.

- **Saying a prayer to the deity.** This can be spontaneous or written beforehand.

- **Performing a dance or music.** This is especially appropriate if the deity is associated with dancing or music.

- **Pouring a libation into a bowl.** If possible, use a substance that the deity is known to be associated with.

- **Dedicating a ritual object.** For example, you might make a thyrsus (a wand with a pine cone on the end) which was traditionally associated with Dionysus, and dedicate it to him.

- **Making a talisman.** You might make a talisman with an image or sigil of the deity and dedicate it to them.

- **Knotting a cord or ribbon.** This could be a magical reminder of the deity.

- **Making prayer beads.** Many Pagans create prayer beads as a focus for devotion to their deities.

The aim of the act of devotion is to deepen your connection to the deity or spirit.

Share consecrated food in the circle and leave a libation for the gods.

Folklore and Mythology

> Humans need fantasy to be human. To be the
> place where the falling angel meets the rising
> ape.
>
> —Terry Pratchett, *Hogfather* (1996)

Folklore and mythology are rich in symbolism and stories. Folklore tends to consist of stories that are local in scope, and that are often about ordinary people. These stories explain why a community does things in a specific way, or how a local feature or animal got its name. Mythology tends to be about gods and heroes—beings with fantastical powers. It often includes creation stories. The protagonists of folk tales are often foolish or at least ordinary. Folklore can also include traditional dances, food ways, herb lore, songs, stories, and folk art such as quilting, wood carving, weaving patterns, or embroidery styles.

Folklore and mythology are of interest to contemporary Pagans because they develop out of the relationship of people to the land, the Earth, and Nature. They provide the depth and color that archetypes alone do not convey.

Pagans often describe our religion as being about connecting with Nature, and we do that by connecting at local, regional, and global levels. Folklore and mythology are ways in which a culture transmits its core values, practices, and knowledge to the next generation. People remember instructions better if they are embedded in a story, as author Philip Pullman once pointed out:

We don't need a list of rights and wrongs, tables
of dos and don'ts: we need books, time, and
silence. *Thou shalt no*t is soon forgotten, but *Once
upon a time* lasts forever.[44]

Stories can also provide complexity, nuance, and a space for
making up your own mind, which a list of commandments cannot
provide. Every symbol that appears in a story has multiple layers
of meaning, like the symbols on the alethiometer in Pullman's *His
Dark Materials* trilogy, which have many meanings depending on
the context. For example, consider the green girdle in the story of
Gawain and the Green Knight.

A mysterious Green Knight arrives at King Arthur's court and
offers a challenge. One of the knights must strike off his head with
his ax and then meet him in a year's time for him to return the
blow. Gawain takes up the challenge and strikes off the Green
Knight's head with the ax. The Green Knight picks up his head
and rides off, telling Gawain to meet him at the Green Chapel in
a year's time, when the Green Knight will return the blow that
Gawain gave him. Gawain rides out to seek the Green Chapel and
comes to Sir Bertilak's house. Sir Bertilak invites him to rest and
recuperate over Christmas, and they will play a game. Sir Bertilak
will give Gawain whatever he gains while out hunting, and Gawain
will give him whatever he receives while staying in the house. Each
day, the lady of the house, Sir Bertilak's wife, gives Gawain a kiss,
which he gives to Sir Bertilak on his return from hunting. On the
last day, she gives a green girdle to Gawain which will protect him
from harm, and Gawain does not give his host the girdle. When
he rides out to the Green Chapel to receive the blow, he is wearing
the girdle to protect himself. The Green Knight realizes that he is
protected by the magic of the girdle when he tries three times to

---

44   'World Book Night: Ten writers' reasons for reading.' The Guardian., 23 April 2013.

strike him with the ax and can only make a small nick on his neck. He reveals to Gawain that he is one and the same as Sir Bertilak, and this whole game has been a ploy to test the honor of the knights of King Arthur.

Gawain is ashamed because he has been caught in a lie—but how many people would not be tempted to keep the girdle if it meant that it would protect them from the Green Knight's ax?

The girdle has multiple meanings. It represents the attempt by Sir Bertilak's wife to seduce Gawain; protective magic; low cunning; the loss of honor; the necessity of pragmatism in the face of imminent death; and the fact that no one is perfect. The green color represents Nature.

The complexity and nuance of the story invites the audience to think about what they would do in a similar situation, and it encourages people not to be judgmental about other people's moral decisions and compromises. The story can mean different things to different people at different times. On one level, it is a spooky story for Christmas; on another level, it is a morality tale; and it also can be seen as a story about the relationship of humanity and Nature.

Another morally ambivalent battle takes place at the winter solstice, in the form of the traditional mummers' play. The protagonists of the play are Saint George and a traditional adversary (variously referred to as Bold Slasher, the Turkish Knight, or Napoleon). Saint George kills his adversary, but Old Father Christmas says that the slain man is his beloved son and calls for a doctor to revive him. A certain amount of banter about the state of the medical profession in the early nineteenth century ensues ("This man's a quack as you can plainly see") and then Jack Vinny arrives to save the day by magically reviving the slain man.

It has been suggested that the battle between the two protagonists represents a fight between a solar hero and the darkness. It is clear from the resolution of the story that both of the combatants are cosmically necessary, and that the killing of Saint George's adversary is frowned upon by the anonymous authors of the mummers' play.

In my view, any good story should have multiple meanings and resist a single interpretation. Otherwise it is merely an allegory or a morality tale.

Another interesting aspect of folklore is that it is a collective endeavor. The stories and symbols and customs have been honed and developed over generations and adapted to fit their circumstances. If you visit any collection of folktales or folksongs, you will find multiple variants of them. It is interesting to compare these variants. For example, the Scottish song "Twa Corbies"[45] is much bleaker than the English equivalent, "Three Ravens."[46] In the Scottish song, the dead knight lies unheeded and unguarded in the ditch, because his hounds and his hawks have gone hunting, and his lady has taken another mate. In the English song, his hound and his hawk are guarding his body from predators, and he is buried by a pregnant fallow doe, or a pregnant lady. There are many variations of these two songs. "Three Ravens" was first printed by Thomas Ravenscroft in 1611 in a collection called *Melismata*, and a distinct variant of it was collected in the early 1800s in Lincolnshire.[47] There are also several variants of "Twa Corbies". The two songs also have very different tunes. This example shows that folklore changes according to circumstance, and that written culture and orally-transmitted culture inform each other. It is interesting that Scottish culture gave us "Twa

---

45   Anonymous, 'The Twa Corbies.' Scottish Poetry Library.
46   'The Three Ravens (English Folk Ballad).' Poem Analysis.
47   26. 'The Three Ravens (or Twa Corbies).' Bluegrass Messengers.

Corbies", and English culture gave us "Three Ravens". It is not clear which song came first, but it is almost as though the one is a commentary on the other.

Folklore can give depth and breadth to our seasonal celebrations as well. There are many folktales and customs associated with seasonal festivals, and these are connected with specific places and communities. For example, wassailing was most practiced in apple-growing or fruit-growing regions, because people's livelihoods depended on there being a good crop. In regions where other crops were more prevalent, people would celebrate Plough Monday instead. Maypole dancing was practiced in Southern England, the Netherlands, and Germany; Beltane fires were specific to Northern England. In the English Midlands, where the story of Robin Hood was very popular, people celebrated the coming of the May with Robin Hood's Games and built bowers for Robin Hood and Maid Marian.

In Scandinavian countries, bonfires were lit at Midsummer rather than May Eve, because the spring arrives later in more northerly latitudes.

Traditional songs and folk plays were associated with specific festivals. There are several variants of a song about John Barleycorn,[48] the fictional personification of barley, who is cut down in his prime and turned into whisky. The most appropriate festival at which to sing this song would be Lammas. Another song, "The Rigs O' Barley"[49] (also known as Corn Rigs"[50]) by Robert Burns references Lammas.

"The Lyke Wake Dirge"[51] would be very appropriate for Hallowstide, as it is a song about the journey of the soul after

---

48   'John Barleycorn (Roud 164; G/D 3:559).' Mainly Norfolk: English Folk and Other Good Music.
49   'The Rigs O' Barley.' Robert Burns.
50   'Corn Rigs—Robert Burns.' BBC.
51   'The Lyke Wake Dirge (Roud 8194; TYG 85).' Mainly Norfolk: English Folk and Other Good Music.

death, which was traditionally sung at a wake (the practice of sitting with a corpse before burial). There were numerous songs sung by people who begged for soul-cakes at All Hallows.[52]

Mummers' plays were traditionally performed at Christmas, but there were folk plays and dances for many different festivals, because they were a great way to collect money from the people who were better off.[53] Wassailing songs were sung in the orchards and around the villages to collect money or cider. People also went caroling from door to door, and sang carols in pubs. This practice still survives in some parts of England, especially North Derbyshire and South Yorkshire, and has also migrated to Canada and the United States. Carols were sung in the street, the pub, or the home because, until the late Victorian period, Anglican churches would not sing any hymns or carols that were not based on Biblical texts (which excluded every carol except "While Shepherds Watched").[54]

The period of time around Christmas is absolutely bursting with minor festivals, customs, folklore, and traditions. These include Saintt Lucia's Day in Sweden, Krampusnacht in Germany, the Jólabókaflóðið (Christmas book flood) and the Yule cat in Iceland, Hogmanay in Scotland, Mother's Night celebrated by the Old English, and many more.

Similarly, there are many customs associated with Easter, which is celebrated in Christianity on the Sunday after the first Full Moon after the Spring Equinox, which is an attempt at continuity with the Jewish festival of Passover (Pesach), the date of which is determined by the Jewish lunar calendar. The Old English pagans celebrated on the April Full Moon with a feast of roast beef, possibly in honor of a goddess of the dawn. Author Adrian Bott

52   Linda Crampton (2023), 'Soul Cakes and Souling: A Musical Tradition From the Past.' Spinditty.
53   Ronald Hutton (2001), Stations of the Sun: A History of the Ritual Year in Britain. Oxford Paperbacks.
54   'The History of Christmas Carols.' WhyChristmas.com.

has researched the origins of Easter extensively, and concluded that the association with hares, rabbits, and eggs is neither especially ancient, nor ubiquitous in Europe, as some regions associated other animals with Easter, like the fox.[55]

Most people instinctively shy away from the fact that Christian Easter is a commemoration of a brutal killing, and prefer to emphasize the spring symbolism associated with the resurrection. Hence the popularity of eggs (first mentioned in a legend about Mary Magdalene meeting the Roman Emperor), chicks, Easter bonnets with flowers on them, and making nests for the Easter bunny to lay its eggs in.

Just as there was simnel cake and Easter eggs at Easter, many regions had special foods that they only ate at specific festivals. People are used to the idea of special cakes and desserts (stollen in Germany, panettone in Italy, Christmas pudding in England, black cake or rum cake in the Caribbean) and specific meals (roast turkey in England and North America, carp in Poland) for Christmas, but there are special foods for other festivals too: parkin (sometimes called tharf cake) for Bonfire Night in Yorkshire and Lancashire; soul cakes for Halloween in many countries; simnel cake and hot cross buns for Easter; a cake with a bean in it to select the Lord of Misrule or Bean King on Twelfth Night; and so on.

The making of cakes for festivals is older than Christianity. The Old English name for February was Sol-Monath, the month of cakes, and people baked cakes to give as offerings to the gods.[56]

Special apotropaic cakes with spikes on them, called witch-cakes, were made to be hung behind doors to keep witches away. These cakes were never eaten. Rich fruit cakes called groaning

---

55   Yvonne Aburrow and Adrian Bott (2015),'Move over Easter Bunny, here comes the Easter Fox.' Dowsing for Divinity.
56   Ben Gazur (2022), 'The weird folklore of British cakes.' Wellcome Collection.

cakes were given to women who had just given birth; they were also placed under pillows to bestow dreams of a future spouse. And the custom of blowing out the candles on your birthday cake and making a wish is still going strong.[57] Birthday cakes were first mentioned by the Roman poet Ovid in 8 CE, while the tradition of placing candles on birthday cakes is said to have been invented by the ancient Greeks, who lit candles to honor the birth of the goddess Artemis on the sixth day of every lunar month.[58] Wedding cakes are still immensely popular, and now there are divorce cakes too (see the section on rites of passage in Chapter 8).

Many of these customs were taken to other parts of the world by European migrants and settlers, who developed new festivals based on the crops, flowers, and fruit that grow in their specific regions.

Traditional stories are very important and often give rise to local customs. They often become source material for Pagan and Wiccan ritual too. These stories include the tales of Robin Hood and his Merrie Men, the Arthurian cycle of stories, *The Mabinogion*, the story of Aradia, folklore and folktales about the Moon, the Wild Hunt, the Lord of the Animals, and the Lady of the Flowers.

Mythological tales that are often referenced include the story of Demeter and Persephone (not forgetting the part played by the goddess Baubo), the lore of the goddess Hekate, and Oðinn's quest for the runes.

You can make your festival celebrations and rituals richer and more satisfying by including seasonal folklore, folktales, mythology, customs, food, and songs. When introducing these to people who are unfamiliar with them, however, it is a good idea to explain the

---

57 Ibid.
58 Cristina Florentina Braia (2020), 'The history of cake: Has it lost its meaning?' Canadian Military Family Magazine.

context and meaning of the folklore you are including, otherwise they may be baffled.

Exercises and Journal Prompts

- **Research the folklore of your region or ethnic group,** and incorporate it into your seasonal festivals. Be sure to avoid cultural appropriation.

- **Research the concept of cultural appropriation** if you are unfamiliar with it. I have written about it extensively[59] (both online and in my previous books).

- **Reflect on what folklore means to you.** Do you feel a connection with it? Is it part of your Pagan practice?

---

59   Yvonne Aburrow, 'Cultural appropriation.' inclusive Wicca.

Meditation: Focus on a Symbol

Get comfortable. Have an example or a picture of your chosen symbol in front of you, if possible. Reflect on the many and varied meanings of your chosen symbol and why it is significant for you. Think back to all the contexts in which you have seen it or used it.

Ritual: Wassailing

Do this when the trees are just about to wake up in the spring. This can vary depending on the local climate.

Gather some friends and some objects for making noise (pots and pans, rattles, drums, shakers, etc.).

Make a wassail bowl (generally mulled cider[60] with stewed apples in it, which are known as lambswool). Add spices such as cinnamon sticks, ginger, and nutmeg.

Make some toast and cut it into small squares.

Choose a wassailing song. My favorite is "The Gower Wassail."[61]

Carry the wassail bowl to your nearest apple tree or orchard.

Sing your chosen wassailing song to the tree or orchard.

Pour some of the mulled cider from the wassail bowl near the roots of the apple tree. Pass the rest around among the wassailers (or use individual cups if you prefer).

Place the squares of toast in the branches of the apple tree (or trees). This is traditionally done as a gift for the robins. Consider replacing this with a seed cake, which will be better for the birds.

---

60   This can be alcoholic or non-alcoholic cider.
61   'Wassail Song / Gower Wassail' (Roud 209). Mainly Norfolk: English Folk and Other Good Music.

The Wheel of the Year

Recognizing these holidays as part of a never-
ending cycle is important. This cycle is repeated
in our weather, our light patterns, and our
growing and harvesting seasons externally.
Internally, it can also be reflected in our own lives.
We must have times of light and times of dark,
times of harvest and times of sowing, times of high
energy and times of quiet reflection. Celebrating
the wheel of the year allows us to recognize this in
our lives as well as balance our own energies with
those of the land.
　　　—Dana O'Driscoll, *The Druid's Garden* (2013)

The Sabbats are the eight points at which we
connect the inner and the outer cycles: the
interstices where the seasonal, the celestial, the
communal, the creative, and the personal all meet.
　　　—Starhawk, *The Spiral Dance* (1979)

An important aspect of contemporary Pagan paths is the
celebration of seasonal festivals. Different traditions name these
differently, or celebrate a different set of festivals—but each of these
traditions honors the principle of cyclicity and the idea that marking
specific holy days is valuable as a way of marking out time, observing
the seasons, connecting with Nature, and becoming aware of
internal changes within ourselves. Pagans observe the same festivals
year after year, but we never tire of them because we are different
every year. The people we celebrate with are also changing, the
ritual touches us differently every time, and the weather is different.

Many people see the wheel of the year as marking not only seasonal changes, but also internal shifts in mood. They tend to be more extroverted and physically active and outdoorsy in summer, and more introspective and quiet and likely to do handicraft activities indoors in the winter. This likely goes back to ancient times, when people spent the summer hunting and gathering to lay up a store of food for the winter, and then stayed indoors or near a fire during the winter.

There are several overlapping cycles reflected in the wheel of the year. There's the vegetation cycle (from seed, through seedling, leaf, blossom, fruit, to seed). There are changes associated with cattle and sheep (when they move from the high pastures in summer, down to the low pastures in winter; when they produce lambs and calves). There's the turning of the seasons (spring, summer, autumn, winter) and the four tides of the year. There are the solstices and equinoxes, reflecting the changes wrought by axial tilt and the Earth orbiting around the Sun. Each of these overlapping cycles contributes to the symbolism of the festivals.

There are also minor festivals that many people celebrate, such as Plough Monday, which is celebrated in areas where arable crops are the norm. It is said that when a farmer wanted to test if his fields were ready for plowing, he would place his bare bottom on the ground. If his butt cheeks did not freeze to the ground, then the field was ready for plowing.

Each festival on the year's wheel is a chance to pause and reflect and take stock of what has been, and to attempt to scry into what is to come. I do not believe in "living in the moment." While it does not help to dwell overmuch in the past, or to worry excessively about what is to come, it is good to reflect—take the omens, and enact rituals that connect us to the great sweeping currents of life and culture that root you in the past so that you can put forth branches into the future.

In the past, life was much more uncertain. You were more likely to witness the death of a loved one from hunger, illness, violence, or childbirth. You yourself might die. So taking the omens at moments of liminality when the veil between the worlds is thin was a matter of survival, not just a quaint parlor game. The same was true of building strong connections with your community: A person who was outcast from the community lost most of the things that made life bearable and survivable.

Now, people mourn the draining of meaning from the cultural commons, the enclosure of meaning in walled gardens, and the loss of cultural memory caused by the commercialization of the holidays, and assimilation to bland, generic whiteness. But you can recover the many layers of meaning and beautiful customs that are available from traditional festivals, and weave their magic and wonder once more into your life.

Imbolc, or Candlemas (February 2)

Imbolc is a festival celebrating the lactation of ewes, the coming of lambs, and the first stirrings of spring. The name is said to mean either "ewes milk" (Oimelc) or "in the belly" (im bolg). At this time in the British Isles, sheep are giving birth to lambs, and the trees start putting forth new growth, whose twigs are often red. Snowdrops are blooming. In other parts of the world, there is still a lot of snow lying on the ground, and flowers are a distant memory, so you may need to adapt the symbolism of your ritual to match your local climatic conditions.

The festival of Imbolc is celebrated by Druids, Wiccan, and many polytheists.

In Ireland, Imbolc is the feast of Brighid, originally a Goddess, and now a saint. The goddess Brighid is associated with healing, poetry, and smithcraft. I associate it with creativity and starting new projects. I usually celebrate it with poetry readings and honoring the goddess Brighid.

Saint Brighid is also associated with healing, poetry, and smithcraft, and with the perpetual flame tended by the nuns of Kildare—which possibly goes back to pre-Christian times. There are numerous folk customs and stories associated with Brighid.

In England, Brigantia (who may be the same goddess as Brighid) is the goddess of sovereignty and the land, so this could be a good time to celebrate regaining one's personal sovereignty or autonomy. There are several known inscriptions to her in the region associated with the Brigantes (a Celtic tribe in the north of England). She was interpreted by the Romans as being associated with victory. There are numerous places named after her all over Europe.·

Candlemas (also on February 2) is the Christian festival of the Purification of the Virgin, when Mary presented Jesus at the Temple forty days after his birth, to complete her purification after childbirth in accordance with the Torah. It is also the traditional date on which the church's candles were blessed for the coming year.

Both these festivals have traditionally focused on the increasing light and life as the days lengthen and the trees start to blossom and bud. They are also a celebration of goddesses.

For more than decade (from 2005 to at least 2017), there was an online poetry slam in honor of Brighid, so there are many poems about her online. You could celebrate Imbolc by holding an in-person poetry slam.

Many people celebrate Imbolc by making representations of Brighid and the traditional Irish Brighid's cross made from woven reeds. Representations of Brighid are traditionally a doll wrapped in white cloth and laid in a small bed with a club to represent the Dagda (the god of magic, druidry, wisdom, fertility, agriculture, and strength). The woven cross has rotational symmetry and is made by folding over reeds and tying them at the ends. If you want to avoid appropriation of Irish culture, you could investigate what sovereignty goddesses existed in your region and what customs were associated with them. You could also investigate the ancient Roman practices of purification associated with the month of February.

Lupercalia—February 15

The theme of February festivals in the ancient world was all about cleansing: honoring the ancestors through the festival of Parentalia[62] (a nine-day festival held in honor of family ancestors, beginning on February 13), and preparing for spring with a clean sweep through the festival of Lupercalia. The festival of Parentalia was celebrated by offering garlands of flowers, wheat, salt, bread soaked in wine, and violets to the spirits of the dead at family tombs, which were outside Rome's sacred perimeter.[63] Parentalia culminated in the rite of Feralia, when the head of the family had to make offerings to appease the dead.[64] It appears to have been organized by a different priesthood than Lupercalia.

Lupercalia was a fertility festival honoring the she-wolf who suckled Romulus and Remus. It also honored Lupercus, god of shepherds. The festivities were presided over by the priesthood of the Luperci, who were dedicated to Faunus. They sacrificed two

---

62   Mary Beard, J.A. North, and S.R.F. Price (1998), *Religions of Rome: A History*. Cambridge University Press, p. 50.
63   Ovid, *Fasti*, 2.534-539.
64   Georges Dumézil (1996), *Archaic Roman Religion: With an Appendix on the Religion of the Etruscans*. Baltimore, MD: Johns Hopkins University Press. p. 366.

goats and a dog. There was then a sacrificial feast, and the Luperci cut thongs called *februa* from the skins of the animals, dressed themselves in the skins of the sacrificed goats, and ran round the walls of the old Palatine city. They struck all those who came near with the thongs. Young women would line up on their route to receive lashes from the thongs. This was reputed to ensure fertility, prevent sterility, and ease the pains of childbirth.

There seem to be several themes running through Lupercalia:

- a celebration of wildness in the form of the wolf
- male bonding (whether in the form of friendship or same-sex love)
- purification and cleansing
- a celebration of Spring, fertility, new life, and childbirth (though fertility doesn't have to mean producing children—it can also mean creating new ideas and projects)
- the celebration of the founding of Rome (which could be extended to the founding of all cities)
- the relationship of city and countryside

The name of the month of February comes from the februa, which was any tool used for purification, including wool (used for cleaning), brooms, pine boughs, and so on. So if the other aspects of Lupercalia do not appeal to you, you could always celebrate Lupercalia by giving your house a thorough spring cleaning. It could also be interpreted as a celebration of consensual kink.

Spring Equinox (March 21)—Alban Eilir

At the Spring Equinox, day and night are equal, and after this the days will lengthen. It's also the time when the coming of spring is becoming apparent: The sap is rising in the trees, lambs are growing, the willow trees are putting out buds and catkins, and primroses are blooming.

The festival of Easter is frequently associated with hares, rabbits, and eggs, but there's some intriguing older symbolism involving foxes. Adrian Bott has researched the origins of this festival extensively and found traditions of the Easter Fox in some parts of Germany.[65]

The Old English did not celebrate the Spring Equinox. Insteads they honored the fourth full moon of the year, at which they ate roast beef.

According to Bede, the Old English heathens honored a goddess called Eostre. She was later conflated with Ostara by the Brothers Grimm, who said she was associated with hares and the Moon and eggs; however, there is no reference to this goddess in any other text, so much of the modern mythology associated with her is extrapolated from Bede, and has no basis in older mythology. That does not mean that it is not valid as mythology, just that people should not claim ancient origins for it.

Many contemporary Pagans celebrate the equinoxes, the time of year when day and night are of equal length. At the Spring Equinox, the days are getting longer; at the Autumn or Fall Equinox, the nights are getting longer. Rituals for this aspect of the festival can include personifications of darkness and light— pointing out that humanity needs both of them.

The Druid name for Spring Equinox is Alban Eilir, the Light of the Earth.[66] Druids associate the shamrock with this festival. It is

65   Adrian Bott (2009), 'Eostre: the making of a myth (part 1).' Cavalorn.

Adrian Bott (2009), 'Eostre: the making of a myth (part 2).' Cavalorn.

Adrian Bott (2013), 'Hunting the spurious Eostre Hare.' Cavalorn.

Adrian Bott (2014), 'Eostre, Ostara, and the Easter Fox.' Cavalorn.
66   Druidry.org (undated), 'Spring Equinox—Alban Eilir.' Order of Bards, Ovates, and Druids.

possible that the shamrock is the symbol of Ireland due to its earlier druidic symbolism, where it represented a sun-wheel or trignetra (also known as a triquetra). It can also be related to the symbol of the Awen, three rays or pillars of light, which is widely used as a symbol of druidry.

Fun activities to enliven your Spring Equinox ritual include painting eggs (a traditional craft all over Europe), an Easter egg hunt, making Easter bonnets, and building a nest for the Easter hare, fox, or other animal associated with Easter eggs in local folklore.

Beltane (May 1)

Beltane is a beautiful festival, the start of the growing tide and the festival of spring, of lovers, and of reawakening. It is a festival of unabashed sexuality, where people dance around a giant flower-bedecked phallic symbol and leap naked over the Beltane fire, hand in hand with their beloved, or their lover of the moment. There are lingering caresses in the woods, under the blossoms and the boughs. Firelight plays on ecstatic dancing bodies, lost in the ecstasy of sexual abandon. The contemporary celebration of Beltane seems to have acquired quite a lot of its character from the Roman festival of Floralia (April 27/28), which also celebrated sexual pleasure and flowers.

In Scotland and the north of England, Beltane was celebrated by leaping over bonfires. In the south of England, it was celebrated by erecting and dancing around maypoles.

Beltane is celebrated by Druids, Wiccan, and many other Pagan traditions.

The symbolism of Beltane should not be heterocentric. Couples and groups of lovers of any gender can jump over the bonfire or dance around the maypole.

Ritual facilitators can devise rituals for people who are asexual which celebrate bees pollinating flowers, and/or the blossoming of new ideas and art.

Some pastoralists would drive their cattle between two bonfires, so you could make the bonfire-leaping more accessible by having two bonfires, allowing those who cannot leap over the bonfire to run/walk/wheel between the two fires.

Beltane rituals can celebrate all forms of love, and they celebrate deities of both same-sex and different-sex love. The tradition of Robin Hood's Games in the English Midlands involved building bowers for Robin Hood and Maid Marian, but you could also build a bower for Will Scarlet and Alan à Dale. Our coven has built bowers for Beltane a few times, and it is a lot easier than erecting a maypole.

But spare a thought for those who do not quite fit into this idyllic picture. What about people who are single? Being single at Beltane is no fun: hanging around the Beltane fire, hoping that romance will be kindled by the energies of Beltane. What about the widowed? Those who have loved long and well and have lost the ones they love? What about the divorced, the abused, and the traumatized? What about asexuals—what are they supposed to do with a festival that harps on and on about sex? And if the focus is mainly or exclusively on cisgender heterosexual lovers, spare a thought for lesbian, gay, bisexual, transgender, and nonbinary people, too, and enlarge the focus of the celebration to include same-sex love. What about the frequent portrayal of the God and Goddess of Beltane as white? How about including some lovers of color? And what about people with disabilities? Other than physicality or communication styles, they are no different from the rest of us in their sexual, emotional, and romantic desires. Beltane, with its themes of excess and wild abandon, can also be difficult for people in recovery, who may feel the need to set boundaries.[67]

Author Molly Khan points out that the theme of sexual love is not understandable to children, and suggests other ways of celebrating Beltane if you have kids. She includes themes of creativity, being passionate about an activity or a cause, and talking about other kinds of love, such as friendship and familial love, not just the erotic or romantic variety.[68]

Midsummer, or Summer Solstice (June 21)—Alban Hefin

Midsummer is a festival celebrating the Sun. At this time of the year, the days are at their longest, so the Sun is said to be at the height of its power. However, after Midsummer, the days will get shorter, so the Sun is said (symbolically) to descend into the underworld. The Sun is a metaphor for our consciousness; as you descend into the depths of winter, the self goes inward and becomes more introspective.

A celebration of Midsummer could focus on the aspects related to consciousness, and emphasize the shift from outward to inward preoccupations.

At Summer Solstice, the Sun rises at the same point on the horizon for about three days, and in the Northern Hemisphere, that point is the northernmost point at which it rises (it's the other way around in the Southern Hemisphere). The name solstice means "Sun stands still" which refers to the Sun rising at the same point on the horizon.

I tend to associate the summer solstice with the Grail Mysteries, which are associated with Parsifal and the Fisher King, a legend in which two men together restore fertility to the land. Our ritual for this festival includes a symbolic journey to the castle of the Grail.

---

67   Jenya T Beachy (2015), 'Danger and Delight in the Season of Sex.' Dirt Heart Witch.
68   Molly Khan (2015), 'Beltane for Kids.' The Pagan Families Blog.

LGBTQIA+ Pride celebrations usually occur at some point during the tide of growing, which is symbolically apt given the growing confidence, pride, and power of the LGBTQIA+ community.

Midsummer is sometimes known as Litha. The name Litha was added to the contemporary Pagan wheel of the year by Aidan Kelly in 1974, but the Old English called the two months either side of Summer Solstice "Aerre Litha" and "Aeftere Litha," so it follows that the Old English probably called Midsummer "Litha," by analogy with the fact that they called the months either side of the winter solstice "Aerre Geola" and "Aeftere Geola," and they called the Winter Solstice Geola.

The Druid name for Midsummer is Alban Hefin, the Light of the Summer or the Light of the Shore. The shore is a liminal place, and the solstice is a liminal time. The tides of the year start to ebb after the Summer Solstice, hence the association with the shore, where the tides of the sea ebb and flow.[69]

Symbols for Midsummer include sunflowers, St John's Wort (John the Baptist was associated with Midsummer in Christian mythology), red and orange fruit, and fire.

Lammas (August 1)—Lughnasadh

The old English name Lammas comes from *hlafmass* ('loaf-mass'). This is the festival of harvesting the oats, wheat, and barley, and it is the start of the reaping tide.

The Irish name Lughnasadh is associated with the god Lugh and his foster-mother Tailtiu, who plowed the whole of Ireland and then died; Lugh established a festival of games in her honor. The Druids celebrate Lughnasadh.[70]

---

69   Mara Freeman (undated), 'Summer Solstice—Alban Hefin.' Order of Bards, Ovates, and Druids.
70   Eilthireach (undated), 'Lughnasadh—Harvest Festival.' Order of Bards, Ovates, and Druids.

Contemporary Lammas rituals often commemorate the death of John Barleycorn, the dying and resurrecting vegetation god. Singing the song about him is very effective. According to Scottish anthropologist and folklorist J.G. Frazer, the corn[71] was believed to be inhabited by the corn-spirit, which was killed at every harvest and resurrected in the planting of the new corn. The harvest is an important symbol of cyclicity, growth, and change. The wheel turns, and what has grown must die, so that the seeds can be planted for the new cycle of growth.

Inspired by this folklore, I devised a chasing game for Lammas, where half the participants are the reapers and half are the corn. One person is the hare, who is the spirit of the corn, hiding from the reapers. The job of the corn people in the game is to hide the hare; the job of the reapers is to catch him.

Another ritual I devised one year was the creation of silent tableaux or mimes representing the themes of Lammas and the story of John Barleycorn. These were very moving.

Many Pagans bake bread and brew beer for the festival of Lammas, and they hold games in honor of the god Lugh and his foster mother. These could include cheese-rolling (rolling a round cheese to see who can get it to go the furthest), gurning (competing to see who can create the silliest or ugliest facial expression), and welly-wanging (lobbing Wellington boots backwards over your shoulder to see who can throw them the farthest). Making corn dollies is also popular.

---

71   In England and Wales, corn is a catch-all term for wheat, barley, and oats. Not to be confused with maize or sweetcorn (Zea mays).

Autumnal Equinox (September 21)—Alban Elued, or Alban Elfed

At Autumnal Equinox, day and night are again equal in length, but the nights are getting longer, so most rituals focus on this and on the importance of balance. A celebration of Autumnal Equinox could focus on the sensual delights of food and the harvest of work and creativity, as well as the balance of light and dark. Many people like to enact the story of Hades and Persephone as a ritual drama.

In British folk traditions, there are three harvests: the corn harvest at Lammas; the fruit harvest at Autumnal Equinox; and the harvest of meat at Samhain, when some of the cattle would have been slaughtered and preserved for the winter. As Autumnal Equinox is the fruit harvest, I associate it with the story of Pomona, goddess of apple orchards, and Vertumnus, god of the turning seasons and the autumn winds. Pomona was courted by several woodland gods, but wasn't interested in any of them. Vertumnus disguised himself as an old woman and came courting her, telling her of what a handsome chap Vertumnus was. Then she was interested, adding some interestingly queer overtones to this story.

The idea of referring to the Autumnal Equinox as "Mabon" was devised in 1974 by Aidan Kelly.[72] He was looking for a northern European myth that resembled the myth of Persephone, which has often been associated with the Autumnal Equinox. Mabon (pronounced with a short "a" as in "cat") is a character from the Welsh story-cycle known as *The Mabinogion*. He was not associated with the Autumnal Equinox by the Celts. Many people now refer to the Autumnal Equinox as Mabon, but it is good to be aware that this practice is not ancient.

---

72 Aidan Kelly (2017), 'About Naming Ostara, Litha, and Mabon.' Including Paganism.

The dance of the seasons illustrates the dynamic balance of opposites. The wheel of the year turns, falling in the autumn and rising in the spring. As it falls in the autumn, and the nights draw in, people turn inward, toward home and hearth and spiritual things; baking and making jam and wine; creative projects.

The Druid name for this festival is Alban Elfed (the light of the water). They celebrate it as a harvest festival.[73]

A great way to celebrate the Autumnal Equinox is to gather apples and blackberries and make apple pie or apple and blackberry crumble or crisp. This is a time of year when everything is shutting down for the winter, so making nourishing foods and storing them for the cold days to come is a very satisfying activity.

Samhain (October 31)—Samhuinn

Contemporary Pagans associate Samhain with death and the ancestors, but the ancient Celts associated it with liberation from oppression. It is also the time when the cattle would be slaughtered and salted down for the winter, so it is the last of the three harvest festivals. It is said to be a time when the veil between the worlds is thin, and the ancestors and beloved dead can come visiting. Many Wiccans use Samhain rituals to honor, remember, and commune with loved ones who have passed on. For LGBTQIA+ people, it can also be a time to celebrate queer ancestors.

In East Anglia, this festival was known as Hollantide. In other areas, it was called Hallowstide.

Samhain is the "harvest of meat" when cattle would be slaughtered before the winter. Samhain is the Irish word for the month of November. The ancient Irish festival held at this time

---

73   Coifi (undated), 'Autumn Equinox—Alban Elfed.' Order of Bards, Ovates, and Druids. https://druidry. org/druid-way/teaching-and-practice/druid-festivals/autumn-equinox-alban-elfed

was about the renewal of freedom; the legends associated with it tell of heroes who freed their people from bondage. So the association with the dead was probably imported by Christianity, as this was the feast of All Saints and All Souls. After the Reformation, of course, the importance of these festivals was downplayed, and by the early twentieth century, folklorists were speculating that the origins of All Hallows were actually Pagan. The first stirrings of the Pagan Revival started in the early twentieth century, so the idea of Samhain being associated with the dead was imported into the Pagan Revival.

Pagans tend to focus on the preciousness of this life—not some future one beyond death. We want to celebrate and remember the lives of our ancestors. Ancestors can be relatives and friends who have died, or people from the past that we admire. We often honor both. These people have shaped who we are now—given us life, given us inspiration, guided us, comforted us, and nurtured us— and it comforts us to remember them and commune with them. The concept of ancestors of spirit overlaps with the idea of queer ancestors, who are LGBTQIA+ people from the past who inspire us with their heroic resistance and moments of joy.

Many people believe in reincarnation, and hold that the consciousness resides in an in-between place between lives. In Paganism, the dead are seen as not being very far away, and many Pagans say that "the veil between the worlds is thin" at Samhain, because the tides of life are on the ebb as winter approaches, and because the encroaching darkness of winter is seen as a time for contemplation, remembrance, and introspection.

Pagans do not see darkness and death as evil, but as part of the cycle of life, death, and rebirth. If there was no death, there would be no growth, no change, and no birth. If there was no darkness, the seeds could not gestate in the warm darkness of the earth; if there was no night, there would be no sleep, and no stars and moonlight. If there was no winter cold, there would be none of the beauty of autumn, the seeds would not germinate, and germs and pests would not be killed by the frost. Darkness is the yin spoken of by the Taoists—one half of the divine dance of the cosmos.

Samhain or Hallowe'en is part of the dance of the elements around the wheel of the seasons, one of the many interlocking cosmic cycles of which our lives are an intimate part.

In many cultures, especially in Mexico, All Souls is the Day of the Dead—Día de los Muertos—when people go to visit the graves of departed family members and set up altars for them in the home. This is not a morbid practice, but an acknowledgment of death in the midst of life, of death as part of the natural cycle.

Why should you reintegrate Samhain or Hollantide into your spiritual practice? Because in Western culture, death is swept under the carpet, ignored and feared. If you acknowledge it (at least once in the year), it becomes an invitation to live more fully and mindfully. If you ignore it, it becomes part of the shadow, the part of your psyche that you reject and that contains your fears and follies. People then project those rejected parts onto other people: the Other, the outsider, the transgressor. If you recognize death as being part of the natural cycle, like the seasons of the year, then you can live a more integrated life.

Samhain is also the time when, as the nights get longer and winter grips the land, people descend into their own depths. Summer is a time for being extroverted, creative and expansive; winter is a time for curling up by the fireside and going within the self to find the poetic, the spiritual and the quiet side of ourselves—the forgotten aspects, or perhaps even the side of ourselves that we have repressed and need to examine.

The presiding deity of winter is the Crone Goddess. She has been feared and denigrated in recent centuries (people speak of old wives' tales, haggard old witches muttering in corners, and so on). But traditionally, old women were the ones who were the keepers of traditional wisdom such as stories, herb lore and midwifery. She is the midwife and the one who washed, anointed and laid out the dead. She is the one who cuts the cord of life and of death. She represents merciful release but she also possesses the wisdom of old age. Wisdom is traditionally represented as a feminine being or quality. Wisdom is the joining together of instinct and experience and knowledge. It is the wisdom of the body, the knowledge of when to act and when to refrain from acting, when to speak and when to keep silent. Wisdom comes from reflection upon experience and knowledge.

The Crone is also the Goddess of the Waning Moon, which represents a time of letting go and ebbing away, so it is traditional at Samhain to let go of aspects of your life that you do not need or want anymore.

In Druidry, Samhain is known by the same name, sometimes spelled Samhuinn.[74] The Cailleach (the Scottish goddess of winter) causes the leaves to fall from the trees, speeding the decay of summer's bounty to feed the new life to come. Many people ask Her to take away the painful aspects of their experiences, so that these too might be transformed like compost.

One of the ways that I like to observe Samhain is to invite people to bring photographs of their beloved dead and share stories about them. Most people find this very healing.

---

74   Susa Morgan Black (undated), 'Samhain—Rituals and Traditions.' Order of Bards, Ovates, and Druids.

Yule, the Winter Solstice (December 21)—Alban Arthan

Yule is a turning point in the year. In a way, this is true of every festival in the Pagan wheel of the year, but it is said that the word Yule means a turning point.

There are many facets of Yule. There is the anarchic element of mumming, Saturnalia, the bean king, boy bishops, the lord of misrule, the inversion of the usual order of things. This aspect seems to be inspired by the concept of turning, and of liminality: being on the threshold, being neither one thing nor the other. The twelve days of Yuletide are intercalary days, making up the difference between the lunar year and the solar year.[75] That certainly contributes to a feeling of liminality.

The most significant thing about Yule for our ancestors was probably that it is dark and cold outside, and the best response to that is to lurk indoors and make lots of nourishing food, light the candles, and snuggle up under blankets and furs. This response to the season still exists in the popular Danish concept of *hygge* (comfort, coziness, and good cheer), and in the urge to deck your house with as many fairy lights as possible. It is the darkest it is going to get throughout the year, and the days will start to get longer after the solstice. Axial tilt is the reason for the season, after all.

Yule is mysterious and uncanny. In many ancient mythologies, the Sun descends into the underworld. A descent into the darkness of the underworld is a chancy endeavor, as the stories of Tammuz, Orpheus, Eurydice, Inanna, and many others make clear. Many other cultures have stories where the Sun does not return and the animals or birds have to bring fire to humans or bring the Sun back.

---

75   Fair Folk Podcast (2022), The Twelve Days: December Almanac.

There are numerous stories of Sun gods being born at Yule, a highly significant event in Northern latitudes where the Sun struggles to get above the horizon.

The uncanny nature of Yule is very well illustrated by the story of *Gawain and the Green Knight*, the mysteries of mummers' plays enacted by Morris sides all over Britain, the first-footing customs of the New Year, the stories of making a king for the duration of Yuletide (probably based on the Saturnalian idea of inverting the usual hierarchy), and the tradition of ghost stories at Christmas (a tradition whose origins are lost, but which makes sense when you consider that the winter solstice is the darkest time of the year[76]).

Yuletide is the turning point of the old year becoming the new. That's why Janus, the doorkeeper, is represented with two faces and is associated with Cardea, the goddess of the hinge. The threshold, the doorstep, is an edgy space—neither public nor private, neither in nor out. That's why wassailers and mummers and carollers and guisers (trick-or-treaters) come only as far as your doorstep. There's a sense that anything could happen; the Otherworld might very well break in upon our world. The light breaks through the crack in the burial mound, the harbinger of the Sun returning from the deep.

Any liminal time is an opportunity for normal constraints to be loosed, and Yule is no exception to this rule. The German custom of letting loose the Krampus is an illustration of this principle, and the anarchic spirit of Krampusnacht seems to feed a yearning in people for this anarchic and chaotic aspect of Yule. And don't forget the wondrous and awe-inspiring Mari Lwyd of Wales, a horse's skull with a white robe carried on a pole, who pokes her bony nose into houses at this time of year.

---

76   Elizabeth Yuko (2021), "How Ghost Stories Became a Christmas Tradition in Victorian England." History Channel.

But that sense of liminality, otherness, and strangeness can also give rise to a more reflective mood. This is where old customs like Modranecht, or the Swedish custom known as the Årsgång (Year Walk), serve to create a space for going inward. On Modranecht, people reflect on female ancestors, known as the Disir—a subtly different practice than focusing on ancestors in general. The Year Walk is a silent walk that is meant to foretell the year to come. Research archivist and author Tommy Kuusela writes:

> In Sweden, one oracular method was a ritual
> known as year walk, and those who ventured
> on this perilous journey were known as year
> walkers. Success meant that the omen-seeker
> could acquire knowledge of the following year;
> it was a ritual that sought answers regarding the
> unbearable uncertainty of being. [77]

The person engaging in the Year Walk must leave the house and walk silently to the nearest graveyard, noting any unusual phenomena that they see along the way. These phenomena will be omens for the events of the year to come, according to Kuusela:

> ...it is said that if someone before firstlight on
> Christmas Eve goes into a forest without saying
> a word, without looking back, without looking
> into a fire, without food and drink, and so far
> that the crowing of a cock cannot be heard,
> they can walk on church roads and see all of
> the funeral procession of the coming year, and
> by looking at the fields, they will see how the

---

[77]   Tommy Kuusela (2016), 'He met his own funeral procession': The Year walk-ritual in Swedish folk tradition.' Academia.edu. Chapter in: Folk Belief and Traditions of the Supernatural. Edited by Tommy Kuusela & Giuseppe Maiello. Beewolf Press 2016, pp. 58–91.

> harvest will turn out and if and where there will
> be fires as well as other things that will come to
> pass. [78]

In other cultures there are divinatory customs associated with Halloween, so it is very likely the liminal quality of festivals that makes them particularly suited to divination.

At Yule, the Sun rises at the same point on the horizon for about three days, and in the Northern Hemisphere, that point is the southernmost point at which it rises (it is the other way around in the Southern Hemisphere). The name Yule possibly means "turning point," in which case it refers to the Sun appearing to move northwards after the solstice. Hence the line in Rudyard Kipling's "A Tree Song": "the sun has come up from the south." One possible ritual is to carry a candle or lamp representing the Sun around the perimeter of the circle, from the South to the East, to represent the apparent journey of the Sun around the horizon.

Because the Sun appears to be reborn at the winter solstice, this festival is often associated with birth and rebirth. But there are many cultures around the world that have a Sun goddess instead of a Sun god, and some people talk about the rebirth of the light instead of a literal birth. One ritual that I like to do is have everyone "give birth" to everyone else, regardless of gender, by having everyone in a ritual form an arch or tunnel, which everyone else walks through. The people at the back of the tunnel go through first and then join the arch at the other end, so everyone gets to go through the same length of tunnel.

Tommy Kuusela (2016), 'He met his own funeral procession': The Year walk-ritual in Swedish folk tradition.' Academia.edu. Chapter in: Folk Belief and Traditions of the Supernatural. Edited by Tommy Kuusela & Giuseppe Maiello. Beewolf Press 2016, pp. 58–91.

In terms of the vegetation cycle, this is the time when seeds are resting, lying in the ground and germinating, so you could work that symbolism into your ritual.

Many of the customs associated with the winter solstice originated in ancient Pagan festivals. Bringing greenery into the house at the solstice was a custom in several ancient cultures. The Christmas tree was first recorded in the 1600s, but the Yule log seems to date to pre-Christian times. The exchange of gifts was practiced by the Romans for Saturnalia. Another ancient custom that derives from Saturnalia is the choosing of the Lord of Misrule. The god Saturn was seen as a bringer of chaos and the inversion of the usual social order, so people would choose a Lord of Misrule to preside over a night of anarchy and playfulness.

The Druid name for the winter solstice is Alban Arthan[79], the Light of Winter. It can also be Alban Arthuan, the Light of Arthur, or the light of the constellation of the Great Bear. The Druid symbolism reflects the rebirth of the Sun or the hero of light, who can be represented as King Arthur.

Yuletide is especially rich in customs and folklore, partly because it was a time to stay indoors, make merry, tell stories, and do divination for the year ahead. One of the German names for the twelve days between Christmas and Epiphany is Rauhnächte (Smoke Nights or Rough Nights) and these nights were held to be a time when people could foretell the future.[80] They were a time when the Wild Hunt would sweep across the land, and Frau Perchte and Herr Wode would appear. Frau Perchte was a mother goddess figure who rode across the fields

---

79   Druidry.org (undated), 'Winter Solstice—Alban Arthan.' Order of Bards, Ovates, and Druids.
80   Kathrin Reikowski and Veronika Baum (2023), 'Zwischen Weihnachten und dem 6. Januar: Rauhnächte—Eine wilde Zeit "zwischen den Jahren."' BR Kinder.

in a golden chariot. Herr Wode was the leader of the hosts of the dead, and people feared being carried off by his procession of spirits. People would burn incense to ward off harmful beings (hence the name smoke nights), but the name Rauhnächte may also refer to the rough hairy beings who walk abroad at this time, like Krampus.

The glittering stars of Yule shine down upon the Mari Lwyd, the mummers, the Wassailers, the Krampuses, the first footers, and the birth of Mithras in a cave. They shine on the holly leaves, the red berries, and the drop of blood in the snow. They shine upon Old Father Frost and the Cailleach and Mother Holda, painting the land with frost and snow. And they shine upon the Christmas Truce of 1914, when the soldiers realized that they had more in common with each other than with the establishments they were fighting for.

May all your Yuletides be blessed with the spirit of anarchy, camaraderie, liminality, the wildwood, the old gods, feasting, and creativity.

Modranecht, Mōdraniht, or Mother's Night—December 24

Modranecht, Mōdraniht, or Mother's Night, the traditional festival honoring the Disir or female ancestors, takes place on 24 December.

Mōdraniht involves communing with the Dísir, the Matronae (ancient European mother goddesses), and our own female ancestors. If you are alienated from your biological ancestors, you can connect with ancestors of spirit (people you admire) instead.

If you have an ancestor altar or a hearth, you can sit by it with a glass of your favorite tipple (even better if it is also their favorite tipple). Don't forget to pour them a glass too, and you can also share food and treats that they especially liked.[81]

Then you can look at photos of your female ancestors, and speak their names, praise their qualities and their deeds, and spend time communing with them.

If you don't have an ancestor altar, you can make one or just cover a table with a clean cloth and place photos of your ancestors on it, together with snacks that they liked and a candle.

Why female ancestors specifically? I think it corrects an imbalance, in that people tend to think more about male ancestors than they do about female ones. In ancient times, women's contribution to society was highly valued. Marc writes on the *Of Axe and Plough* blog:

> Female figures in Anglo-Saxon lore and culture
> are commonly associated with similar themes:
> of hospitality (women offering drink, regardless
> of their social station), magic, prophecy and
> fate, spinning, representations of wealth, and
> the maintenance of societal or family order,
> all of which reflect a cross-cultural continuity
> across the Celto-Germanic spectrum.[82]

The first time my husband and I celebrated Mōdraniht, we came up with the idea of connecting with your last Pagan ancestor—the last member of your direct ancestry who was a practicing ancient pagan. You will never know their name, but you can connect with them in spirit.

---

81   Joanna van der Hoeven (2020), 'Mothers' Night/Mōdraniht.' (Heathen on the Heath Series).
82   Marc (2017), 'Mōdru and Mōdraniht.' Of Axe and Plough.

Marc at the *Of Axe and Plough* blog also suggests honoring Frīg Heorþmōdor (Frigga Hearth-Mother), "as fate spinner and seeress, in hopes of a fortuitous coming year and a healthy passage through the winter season."

New Year's Eve—December 31

New Year's Eve is a liminal moment: the end of one year and the beginning of another. It is strange then that our culture has forgotten many of the customs and traditions that made this turning-point memorable.

New Year's Eve is not one of the major festivals of the contemporary Pagan wheel of the year (many people regard Samhain as the Pagan New Year), but it has many fascinating customs associated with it.

New Year's Eve can be an occasion to honor Janus, the Roman god of January, who looks forward and backward, and a related goddess, Cardea, the goddess of the hinge.

I have two favorite New Year rituals: First Footing and Bridge of Light.

At Bridge of Light, people light a rainbow of candles, each one representing an aspect of consciousness, kindled in the liminal time between the end of the one year and the beginning of the next. The festival creates a space for the celebration of queer spirituality, queer lives, and queer joy.

Bridge of Light was founded by Joe Perez in 2004, and further developed by Kittredge Cherry. Cherry is an author, art historian, and minister in the Metropolitan Community Church (a church founded by and for LGBTQ+ people) and Perez is a writer on queer spirituality and author of Soulfully Gay. It is intended as an interfaith celebration; you do not have to belong to any particular tradition or subscribe to any belief system to practice it; it is a celebration of queerness. If cisgender and heterosexual people want to do it, they should acknowledge and affirm and celebrate its queer origins.

First Footing is a custom in Scotland, the Isle of Man, and Northern England.[83]

Since the first person to set foot over your threshold after midnight is a portent of the year to come, you want them to be a person of good omen, bringing magical items to ensure a successful year ahead. Hence the custom of the first foot and the New Year luck bag.

The New Year luck bag should contain:

- A piece of coal (or wood) so that you'll have enough fuel for heating throughout the year
- A leaf of holly (or other evergreen) so you'll have luck throughout the year.
- Some money, so you'll have money throughout the year
- A piece of bread, so you'll not go hungry throughout the year

The bag should be brought over your threshold by the first person to set foot in your house after midnight. This person is called the first foot, and is traditionally a man with dark hair. This is a Scottish tradition but it seems to be fairly widespread.

You can keep the money and the coal for next year's bag, but replace the bread and the holly each year. I usually add a bit more money each year.

Keep the bag in whatever you consider to be the heart of your house (kitchen, hearth, airing cupboard, or furnace)

---

83 Jacqueline Simpson and Steve Roud (2000), 'New Year.' A Dictionary of English Folklore. Oxford University Press.

There are many different New Year's traditions from around the world that can be categorized as taking the omens for the following year; seeking to ensure that you will have luck for the year; and sending the spirit of the old year away, and welcoming in the new.

Many people sing "Auld Lang Syne" at New Year (especially if they have a connection to Scotland). Hogmanay is the Scottish celebration of New Year, and First Footing is an important part of the Hogmanay celebrations.

In Spain and other Spanish-speaking countries, they have the Twelve Lucky Grapes, or *las doce uvas de la suerte*:

> To ensure good luck for the next year, people eat one green grape for each of the upcoming twelve months. However, you cannot just eat the grapes during the first day of the new year any time you feel like it. You must eat the twelve grapes starting at the first stroke of midnight on Nochevieja ("Old Night," New Year's Eve) as one year changes to another. And you have to keep eating: with each toll of midnight, you must eat another grape, giving you about twelve seconds to consume all of them. If you can finish all dozen grapes—you can't still be chewing on them!—before the last bell toll fades, you will have a luck-filled new year.[84]

It is also a custom that you have to be wearing red underwear that was given to you as a gift, though no one is sure how that started.

The Southern US custom of eating Hoppin' John with collard greens possibly stems from the more general idea that you should

---

84   '12 Grapes For 12 Months: An Unusual New Year's Tradition.' Advantage Air Tech blog.

eat round foods (especially fruit) at New Year.[85] It is also an example of the creative food ways brought to North America by Africans.[86]

In Denmark, people leave broken crockery on each other's doorsteps (sometimes it gets thrown at the house). People save their broken crockery throughout the year to use it for this custom on New Year's Eve.[87]

In Italy, people throw their old furniture out of the window (usually soft items like cushions and blankets).

In Ecuador, people fill scarecrows with paper at midnight on New Year's Eve and then set fire to them, along with any old photographs that represent bad memories. This is thought to help banish the misfortunes of the past year.

In Greece, people hang bunches of onions outside their front doors for luck on New Year's Eve and then wake their children on New Year's morning by gently bumping them on the head with the onions. New Year's Day is the feast day of Saint Basil, so families get together and eat a sweet cake called Vasilopita. A coin is hidden in it, and whoever gets the slice with the coin gets the luck.[88]

There's a custom in many countries of opening the windows to let the old year out. This could be a bit chilly in some climates.

Many countries have customs for driving away bad spirits at New Year. In Ireland, they bang Christmas bread against the walls of the houses; in Puerto Rico, they dump a bucket of water out of the window.

---

85   Stephanie Butler (2012, 2020), 'Hoppin' John: A New Year's Tradition.' HISTORY.
86   Jessica B. Harris (2012), High on the Hog: A Culinary Journey from Africa to America. Bloomsbury USA.
87   Lisa Joyner (2020), '8 Unusual New Year's Eve Traditions From Around The World.' Country Living.
88   Victoria Loutas (2020), 'All you need to know about Greek New Year's Eve customs and traditions.' Greek Herald.

In ancient Rome, the early part of January was called the Kalends of January and was associated with three deities: Cardea, the goddess of hinges, Forculus, the god of doorways, and Limentinus, the god of thresholds. These deities were associated with marking out space and boundaries—an important consideration in agricultural societies.[89]

It has been suggested that these three deities were the doorkeepers who guarded the doorways between the earthly realm and the otherworld. These heavenly doorways were called the *ianuae coeli*, and identified with the solstices.[90] As well as referring to the hinge of a door, the cardo was an important concept in Roman surveying and city planning. The main north-south street of a town or an army camp was called the *cardo*. When surveyors first laid out a town, the surveying of the *cardo* was accompanied by rituals and auguries to align earth and heaven. The gates of the town or camp were aligned with the cardinal points of the compass and the word cardinal is derived from *cardo*.

So here you have the idea that the plan of a city, and even the plan of a military camp, should echo the design of the heavens: the microcosm reflecting the macrocosm. This seems to be a key idea in ancient Pagan and animist thought, that harmonious living involves the ritual repetition of cosmic themes. This is the reason that Wiccans cast a circle and call the quarters—to create a harmonious microcosm in which we can perform our magic.

The principles of animism are also apparent in this description of the door deities and spirits—there's a deity of the threshold, the hinges, the door, and the doorway. Animism is the view that everything has a spirit, so why not a spirit presiding over each aspect of the door and the doorway?

---

89 CM McDonough (1997), "Carna, Proca, and the Strix on the Kalends of June", Transactions of the American Philological Association, 127.
90 Stefan Weinstock (1946), "Martianus Capella and the Cosmic System of the Etruscans", Journal of Roman Studies 36, p. 106. https://www.jstor.org/stable/i213258

Janus is the god with two faces who looks forward to the New Year and backward to the Old Year, so he is the doorkeeper of the year and the god of doorways more generally. The month of January is named for him. He is also the god of beginnings, gates, transitions, time, birth, journeys, duality, doorways, passages, frames, and endings. He was associated with Portunus, a similar harbor and gateway god concerned with travel, trade, and shipping.

Janus ruled the beginning and ending of conflict, and hence war and peace. There was an enclosure with gates at each end in Rome named after him whose gates were opened at the start of a war and closed in times of peace.

There are many traditional practices associated with the New Year, including house cleaning and tidying, taking stock of the old year, and making New Year's resolutions.

You could honor Cardea by oiling the hinges on your doors, Limentinus by sweeping your threshold clean, Forculus by polishing the doorknobs, and Janus by going for a walk on New Year's Day. And Janus can be honored all year round.

I find these minor Roman deities very interesting, perhaps because they represent an intricate mythological representation of the cosmos, but also because of the possibilities for developing an animistic worldview.

The Four Tides of the Year

- **Resting** (from Samhain to Imbolc): during the late autumn/early winter, when everything lies still in the earth. Psychologically, this is when people sit by the fireside and tell tales, going within themselves.

- **Cleansing** (from Imbolc to Beltane): during the late winter/early spring, when the frost breaks down the earth and decayed matter. February was the month of cleansing in ancient Rome. Psychologically, it's time for a clearing of old habits, for a spring-cleaning of the house.

- **Growing** (from Beltane to Lammas): late spring/early summer, everything is growing. Psychologically, it's the time of new projects, of branching out into new ideas, of being creative and extrovert.

- **Reaping** (from Lammas to Samhain): the time of harvest, when the fruit and corn ripen and can be gathered in. Psychologically, it's the time of bringing things to completion and fruition.

The wheel of the year is a modern construct—no ancient cultures celebrated all of the festivals celebrated by contemporary Pagans—but it is a deeply satisfying way of engaging with the seasons, marking the passing of time, and getting in touch with Nature.

Meditation: The Turning Wheel

Visualize a wheel, or use an actual physical wheel. Turn the wheel in your hands. As you turn it, visualize the ebb and flow of the seasons and the movement of the sun around the horizon. If you have a situation in your life that feels stagnant to you, you can visualize the wheel getting unstuck from a rut and moving to ease the flow of the situation that needs resolving.

Exercises and Journal Prompts

- **Keep nature notes.** When you go for a walk, make a note of the flowers, fungi, birds, butterflies, animals, and trees that you see. Note the date, the temperature, and the weather conditions. What is in bloom? What birds have arrived on their migrations? Did a particular flower or tree bloom earlier or later last year?

- **Localize your seasonal rituals.** Include your local flora and fauna and climatic conditions in your rituals.

- **Make or obtain a wheel.** You can then use this to "turn the wheel" during your seasonal celebrations.

- **Identify your ancestors.** Research your family ancestors—these are your "ancestors of blood." Find out about the queer ancestors, the LGBTQIA+ people of the past, their stories, and their struggles. Identify people whom you admire—these are your "ancestors of spirit." Find out about the people who lived in the area where you live now—these are your "ancestors of place." Gather images to represent these ancestors, and build an altar for Samhain.

- **Research seasonal customs and foods.** Find out about the seasonal rituals, customs, stories, and food of your ancestors of spirit, blood, and place. Build these stories, practices, and foods into your seasonal rituals.

- **Be inclusive.** Does your ritual practice and symbolism include everyone who wants to take part? Check to make sure it is not ableist, racist, sexist, ciscentric, or heterocentric.

Ritual: The Three Norns

Roles: Urð, Skuld, Verðandi, Heimdall, the völva, traveller.

Setup: Create your ritual space as you normally would. If you do not have a usual method of setting up your ritual space, you can start the ritual with soft drumming.

> **The völva:** You stand upon a cliff
> At the edge of Middle-Earth,
> looking out across the yawning gap.
> Here ice and fire met, mingled
> and brought forth life.
> The rainbow bridge spans the gap,
> an arch of many-coloured light.

[drumming]

> **Heimdall:** I am the guardian of the bridge.
> My hearing so acute that I can hear the grass growing,
> My sight is so keen that I can see all the way to the end of the world.
> I carry the yelling horn to warn of doom,
> the horn that drew water from Mimir's Well.
> If you wish to pass, you must tell me your name.

All tell Heimdall your names.

> **The völva:** You stand now at the Well of Wyrd,
> where the Three Norns weave the fate of the worlds.

(one person can be all three Norns, but wear three different masks—turn away from the rest of the group and change masks in between speeches)

Urðr: I am the Norn of fate,
I see the hidden causes of events.
I weave the web of wyrd.

[drumming]

Skuld: I am the Norn of debts,
I weave the threads of the past
Into the design of the future.

[drumming]

Verðandi: I am the Norn of becoming,
I weave the present moment
in its many hidden happenings.

[drumming]

The völva: You may gaze into the Well of Wyrd
Where the swans float on the surface of the
waters.Every day the gods come here to hold
court,
forging the shapes of wyrd.
Here you may see the swirling shapes of your fate
swirling in the waters of the well.

[soft drumming]

Pause for private conversation with the Three Norns.

End the ritual with the striking of three bells to disperse the energy.

Drink mead and feast.

The Cycle of Birth, Life, Death, and Rebirth

> Behold we arise with the dawn of time from the
> grey and misty sea, and with the dusk we sink
> in the western ocean, and the lives of a man are
> strung like pearls on the thread of his spirit.
> —Dion Fortune, *The Sea Priestess* (1938)

> A child is born, the old must die.
> A time for joy, a time to cry.
> —Ric Masten, "Let It Be a Dance" (1972)

Cyclicity is a very important concept in contemporary Pagan traditions. The cycle of the seasons mirrors the cycle of birth, life, death, and rebirth. At Imbolc, the ewes begin to lactate, and they give birth before Spring Equinox. Beltane is a celebration of love-making and mating. At Lammas, the harvest, the wheel turns, and many Pagans honor the death of John Barleycorn. At Samhain, people honor and remember their ancestors and their loved ones who have died.

The vegetation cycle is mirrored in the seasonal festivals. At Imbolc, the seeds germinate, and the young plant pushes up out of the earth. At Spring Equinox, the flower begins to form. At Beltane, it is fertilized. At Midsummer, the fruit begins to form. At Lammas, the fruit is ripe. At the Autumnal Equinox, the fruit falls to the ground. At Samhain, the fruit rots and releases the seed. At Yule, it is lying dormant in the earth. The cycle of death and rebirth is everywhere in Nature. These parallels are frequently mentioned in Wiccan rituals, so that it becomes ingrained to look at the world, and our lives, as a series of interlocking cycles. The North represents death and the moment of birth; the East represents adolescence; the South represents midlife; and the West represents old age.

Many Pagans believe in reincarnation, and regard death as part of the cycle of life, death, and rebirth. The souls of the dead rest awhile in the Summerlands (the Pagan afterlife) before returning for another reincarnation. There is no doctrine of sin and redemption, rather, everyone must evolve spiritually throughout their successive incarnations. Many souls return to Earth again and again, either because they love and cherish the planet, or because they wish to help others. In Buddhism, these souls are known as bodhisattvas. In Paganism, however, unlike in Buddhism, there is no sense that the goal is to cease reincarnating.

Humans fear death because it appears to be the end. The ego cannot face the prospect of its own annihilation and fears dissolution in the ground of all being. Therefore, Western culture hides death away, and banishes the dying to anonymous hospital rooms. The art of dying well has been lost, and with it, the art of living. If people face the prospect of their own death without fear, it becomes possible to live life to the fullest.

But death is a gateway through which all must pass; the seeds of our death are contained in our life. Pagan psychopomp[91] deities guide us through the gates of death and into the realms beyond. Without death, there could be no process of change—there could be no aging, no experience, no birth, and no rebirth.

The Pagan wheel of the year expresses this process. The year begins at Samhain, now celebrated widely as Hallowe'en. This is a

---

91   "A psychopomp is a guide, whose primary function is to escort souls to the afterlife, but they can also serve as guides through the various transitions of life." — Laura Strong (2023), 'What is a Psychopomp?' Psychopomps.

time for remembering the dead and recognizing the transformative powers of Nature. It is balanced by Imbolc, a spring festival of birth dedicated to Brighid, the goddess of healing, smithcraft, and poetry.

It is possible to gain some idea of what death meant to ancient and medieval people by examining the personification of Death in the Tarot. When it appears in a divinatory spread, it does not usually signify the actual physical death of the querent. Instead it represents a radical transformation—the end of one phase and the beginning of another. When the Tarot was created (around the fourteenth century), death was a very visible part of life. You could not ignore death in the past; most people would have seen a loved one die, either in battle or of an illness.

If you have ever seen a corpse, you will know that it is very clear that the person has gone. The life that animated the body has gone somewhere else.

Most cultures have rituals relating to death and grieving. The bereaved person is held and supported by communal rituals (such as wearing a dark-colored toga in ancient Rome, sitting shiva in the Jewish tradition, or chanting hymns to help the dead person's soul to travel onwards in Hindu tradition).

Rituals for the dead and the ancestors seem to be greatly diminished in Western cultures. One theory that might explain this is that it was during the times of bubonic plague. Before this, people would wash and prepare their family members for burial, but this was no longer possible when they could be infected with the plague by handling the corpse.

Another possibility is that these customs were disrupted when people moved to the cities and lost contact with their family and regional traditions. In addition to this, the move away from organized religion and toward non-belief or individual spirituality makes it difficult to organize communal grieving practices.

Traditional cultures have many stories about death and dying. There are ceremonies to ease the transition into the next world, while someone is dying and after they are gone. There is also space for the experience of grieving, and the possibility of giving oneself up to grief completely for a while as a cathartic and healing process. Western society has largely lost these ceremonies, but people are beginning to rediscover them, to reclaim them, and to create new ones out of our own response to death and dying, through death doulas, death cafes, keening, and related practices.

A death doula (sometimes called an end-of-life doula, end-of-life coach, death midwife or death coach) is a trained practitioner who helps a dying person and their loved ones before, during, and after death by offering physical and emotional support, education about the process of dying and how to prepare for death, and guidance for the grieving process.[92] They are not licensed medical practitioners. Rather, they advocate for the dying person and co-operate with health care providers.

A death cafe is a gathering to talk about death in a guided way:

> At a Death Cafe people, often strangers, gather
> to eat cake, drink tea and discuss death. Our
> objective is "to increase awareness of death with
> a view to helping people make the most of their
> (finite) lives." A Death Cafe is a group directed
> discussion of death with no agenda, objectives

---

92   Cleveland Clinic (2023), 'What an End-of-Life Doula Can Do for You.'

or themes. It is a discussion group rather than a
grief support or counseling session.[93]

The cafes are organized around guiding principles developed by
the movement's founders, Jon Underwood and Sue Barsky Reid,
based on the ideas of Swiss sociologist and ethnologist Bernard
Crettaz.

At Samhain, I have often facilitated an opportunity for people
to talk about a person they have loved who has died. They can
also talk about an ancestor of spirit (a person they admire but are
not related to). Each person brings a photograph or an object to
represent the dead person and talks about why they love them. It is
very helpful to be able to remember the dead in this way.

Another important grieving practice that is being revived is
the practice of keening. This was a form of unstructured singing,
usually by women who did it semi-professionally. It often employed
traditional songs as the basis of the keening ritual. It was believed
that keening was necessary to release the soul from the body. The
keeners would utter a sound like "wheesht" and this would be
received as permission for the soul to go.

Keening or Caoineadh was the name of this practice in Ireland
and Scotland, but it was also practiced in other cultures, for
example the mirologoi in Greece.

The traditional English song "The Lyke Wake Dirge" was part
of the English keening tradition. The name of the song contains
the old word for a corpse, lyke (related to the German word Leich).
The song contains elements of ancient pagan beliefs about the
journey of the soul after death. It must travel across Whinny-
Muir (a moor covered in gorse) and will be able to travel across

---

93   Death Cafe (undated), 'What is Death Cafe?'

it without harm if the person gave clothing and shoes to the poor during life (an echo of Jesus' commandment to give alms to the poor). Next it must traverse the Bridge of Dread, and then the fires of purgatory. If the deceased ever gave drink to anyone, the fires of purgatory will not harm them. A letter from the late seventeenth century in the Cotton collection confirms that this song was sung at wakes "by certain old women":

> When anyone dies, certain women sing a song
> to the dead body, reciting the journey that the
> deceased must go, and they are of the belief,
> such is their fondness, that once in their lives
> it is good to give a pair of new shoes to a poor
> man; forasmuch as after this life they are to pass
> barefoot through a great land full of thorns &
> furze, except by the merit of the alms aforesaid
> they have redeemed their forfeit; for at the edge
> of the land an old man shall meet them with the
> same shoes that were given by the party when
> he was living, and after he hath shod them he
> dismisses them to go through thick and thin
> without scratch or scale. [94]

The concepts of perilous regions traversed by the soul, and having been charitable in life assisting the deceased soul to cross these regions, also appear in a traditional Norwegian poem[95] about the journey of the soul after death, and in traditional German folklore.

If you wish to explore more perspectives on death and dying, an excellent resource is *The Pagan Book of Living and Dying*, by

---

[94] Ian Pittaway (2016), 'The Lyke-Wake Dirge: the revival of an Elizabethan song of the afterlife.' Early Music Muse.
[95] The Dream Song of Olaf Åsteson. Translated by Eleanor C Merry. Rudolf Steiner Press.

Starhawk, M. Macha NightMare, and the Reclaiming Collective. A variety of rituals, songs, reflections, and resources is offered that covers the grieving process and deaths in different circumstances, including death by violence and premature death.

Along with the revival of traditional practices and the development of new rituals around death and dying, people are also beginning to turn toward community support for birth.

Birth doulas are trained professionals who offer "continuous physical, emotional, and informational support to a mother before, during, and shortly after childbirth, to help her achieve the healthiest, most satisfying experience possible."[96] They are distinct from midwives in that midwives are medical practitioners who support the biological process of giving birth, whereas a doula provides non-medical support.

Midwives have existed since the Paleolithic era (40,000 BCE) and are found in every culture. The Greeks, Romans, and Egyptians all had midwives and developed obstetric knowledge.[97]

Every culture also has rituals for welcoming the newborn child to the community, including naming ceremonies and rituals to prevent them being harmed by dangerous spirits or stolen by the Fae. As American anthropologist Robbie Davis-Floyd writes:

> Across cultures and throughout history, humankind has used rites of passage to transmit cultural beliefs and values to the individuals participating in those rites. In non-Western cultures, specific rituals, often involving the entire community, accompany such life-changing events as birth, puberty, and death. Such rituals

96   The Society of Obstetricians and Gynaecologists of Canada. 'Doulas—Pregnancy Info.'
97   'The Origins of Midwifery.' The International Confederation of Midwives.

generally serve to imbue individuals in transition
with a sense of the cosmic importance of the
group and of the place of the individual within
that group.[98]

Because of the tendency to move away from communal
approaches to life, partly caused by the upheaval of
industrialized society and partly because of the trend toward
individualism, Western cultures lack shared communal rituals
and understandings of the meaning of childbirth and other rites
of passage. These are being gradually reclaimed or rediscovered
(and in some cultures, they were never lost, despite colonialism's
attempts to eradicate them).

It is important to remember that it is not only cisgender women
who give birth. Nonbinary people, two-spirit people[99], and
transgender men can also give birth. If people exclusively refer to
women giving birth, it makes it harder for nonbinary people and
trans men to obtain care around their pregnancies.

Everyone should have access to ways of making the experience
of giving birth meaningful and beautiful within their spiritual or
religious paradigm. The existence of support services like birth
doulas makes this easier but we should also consider creating
meaningful rituals for ourselves and our communities—preferably
ones that are inclusive of all genders, sexual orientations, and
family types (polyamorous parents, extended families, and so on).

Each rite of passage should include three phases: a separation
from the previous stage of life, a journey across the liminal
space between phases, and an entry into the new stage of life.

---

98   Robbie E. Davis-Floyd (2003), Birth as an American Rite of Passage. University of California Press.
99   Two-Spirit is a modern, pan-Indigenous term used by some Indigenous communities to refer to people who fulfill a traditional gender-variant ceremonial and social role in their cultures. The term was created in 1990 at the Indigenous lesbian and gay international gathering in Winnipeg, Canada, and does not diminish the specific names, roles and traditions of various First Nations. If you are not Indigenous, you cannot call yourself two-spirit. 'Glossary.' inclusive Wicca.

In the case of giving birth, the parent-to-be starts out as an individual and/or a member of a couple or a throuple. As soon as it becomes apparent that they are pregnant, they start to think of themselves as a parent, and a sort of dyad forms between the pregnant person and the baby. After giving birth, this closeness continues until the child starts to become more independent. Parents who are able to discuss their understanding of birth in relation to their spirituality and religious tradition are more likely to experience giving birth in a positive way. Giving birth is sometimes accompanied by a transcendent or peak experience, and it can lead to a transformation of the new parent's concept of self. Understanding and including the psychological and spiritual as well as the biological dimensions of giving birth can make the whole experience more positive and enable it to be experienced as a transformative peak experience.[100]

A Pagan understanding of giving birth often describes it in terms of the Triple Goddess and a transition from the maiden to the mother aspects of the Triple Goddess. This can be very meaningful for some cisgender women, but it may not be all that helpful for nonbinary people and trans men who give birth. Instead, we might look to stories of nonbinary or genderfluid beings who give birth, such as Loki or Lilith.

It would also be helpful to develop better rituals and support for people who have abortions, miscarry, or lose newborn babies. Abortion is healthcare, and is often necessary to save the life of the pregnant person. The feelings around each of these situations are entirely valid, and they need to be acknowledged, held, and supported.

---

100   George Jacinto, Julia W Buckey (2013), 'Birth: A Rite of Passage.' The International journal of childbirth education: the official publication of the International Childbirth Education Association 28(1):38–42. (note that this article does not use inclusive language)

Rites of passage for other significant events in life are also important. Divorce is an increasingly significant rite of passage, and there are now divorce doulas and divorce coaches to help with the difficult emotional and practical aspects of divorce.[101] Better ritual to support the process of divorce would be helpful. When we separated, my ex and I posted our updated relationship status to Facebook at the same time and removed our wedding rings. We were also very considerate of each other in dividing up our assets. When the decree absolute came though, I bought cake for colleagues at the office. Divorce cakes are very popular, and many of them are hilarious, with slogans like "I do. I did. I'm done," or "May divorce be with you" (for *Star Wars* fans). Marking your divorce with a celebration can provide a sense of closure, strengthen your friendships by reassuring your friends that you still want them in your life and affirm your new role as a single person (possibly even "single and ready to mingle" as one cake slogan put it).[102] Injecting humor into a stressful situation can be very therapeutic, provided that the humor is not vindictive or misogynist. Many divorces are acrimonious and traumatic, requiring complex legal process, therapy, and mediation to resolve them and come to an amicable arrangement regarding children, companion animals, and the division of property.

One of the strengths of contemporary Pagan religions is that they have embraced the concept of handfasting, which allows for the possibility of separation and divorce. The traditional concept of handfasting is that it was a trial marriage for a year and a day, after which the couple could separate if they wished. Many contemporary Pagan couples renew their handfasting vows each year. I do this with my husband (and I did it with my previous husband) and I find it to be a beautiful and meaningful ritual.

---

101   Madeleine Aggeler (Nov. 28, 2023), 'Divorce doulas: "like having that best friend you've always wanted, but you're paying for."' The Guardian.
102   Emily Lou (2023), '99 divorce cake ideas you have to see to believe!' Divorce Club.

(The divorceclub.com website has many online events and resources to help with the process of divorce.)

Transitioning to a different gender than the one you were assigned at birth is another significant rite of passage. It can be a long, drawn-out process with many significant milestones (social transition, changing your pronouns, changing your documentation, coming out at work, starting hormones, getting surgery—though it is important to bear in mind that not all trans people do get surgery or hormones, and that their gender is just as valid as the gender of those who do). Each of these milestones is worthy of celebration and affirmation by the wider community. The process of transitioning is different for each transgender and nonbinary person, and the steps listed above may not happen in the same order for everyone.

Coming of age is another important rite of passage, where the person transitions from childhood into adulthood. Many traditional cultures retain their coming-of-age rituals (like the Bar Mitzvah and Bat Mitzvah ceremonies in Judaism). These rituals generally acknowledge the person's changed role in relation to their community, leaving behind the status of child and taking on adult responsibilities. There are some remnants of this ritual in Anglo culture, such as learning to drive, getting your own house, going to university, or getting your first job—but there is no single ritual that celebrates the shift from child to adult; instead there are multiple rituals, such as being given a key to the front door or getting a driving license. Some Pagan groups have created their own rite of passage for this shift, but it is not universal (and not all adolescents would necessarily want such a ritual, in any case). I discussed this with a group of twentysomethings, and they all agreed that a rite of passage for the transition from childhood to adulthood would be helpful. We must be wary of appropriating other cultures' rites of passage for this, however. Such a ritual might include the symbolic crossing of a threshold and having adults welcome the adolescent into adulthood with gifts or words of wisdom.

I find it very helpful to think of all these life events as part of the cycle of birth, life, death, and rebirth. Positioning myself in a cycle of change that I can relate to the seasons is deeply reassuring because spring always comes after winter; rebirth always comes after death. Every phase is part of the dance.

Note that the following meditation may be distressing for people who have a deep fear of death and dying.

Meditation: Entering the Cycle

Lie down on the floor and visualize yourself being dead. Visualize your body crumbling away into dust, its nutrients returning to the land to feed other animals. Notice that you are still present, even though your body is not. Take the time to really feel yourself as a spirit without a body. Visualize yourself traveling across Whinny-Muir (the moor of gorse and thorns), and the Bridge of Dread, to reach the Summerlands. Now visualize yourself being reborn: You are a small baby, returning to the world. Really take the time to enter into the emotional states associated with each of these phases of the journey.

Exercises and Journal Prompts

- **Write your will and an accompanying letter of wishes.** Include what you would like to happen to your body (cremation or burial), and what should happen to your possessions.

- **Appoint executors** who will ensure that your wishes are carried out.

- Keep the details of your will and executors up to date.

- **Plan and write your funeral.** There are many resources for Pagan funerals available on the internet. Remember to include a section for the main ceremony, and one for what should happen at the burial or cremation.

- **Organize or attend a death cafe.** Use the Death Cafe website to help you plan this event.

- **What other significant changes have occurred in your life?** These could include coming of age, first menstruation, first sexual experience, giving birth, gender transition, gender confirmation surgery, marriage, divorce, the death of a parent, the death of other loved ones, including companion animals. Reflect on these experiences and how the rituals around them supported you through the experience (or how they could have supported you better).

Ritual: A Keening Ritual

Roles: keeners, mourners.

Setup: Create your ritual space as you normally would. If you do not have a usual method of setting up your ritual space, you can start the ritual with soft drumming.

> **Keener 1** *(facing North)*: At the moment of death and rebirth, the space between the last breath and the first breath, we call to the spirits of the North.
>
> **Keener 2** *(facing East)*: At the moment of awakening, the hour of dawn, the first fire on the horizon, we call to the spirits of the East.
>
> **Keener 3** *(facing South)*: At the zenith of the day, the full fruitfulness of Earth beneath the noonday Sun, we call to the spirits of the South.
>
> **Keener 1** *(facing West)*: At the waning of the day, at the ebbtide of the year, as the waters ebb and flow, we call to the spirits of the West.
>
> **Keener 1:** We come to mourn those we have not mourned,
> We come to shed the tears we have not shed,
> We come to release the souls of those who have not gone beyond.

All hum / wail / keen / ululate.

> **Keener 2:** We come to praise the beloved dead,
> We come to sing the songs of the ancestors,
> We come to keen over those we have lost.

All hum / wail / keen / ululate.

> **Keener 3:** We come to guide the travelers,
> We come to bring solace to the unconsolable,
> We come to wail and keen and lament.

All hum / wail / keen / ululate.

All three keeners sing a version of the "Lyke Wake Dirge":

> This one night, this one night
> Every night and all
> Fire and fleet and candle-light
> The Gods receive thy soul
>
> When from this earth your soul has passed
> Every night and all
> To Whinny-Moor you'll come at last
> The Gods receive thy soul
>
> If ever you gave out clothing or shoes
> Every night and all
> Then sit you down and put them on
> The Gods receive thy soul.
>
> From Whinny-Moor when you have passed,
> Every night and all,
> To Bridge of Dread you'll come at last;
> The Gods receive thy soul.
>
> If ever you gave out drink or bread,
> Every night and all,
> You shall reach the far side of the Bridge of
> Dread,
> The Gods receive thy soul.

If drink or bread you never gave none,
Every night and all,
You'll meet the Wild Hunt's hungry hounds,
The Gods receive thy soul.

At this point, all those assembled may call out the names of loved ones who have died, light candles for them upon the altar, wail, keen, cry, rock, and ululate.

The ritual concludes when catharsis has been achieved. All present share bread and milk.

Keener 1: We have praised the beloved dead,
We have sung their songs and named their names.

Keener 2: We have feasted at the crossing place between the seen and unseen,
With the beloved dead.

Keener 3: We have gathered to mourn those we left unmourned.
We release them now into the loving arms of the Great Mother.

All: We release them! We release them! We release them!
Wheesht! Wheesht! Wheesht!

Return your ritual space to ordinary time. Say farewell to the quarters.

Keener 1 *(facing West)*: Farewell to the land of the blest in the uttermost west,
And the ocean of tears that carries the dead to their rest.

Keener 3 *(facing South)*: Farewell to the earth that gave us our birth,
And the mirth of our lives, and the rest found in death.

Keener 2 *(facing East)*: Farewell to the fire, the spark of all life,
The light of the dawn, and the hope of those who mourn.

Keener 1 *(facing North)*: Farewell to the breath, the last and the first,
The breath that inspires, and the kiss that we share.

Gender and Sexuality

Heterosexuality isn't normal, just common.

—Derek Jarman,

At Your Own Risk: A Saint's Testament (1992)

Gender and sexuality have been key concerns for modern and contemporary Paganisms, ever since the first stirrings of the Pagan Revival were felt in the nineteenth century. Two key ideas from the perspective of the women's movement were the reclaiming of the concept of the witch and the reinstatement of the divine feminine. LGBTQ+ practitioners were initially inspired by the idea of sexual freedom in ancient Greece, epitomized for women by Sappho and for men by the god Pan and the satyrs, and later by the discovery that many ancient cultures were accepting of a variety of sexual orientations.

Professor and author Alex Owen emphasizes the importance of the Hermetic Order of the Golden Dawn for the creation of modern occultism, and the centrality of modernist discourse in their views.[103] The Golden Dawn was largely a magical order, but it combined so many forms of mysticism and magic that a wide variety of people got involved. Samuel Liddell MacGregor Mathers, the founder of the Golden Dawn, was married to Moina Bergson, sister of the philosopher Henri Bergson. W.B. Yeats, Arnold Bennett, and other well-known figures were members. If you were anyone who was anyone and you weren't in the Golden Dawn, you were probably a Theosophist instead—Oscar Wilde was a member of the Theosophical Society. One of the stated aims of Golden Dawn practice was to achieve psychological androgyny (though this did not necessarily mean they were tolerant of same-sex love). Many of its most enthusiastic members were women (and

---

103   Alex Owen (2004), The Place of Enchantment: British Occultism and the Culture of the Modern, Chicago: University of Chicago Press.

treated as equals by their male colleagues) and were also prominent in the socialist movement and the suffragette movement, along with members of the Theosophical Society. The order also created a highly eclectic synthesis of previous magical traditions that became the basis of much subsequent magical and Pagan practice in the twentieth century, including Wicca and Thelema.

In 1899, *Aradia, or the Gospel of the Witches*, was published, by Charles Godfrey Leland. He claimed to have discovered a secret witch cult in Tuscany that was worshiping Diana, Lucifer, and Aradia (the pronunciation of Herodias in Italian; Herodias was alleged by the Inquisition to have been worshiped by medieval "witches"). It is not known whether his sources, Maddalena and Marietta, had fabricated the material they gave him—but the material seemed to be a palimpsest of Catholic and ancient pagan material, as one might expect from something that came from folk tradition. This seems to suggest that it was genuine.[104]

Another key source in the development of modern Paganisms is the writer Edward Carpenter (1873–1920). Although few remembered him until recently, he is enjoying a revival among gay Pagans. He influenced E.M. Forster and D.H. Lawrence, and thereby the wider culture. In 1889, he called for a return of cosmic consciousness to modern Man [sic]:

> The meaning of the old religions will come back
> to him. On the high tops once more gathering he
> will celebrate with naked dances the glory of the
> human form and the great processions of the stars,
> or greet the bright horn of the young moon.[105]

104　Craig Spencer (2020), Aradia, A Modern Guide to Charles Godfrey Leland's Gospel of the Witches. Llewellyn.
105　Edward Carpenter (1889), Civilisation: its cause and cure.

Carpenter was a poet who campaigned against air pollution and vivisection and promoted mystical socialism, vegetarianism and rational dress. He was a pacifist, a campaigner for gay rights as early as the 1890s (he lived openly with his partner, George Merrill) and an advocate of Pagan and pantheist ideas.

In 1921, anthropologist Margaret Murray published *The Witch-Cult in Western Europe*, expressing the view that pagan witchcraft had survived into the Middle Ages. This was the beginning of the idea that the witch hunts of the Reformation period had actually been persecuting genuine pagan witches, as opposed to non-witches who were accused by their neighbors of maleficent witchcraft. This view was very prevalent in popular discourse and was seized upon with enthusiasm by Gerald Gardner, who used it to great effect in his 1949 novel *High Magic's Aid* and his 1954 non-fiction work *Witchcraft Today*—both founding texts of Wicca. It appears, from research by Philip Heselton, that modern Wicca was effectively founded as early as the 1920s by three women drawing upon various classical and magical sources, and that Gardner stumbled upon this in the mid-1940s.[106]

Ideas about the persecution of witches and how this linked in with the wider oppression of women fed into feminist discourse and the Goddess movement in the sixties, seventies and eighties.

Many writers (Jessie Weston, Jane Ellen Harrison, and Jacquetta Hawkes among them) who were influenced by J.G. Frazer's *The Golden Bough* were promoting the idea of a prehistoric cult of the Great Mother Goddess. While this idea has long been discredited in academia, it retained its popularity in popular discourse until quite recently, when the work of Ronald Hutton, a historian of the recent revival of Pagan traditions, rendered it an untenable position.

---

106   Philip Heselton (2003), Gerald Gardner and the Cauldron of Inspiration: An Investigation into the Sources of Gardnerian Witchcraft.

The early advocates of the Great Mother Goddess theory were social conservatives. Hawkes, a prominent enthusiast for the theory, believed that women and men were fundamentally different and that the role of women was to remain in the home and bring up children. This is rather ironic in view of the theory's next generation of advocates, the separatist feminists of the sixties and seventies. Gardner, the founder of modern Wicca, was influenced by the idea of the Great Mother Goddess. This is apparent from much of the material that he wrote for use in Wiccan ritual. He was also (embarrassingly for most Wiccans who are largely left-leaning) a member of the Conservative Party. However, the women he portrays in his two novels are very feisty and independent characters.

In 1954, Gerald Gardner's book *Witchcraft Today* was published. It (and his 1949 novel, *High Magic's Aid*) drew heavily upon Margaret Murray's popular work, *The Witch-Cult in Western Europe*. Murray wrote the foreword to *Witchcraft Today*. Many people were attracted to witchcraft by both Murray's and Gardner's work.

Gardner felt safe to publish the book and start publicizing Wicca because of the repeal of the 1735 Witchcraft Act, which was replaced by the Fraudulent Mediums Act in 1951. The 1735 act was aimed at people who pretended to have the power to call up spirits, foretell the future, cast spells, or discover the whereabouts of stolen goods. The last person to be imprisoned under this act was Helen Duncan, a spiritualist medium, in 1944.

It is not known when the members of the newly formed Wiccan tradition first became aware of the book *Aradia, or the Gospel of the Witches*. Doreen Valiente began rewriting the Wiccan rituals around 1953, when she became Gardner's High Priestess, and drew upon Aradia for her extensive reworking of Gardner's version of the prose poem, "The Charge of the Goddess". The piece also draws upon classical texts.

"The Charge of the Goddess" is a key text in Wicca, as it contains many of its core ideas, especially the line "All acts of love and pleasure are My rituals," which is widely taken to mean that the Goddess approves of all consensual sexual interactions. "The Charge" also emphasizes the nurturing aspect of the Goddess:

> I am the Gracious Goddess, who gives the gift
> of joy unto the heart of man. Upon earth, I give
> the knowledge of the spirit eternal; and beyond
> death, I give peace and freedom and reunion
> with those who have gone before. Nor do I
> demand aught in sacrifice; for behold, I am the
> Mother of all living, and my love is poured out
> upon the earth.

It explicitly identifies a number of diverse goddesses with the Great Mother, as it begins with the words:

> Listen to the words of the Great Mother; she
> who of old was also called among men Artemis,
> Astarte, Athene, Dione, Melusine, Aphrodite,
> Cerridwen, Cybele, Arianrhod, Isis, Dana, Bride
> and by many other names.

Gardner handed on his writings to several of his priestesses, including Monique Wilson, who went on to found the Long Island Line in the US; Madge Worthington, who went on to found the Whitecroft tradition; and Patricia Crowther, who also has many initiatory descendants.

Valiente, Crowther, and Lois Bourne proceeded to write further books about Wicca, which made it even more widely known.

The witch archetype, the story of the "Burning Times" (the persecution of witches) and the idea of the Great Mother Goddess were enthusiastically advocated by sections of the feminist movement on both sides of the Atlantic, though mainly in the United States.

A parallel development was the growth in popularity of the idea of the divine feminine in Christianity (via the Sophianic tradition, though it may also have been influenced by Goddess-oriented feminism). To demonstrate the centrality of these notions to the identity of adherents of the Goddess movement, Ronald Hutton quotes Cynthia Eller, a historian of feminist spirituality:

> The European witch burnings work both as a persecution history for women and as a symbol of the resilience of women and their goddess-loving religion. As a persecution history, the witch burnings intensify spiritual feminists' sense that they are anathema to the patriarchal powers; it bolsters their conviction that feminism is a question of life and death, of the very survival of women.[107]

Note that this passage refers to the centrality of goddess-religion, the idea that the victims of the witch craze were goddess worshippers, and the idea that they worshiped a single goddess, not a multiplicity of deities. Fine sentiments (though the reader might feel a little manipulated by the appeal to their sense of persecution paranoia), but nonetheless based on spurious history.

Spurious history notwithstanding, the idea of the witch is an empowering one for women, as many feel that it represents the aspects of women that are suppressed in patriarchal society:

---

[107] Ronald Hutton (1999), The Triumph of the Moon: A History of Modern Pagan Witchcraft.

wildness, independence, magic, freedom, power, strength, intellect, intuition, sexuality and cunning.

Sex, Gender and Sexuality

Psychologically speaking, sex and gender are two different things: Sex is your biological characteristics (chromosomes and genitalia) and gender is your psychological role—in which case there are as many genders as there are people. Many Pagan deities do not fit into patriarchal gender stereotypes, and now that many cultures are emerging from the era of patriarchy, people are finding that they do not have to conform to the narrow and shallow definitions of male and female purveyed by patriarchal traditions.

It has been pointed out by some feminists (e.g. Judith Butler) that sex is also socially constructed, given that dividing the world into the two categories of male and female is unnecessary, and that women's and men's bodies are differently developed according to gender stereotypes (e.g. men are encouraged to develop their muscles, and women are not). The way in which society organizes everything along gendered lines is also a social construct.

Lou Hart[108] has explored a variety of models of gender from other societies, and concluded that the conflation of sex and gender is a peculiarly Western idea. For example, in some societies, you could be a woman-man (woman living as a man), a man-woman (man living as a woman), transgender, a man, or a woman.[109]

People's theological stance can affect their views of gender. There are various models available in magical discourse.

---

108   Lou Hart is a queer witch, priestess, artist, musician, writer, and a Radical Faerie. [Queer Spirit: Profile of Lou Hart]
109   Lou Hart (2005), Magic is a many-gendered thing.

One of these is duality. As I understand it, duality is the presentation of things as opposites with no shared characteristics (dark and light, evil and good, left and right, etc.) where the different halves of the pairs then become conflated with each other (e.g. left = passive = female = dark = evil, hence the word sinister, from the Latin for left).

Another is polarity, which I have always understood as being either end of a continuum. The two poles are attracted to each other and a dynamic exists between them. Not only that, but each end of the continuum contains the other within itself (hence the yin-yang symbol has a black dot within the white half and a white dot within the black half to represent Yin within Yang and Yang within Yin). This is sometimes also called complementarity.

A further possibility is multiplicity—the idea that there are many different forces and energies in the universe, just as there are many gender roles and many forms of sexuality. These could be represented as a scatterplot, a landscape, or many interconnected rhizomes or bubbles.

Gender and Sexuality in Wicca

In the first decades of Wicca's existence, it was a radical idea to have women on an equal footing with men, and to have a Goddess for women to identify with. When I first became interested in Wicca and Paganism, this was a very important part of my interest in it. The Goddess is still really important to me, but I also worship deities that represent a whole range of genders. I do not see the need to organize every aspect of Wiccan ritual by gender roles, however.

In inclusive covens, people have largely moved on from the very gendered nature of earlier Wiccan ritual. We are much more likely to see gender as fluid and changeable and be welcoming to nonbinary and transgender people. We do not ascribe specific qualities to specific genders (any gender can be nurturing, any gender can be a warrior, and so on). Inclusive practices include not making participants stand alternately male and female in the circle; not consecrating participants in a gendered way; inviting people of any gender to invoke a deity of any gender onto another person of any gender. Another important practice is inviting two people of any gender to consecrate cakes and wine, using the words "as the athame is to the lover, so the cup is to the beloved," which were created by Crow Dewhurst and Marget Inglis in the early 1990s.

In heteronormative covens, there is a tendency to work magic by using the polarity of sexual tension. As the majority of members are heterosexual, this can lead to feelings of exclusion on the part of LGBTQ+ members. Some Wiccans are duotheist, that is, believing that "All the Gods are one God and all the Goddesses are one Goddess." As the divine couple are then understood to be lovers, this again excludes LGBTQ+ practitioners. It is also a problem for those people of either gender who do not particularly identify with or relate to the predominant archetypes associated with the divine couple. In the past, some Wiccans even went so far as to suggest that because the primary dynamic of the universe was the sexual interaction between the God and the Goddess, this meant that homosexuality was "unnatural." This was counteracted by other people pointing out the words from "The Charge": "All acts of love and pleasure are My rituals."

Polytheist Wiccans see the Horned God and the Moon Goddess (the two deities of the divine couple) as patron deities of Wicca, with a special relationship with the religion, rather than a conflation of a multiplicity of different deities.

Over the past decade or so, the Wiccan community has begun to examine their ideas about gender and sexuality, and has reduced the heterocentricity of Wiccan rituals.

There is no implication in any Wiccan ritual that I have ever seen that all magical acts are about fertility (and even if they were, there's no need to take it literally and assume that it means the fertilization of an ovum by a sperm, otherwise there would be a population explosion). I also think that 'fertility' should be interpreted in its widest possible meaning, namely fertility of ideas, spirit, etc., rather than being about just physical reproduction.

According to Dion Fortune (another important influence on Wicca), the female is passive on the outer planes and active on the inner planes, while the male is active on the outer planes and passive on the inner planes. She also emphasizes that each of us has both male and female within us. While I do not necessarily find her model of magical dynamics helpful, it is interesting how it imagines the "male" and "female" roles to change as you proceed from plane to plane, presumably to infinity.

Wicca is generally very empowering for women. In the early days of Wicca, it was standard practice for women to lead rituals and the Goddess was generally viewed as the "senior partner" of the divine couple. This was heady stuff in the 1950s, 1960s, and 1970s. However, not everything was rosy in the garden: In 1957, Doreen Valiente left Gardner's coven when he produced the "Laws of Witchcraft" (a document that he claimed was ancient, but which he had clearly just written). Among the laws was the statement that a High Priestess must step down when she gets too old and is no longer glamorous. Valiente understandably objected to this law. She joined the other form of witchcraft available at the time, that of Robert Cochrane, who, like Gardner, was inspired by Robert Graves' book, *The White Goddess*.

There is some mention of the divine androgyne in Wicca, and the third degree initiation is about achieving the *hieros gamos*, the internal union of masculine and feminine aspects of the psyche. So there is a resolution of the duality of masculine and feminine.

One of the key ideas in Wicca is the balancing of "masculine" and "feminine" aspects of the psyche (the anima and animus identified by Jung). This idea can be seen as problematic if there is a rigid identification of a gender with specific qualities; but as the idea is to bring all these aspects into balance and achieve psychological androgyny (an idea borrowed from the Golden Dawn and alchemy), perhaps this is not too much of an issue.

It seems to work to some degree, either because people who like the idea of psychological androgyny are attracted to Wicca, or because it makes it easier for practitioners to express the side of themselves that is usually associated with the opposite gender.

Gender and Sexuality in Druidry

As magic is less important in the practice of Druidry, the rituals place less emphasis on gender. However, some Druidry focuses on the divine couple and the divine child, but as belief in these is optional (as it is in Wicca), and some druids are also Christians, there is such a variety of theological positions among druids that it is probably less of an issue. The divine child is the product of the union of masculine and feminine, and perhaps also offers a resolution to this duality—though as an external product of a heterosexual union, rather than an internal product of a mystical union (i.e., the *hieros gamos* in Wicca).

An excellent article by Joanna van der Hoeven on the OBOD website pushes back against the anthropomorphization and gendering of everything in Nature:

> So much within nature is not defined by gender—scientifically or socially speaking. There isn't always a male/female coupling in the natural world—there exists gender neutral or genderless beings, hermaphrodites and homosexuality throughout. Too much focus can be placed on a male/female union, or ritual, wherein we essentially become defined based upon what plumbing we are born with. For me, it is far too restrictive. Some of my deities are gendered, some aren't—I am inspired and learning from Brighde at the moment, but then there is also the deity of the heathland and forest where I live. This local deity has no gender—it simply is. It is everything, therefore how can it be gendered? The clouds—are they gendered? What of the sun and moon—so often gendered within Paganism (and of different genders, depending upon the tradition). Why do we feel the need to engender such entities?[110]

---

110   Joanna van der Hoeven (2020), 'Paganism, Anthropomorphisation and Gender.' Order of Bards, Ovates & Druids.

Gender and Sexuality in Heathenry

Heathenry is a revival of Northern European Paganism, and it draws on the practices, writings, and beliefs of the Old English, Norse, and other Germanic tribes. It includes a form of magic known as seiðr, which was originally largely practiced by women, though also by ergi men (the Norse term for a "passive" partner in homosexual sex). Men regarded seiðr as "women's magic"—cunning and underhand. Seiðr has been enthusiastically researched and revived by Heathen women, and by some gay men.[111] There is also a certain amount of gender-fluidity in Norse myth. When Oðinn was initiated by the goddess Freyja into Seiðr, he became more feminine. Loki transformed himself into a mare, and Thor disguised himself as a giantess.

Heathens do not view the universe as having a primary duality; they are more likely to believe in a multiplicity of beings.

Conclusion

In general, Pagans are very accepting of variation in gender and sexuality and are very willing to challenge received societal norms on this and many other issues. There is also strong evidence that ancient paganisms tolerated a variety of gender and sexual roles, and much Pagan mythology reflects this. Although there has been some difficulty in Wicca with adapting the rituals to be more inclusive, this has by and large been achieved, with new versions of traditional forms of words being introduced.

---

111   Jenny Blain (2001), Nine Worlds of Seid-Magic: Ecstasy and Neo-Shamanism in North European Paganism, Routledge.

Exercises and Journal Prompts

- Gather images and stories of LGBTQ+ people, gender-variant people, and women from different religions.
- Make a shrine for gender-variant, queer, and female spiritual ancestors.
- Tell their stories to others.
- Make a list of heterocentric, ciscentric[112] and patriarchal rituals, practices, stories, and symbols in your tradition, and rewrite or reimagine them to be affirming of gender equality and diversity.
- Gather images and stories of sex-positive people of faith.
- Make a shrine for queer spiritual ancestors.
- Tell their stories to others.

---

112   Ciscentric: Centering on or overemphasizing cisgender people and identity.
    Cisgender: Identifying with the gender you were assigned at birth.

Ritual: A Coming-Out Ritual

The circle or sacred space is opened in the appropriate manner for the tradition celebrating this ritual. If quarters are called, then they are addressed in a nonbinary way: e.g., Mighty Ones of the [direction], Powers of the [element]. All those gathered to celebrate bring a small gift for the person coming out. The one who has recently come out as queer wears a cloak and a veil. Replace pronouns below with the pronouns of the person who is coming out.

> **Celebrant 1:** Today we have gathered to
> celebrate the coming out of [name] as [gender or
> sexual orientation].
> They have been hidden, like a bulb hidden in the
> earth,
> waiting to put forth the first green shoots in
> spring.
> They have been hidden,
> like a bud waiting for the first rays of the Sun to
> open.
> They have been hidden,
> Like a shy animal in their burrow,
> waiting for the dusk to emerge and explore.
> They have been hidden,
> like a butterfly in the chrysalis,
> waiting for the right time to emerge.

Celebrant 2: But now [name] has come out,
and emerges into the world like a bulb putting
forth a green shoot,
like a flower opening to the sun,
like an animal emerging from the burrow,
like a butterfly emerging from the chrysalis!
Come out, [name], and be welcome in your full
glory.

All: Come out! Come out! Come out!

The coming-out person now emerges from the cloak and the veil, and steps forward.

All: Hail and welcome!

Each person now steps forward and gives a small gift to the coming-out person, either offering their own personal blessing, or saying: "I welcome you in your full glory as a [lesbian/gay/bisexual/transgender/nonbinary/queer] person, and celebrate your unique beauty and strength."

Celebrant 1: By coming out of the closet, you
have come IN to the queer community.

All: Welcome in!

Celebrant 2: By coming out of the closet,
you have come IN to the Pagan community.
Paganism encourages us to find our true and
authentic self, and to be that to the best of our
ability. By coming out as [identity], you have
revealed more of your true self, both to yourself
and to others.

Celebrant 1: There are as many ways to be
queer as there are queer people, but we now

present to you ten queer archetypes, who may help you and guide you on your way.[113]

The Catalyst: I am the catalytic transformer.

(Lights a flame)

I bring change.
I hunger and thirst for social justice.
I light the fire in the human heart,
The fire that rages against injustice,
The flame that burns bright to herald a new dawn.

The Mirror: I am a mirror, presenting an inverted image to society.

(Holds up a mirror)

I am the Molly and the Drag Queen.
I am the one who queers everything.
I comfort the afflicted and afflict the comfortable.
I overthrow power structures with my parodies.

The Shaman: I am the queer shaman,

(beats drum)

the consciousness scout.
I find the way between the worlds,
I travel the roads of the dead.
I am a child of the Moon,
a devotee of the lunar mysteries.

---

113   Christian de la Huerta (1999), Coming Out Spiritually: The Next Step..

The Trickster: I am the Trickster,

(presents the coming-out person with a flower)

> The eternally playful one.
> I am Peter Pan, always youthful.
> My tricks expand your consciousness,
> my dreams bring sparkle to the world.

The Beautiful One: I am the keeper and maker of beauty,

(sprinkles glitter)

> making music, and art, and sacred drama.
> I am the queer eye, discerning beauty wherever it roves.
> I am the one who makes all things beautiful.

The Caregiver: I am the one who cares

(caresses the coming-out person)

> for the suffering, the lost, and the outcast.
> I bring joy to those who are on the edge,
> Lost in the liminal spaces.

The Mystic: I am the mystic one,

(holds wand/thyrsis/caduceus)

> The in-between one,
> the shaman, the traveler between the worlds.
> I travel between the seen and the unseen,
> I mediate between the worlds of flesh and spirit.

The Consecrated One: My sexuality is holy,

(sprinkles blessed water or mead)

my being is holy. I stand before the divine ones,
and I lead the people toward the union of matter
and spirit.

The Androgyne: I am the Divine Androgyne,

(holds wand and chalice in each hand)

including and transcending all genders.
I am change and I am growth.
I am space and time.
I am spirit and matter.
I am the inbreath and the outbreath.

The Gatekeeper: I am the gatekeeper,

(makes gesture of opening doors)

who stands at the door of the sacred realm,
welcoming all who come to enter the portal,
the door to the unseen realms.
I welcome you to the place between the worlds.

All: Hail and welcome, [name of coming-out
person]

The ritual is concluded with cakes and wine, mead, an
eisteddfod, or whatever closing is appropriate to the tradition.

The Structures of Pagan Religions

I love large group rituals. I love leading them and
I love participating in them (on the rare occasions
when I can be an ordinary participant). They're
a ton of work to plan, facilitate, and present,
but when they're done right, they help people
experience the Gods and magic and participate
in community in a way that can't be done alone.
My deepest and most meaningful religious
experiences have happened in small groups—
three or five or nine people in someone's back
yard, working spells and pouring offerings and
opening ourselves to the presence of the Gods and
spirits. The core of my Paganism is my daily and
weekly spiritual practice: meditation, prayers, and
offerings.

—John Beckett[114]

There are many different Pagan traditions and organizations,
and they all have slightly different structures, based in part on their
ritual style and levels of commitment available to members. Some
are organized as occult orders, with membership fees and grades.
Some are organized like churches (and some even call themselves
churches, which is odd as the word church is derived from Greek
kyriakos, meaning "the house of the Lord"). Most Pagan traditions
and organizations bear very little resemblance to churches, which I
think is a very good thing, because institutions like churches can lead
to hierarchy and authoritarian behavior.

---

114   John Beckett (2023), 'The Future of Paganism.' Under the Ancient Oaks.

Pagan Traditions

One of the earliest Pagan traditions to be revived is Druidry. The first Druid organizations appeared in the late eighteenth century, although they did not identify as Pagan at that stage. There are two main strands of Druidry: cultural druidry, which organizes eisteddfods (cultural events) in Wales, and is not religious; and religious Druidry, which is a global phenomenon, and celebrates the festivals of the wheel of the year. There are several Druid orders that are mainly Pagan in character (people from other spiritual traditions are welcome to join them). One of the oldest is the Order of Bards, Ovates, and Druids (OBOD), founded in Britain in 1964 by the poet and historian Ross Nichols, with assistance from the writer and Tolkien Society founder Vera Chapman, and fellow members of the Ancient Druid Order (a more universalist druid order). OBOD offers training courses, and its members meet in groups called groves and seed groups. Another well-known order is the British Druid Order, which describes itself as "a contemporary living spiritual tradition based on the earliest native spirituality of Britain and Europe of which any written record survives."

A third British Druid group is The Druid Network (TDN), which is not a druid order but a group that aims to support Druid spirituality and share resources promoting a "conscious support of individuality, community, local diversity and environmental sustainability, promoting awareness of the divine within nature."

In North America, the main druid organization is Ár nDraíocht Féin: A Druid Fellowship (ADF), which describes itself as "a modern tradition of neopagan Druidry," incorporating practices from ancient and modern Indo-European cultures including Celtic, Norse, Slavic, Baltic, Greek, Roman, Persian, Vedic, and more. It is also non-sexist, anti-racist, and inclusive.

The next oldest among contemporary Pagan traditions are Wicca and folkloric witchcraft (sometimes called traditional witchcraft).

There are many traditions within Wicca. The oldest is Gardnerian Wicca, followed by Alexandrian Wicca.

When Gerald Gardner coined the term "the Wica" (originally spelled with one C), he seems to have intended it to refer to any and all witches. Subsequently, the term has come to be used by some people to mean only witches initiated into Gardnerian and Alexandrian Wicca, and it has been used by others to mean anybody who identifies as Wiccan, and a whole spectrum of meanings in between those two terms. This can make it confusing for people to understand what is meant by any one person using the term Wicca.

In an attempt to clear up the confusion, Gardnerians and Alexandrians in North America (by which they mean anyone who can trace their initiatory lineage back to Gerald Gardner or Alex Sanders respectively) have started referring to themselves as "British Traditional Wicca." This seems to have happened in part because there are so many other traditions that are called Wiccan, but that cannot necessarily trace their lineage back to Gardner or Sanders. The term "British Traditional Wicca" has not been widely adopted in Britain, where there are fewer variant traditions of Wicca. In Britain, people generally refer to Gardnerian and Alexandrian Wicca as "initiatory Wicca," but even this term is misleading, as there are other witches with a lineage and initiations who identify as Wiccan in the UK. So the terminology remains fluid and confusing.

Gardnerian Wicca was founded by Gardner in the early 1950s and traces its roots back to the New Forest coven, which included

Dafo, Mother Sabine, and the Mason family. Much of its early liturgy was written by Doreen Valiente. There are numerous lineages within Gardnerian Wicca, with considerable variation in ethos between them. The emphasis of Gardnerian Wicca tends to be less ceremonial than Alexandrian Wicca.

Alexandrian Wicca was founded by Sanders in the 1960s. Sanders was initiated into Gardnerian Wicca, though whether he was elevated to second degree or not is disputed. It tends to include more ideas from ceremonial magic than Gardnerian Craft. In the UK and Europe, Gardnerian and Alexandrian initiates may visit each other's circles without the need for re-initiation.

There is a major distinction between folkloric witchcraft traditions and Wiccan traditions. Folkloric witchcraft does not identify as Wiccan, and it tends to be happy to explore Luciferian and Christian mysteries alongside Pagan mysteries. Wiccans tend to focus on the Horned God and the Moon Goddess, and they do not use the term "the Devil." Wiccan covens are led by a high priestess and a high priest. Folkloric witchcraft covens generally have a Magister and a Maid.

The Clan of Tubal Cain is a folkloric witchcraft tradition. The Clan are the lineage bearers of the Robert Cochrane tradition through Evan John Jones and are also known as the People of Goda. They are a closed initiatory group aligned to the Shadow Mysteries within the Luciferian stream dedicated to experiential gnosis. The sacred tenets of the Clan of Tubal Cain are Truth, Love and Beauty.

The 1734 tradition was founded by Joe Wilson after a lengthy correspondence with Robert Cochrane, founder of the Clan of Tubal Cain. It is a folkloric witchcraft tradition, and it often uses riddles to convey its mysteries.

In North America, the Feri Tradition is a form of American Traditional Witchcraft derived from the teachings of Victor and Cora Anderson and passed down through their various initiates. Feri seeks to transform the individual through practices of ritual magic, meditation, and energy work. The influences of the tradition include Huna, Conjure, Voodoo, Tantra, Celtic folklore, Christian mysticism, Yezidi mythology, and Greek gnosis.

Another important form of witchcraft is Reclaiming, which is a community of people working to unify spirit and politics. Their vision is rooted in the religion and magic of the Goddess, the Immanent Life Force. They see their work as teaching and making magic: the art of empowering themselves and each other. In their classes, workshops, and public rituals, they train their voices, bodies, energy, intuition, and minds. They use the skills that they learn to deepen their strength, both as individuals and as a community, to voice their concerns about the world in which we live and to bring to birth a vision of a new culture. Founded around 1980 in the San Francisco Bay Area, the Reclaiming tradition now includes several dozen regional communities across North America and in Europe and Australia. The founder of Reclaiming, Starhawk, was trained in the Feri Tradition by Victor and Cora Anderson.

There are several traditions that focus on lesbian and gay mysteries, such as the Minoan Brotherhood, the Minoan Sisterhood, and Dianic Wicca.

The Minoan Fellowship is an offshoot of the Minoan Sisterhood, and is open to women and men of any sexual orientation. (The Minoan Brotherhood does not recognize it as part of their tradition.) The Fellowship seeks to be inclusive of all genders and sexual orientations.

Progressive Wicca was started in the UK in the early 1990s by Karin Rainbird, Tam Campbell, and David Rankine. It was a strand within Gardnerian and Alexandrian Wicca, and it emphasized valuing the contributions of all members of the coven and ensuring that all members received thorough training, and it tended to have a stronger emphasis on environmentalism. Progressive Wiccans are happy to experiment and incorporate more eclectic material into their rituals.

Progressive Witchcraft emerged from Progressive Wicca, and was made famous by Janet Farrar and Gavin Bone in their book of the same name. Its ethos is egalitarian, exploratory, and experimental. Janet and Gavin have started their own witchcraft tradition (The Temple of the Cailleach) whose initiation rituals and tenets are distinct from Gardnerian and Alexandrian Wicca.[115]

The inclusive Wicca movement (small i) is not a separate tradition but a strand within existing traditions. Any Wiccan may identify as inclusive and work to make their practice more inclusive of LGBTQIA+ people, disabled people, neurodivergent people, Black people, Indigenous people, racialized people, and other marginalized groups. An inclusive approach to Wicca encompasses eco-spirituality, science, attitudes to truth, the sacred, sexuality, consent culture, group dynamics, coven leadership, ritual, ethics, and Wiccan theology and practice, tradition, and magic—and how these concepts can be explored as part of a liberal religious approach to Wicca.

Heathenry is another important strand of the Pagan Revival. Many Heathens do not identify as Pagan, but as it is possible to be a Heathen and a member of any other Pagan tradition, they

---

115   Tempio di Callaighe in Italian. https://fdrtempiodicallaighe.com/

can be viewed as part of the same spiritual landscape. There are many different Heathen organizations. Some are inclusive of LGBTQ+ people and people of non-European ancestry; some are not. If you are planning to join a Heathen group, look for the word inclusive on their website. They may also have signed on to Declaration 127, an anti-racist declaration, or joined Heathens against Hate.

Good places to start looking for an inclusive Heathen group are Heathens United Against Racism, the Alliance for Inclusive Heathenry, or Heathens Against Hate, which hosts a list of inclusive Heathen groups.

To the best of my knowledge, the first person to use the term "inclusive Heathenry" was Jenny Blain (author of Nine Worlds of Seið Magic), around the turn of the millennium.

There are also many polytheist groups, such as Toutâ Galation (a Gaulish polytheist group), Religio Romana (for Roman polytheists), Romuva (ancient Lithuanian religion), Kemeticism (ancient Egyptian religion), Hellenic (ancient Greek) polytheism, Celtic polytheism, and more. Again, look for groups with explicitly inclusive and anti-racist statements of values.

Pagan Organizations

Pagan organizations are important because they represent Pagans to the wider world and connect members of the Pagan movement together. Through them you can find out more about your chosen tradition and meet other Pagans to celebrate with. Pagan organizations do not claim to represent all Pagans, only their members—but the more people who join these organizations, the stronger and more diverse the Pagan voice in the public square will be.

The Covenant of the Goddess is one of the largest and oldest Wiccan religious organizations. CoG was incorporated as a nonprofit religious organization on October 31, 1975. The Covenant is an umbrella organization of cooperating autonomous Witchcraft congregations and individual practitioners with the power to confer credentials on its qualified clergy.[116] It fosters cooperation and mutual support among Witches and secures for them the legal protections enjoyed by members of other religions. The Covenant is non-hierarchical and governed by consensus. Two-thirds of its clergy are women.

The Pagan Federation (UK) was founded in 1971 and seeks to support all Pagans to ensure that they have the same rights as the followers of other beliefs and religions. It aims to promote a positive profile for Pagans and Paganism and to provide information on Pagan beliefs to the media, official bodies and the greater community. The Pagan Federation International (a separate but related organization) has branches in many countries.

The Pagan Heathen Symposium is a group of Pagan and Heathen organizations in the UK that actively co-operate on a variety of issues and projects.

The Covenant of Unitarian Universalist Pagans (CUUPS) is an organization in the US dedicated to networking Pagan-identified Unitarian Universalists (UUs), educating people about Paganism, promoting interfaith dialogue, developing Pagan liturgies and theologies, and supporting Pagan-identified UU religious professionals. CUUPS was chartered by the Unitarian Universalist Association at its General Assembly in 1987.

The Unitarian Earth Spirit Network (UESN) is an association

---

116   Clergy is the term used by the Covenant of the Goddess

of Unitarians based in the UK that seeks to represent a Nature-centered religious voice within the Unitarian church. The UESN provides a forum for this group and is a recognized, credible part of the British Unitarian movement.

Types of Groups

Various structures are available to Pagan groups. Different structures will suit different styles of ritual and practice.

There is the network, a distributed organization of autonomous groups and individuals that come together at gatherings and networking events but do not have a recognized leader or committee structure. Most Wiccan traditions are networks that operate by a set of norms agreed by the founders of the tradition, but which are often flexible and evolving.

There is the order, which can be structured in a variety of ways. Some Druid orders have a chief, and Druid groups can become recognized groves of the order through a predefined process. Orders tend to have a central body, but also semi-autonomous groups that belong to the order.

At the local level, Pagan communities tend to offer a pub moot, which is a gathering that anyone can attend to socialize and find out more about Pagan traditions. There are also Druid groves, Heathen hearths, Wiccan covens, and sometimes polytheist groups.

There are also numerous Facebook groups and Discord servers where you can find out more about traditions that you might be interested in.

Most areas also have Pagan summer camps where people get together for a weekend or a few days of talks, workshops, and socializing.

Organizing large rituals and groups takes work, and can result in burnout for the organizers if they do not delegate. Many groups are quite small—partly by design and partly because they are constrained by the size of the average living room (most small groups meet in the organizer's home).

It is unlikely that Pagan religions will develop into large-scale organized religions—partly because most people who are leaving Christianity are not looking for a new religion and partly because Pagan religions tend to operate in do-it-yourself mode, and do not offer certainty, because they are not fundamentalist.[117] There is a huge range of theological positions and preferences for ritual style within Pagan and polytheist traditions, so they are unlikely to merge into a single unified tradition. I believe this is a good thing, because diversity is strength and because people do not all want the same things from their religious traditions. Some people want ecstatic and magical practice, others want reflective, meditative, calm liturgy.

Meditation: The Trees and the Forest

As you sit in a quiet place, breathing softly, with your own particular concerns, be aware of our common humanity. Each of us has our own hidden wellspring of joy, our own experience of sorrow, and our unique perspective on the Divine and its relationship with the world.

Let us celebrate the diversity of dreams and visions.

Think of the trees in the woods: Each grows into its individual shape to fit its particular place and the events that have shaped its growth, but each is recognizable as one of a species—oak, birch, holly, maple, yew, beech, hawthorn.

Religions are like that too: Each has its own unique characteristics, shaped by place, culture, and history; but all of them have their roots in the fertile soil of human experience, and all seek the living waters of the divine presence.

Let us honor the beauty and diversity of religions in the world, while loving and cherishing our own particular visions and traditions, recognizing that we, too, are rooted in our common humanity, all seeking the nourishment of the endless outpouring of love and wisdom that we call by many names, all of them holy.

Exercises and Journal Prompts

- **Research the various Pagan and polytheist traditions.** Do any of them appeal to you? Note what attracts you, and what does not appeal to you, about each of them.

- **Do you prefer small-group ritual or large-group ritual?** Try attending both and evaluate your feelings about each of them.

- **Were you drawn to fantasy or Nature writing as a child?** Did you identify with witches, wizards, or some other magical being?

- **Create an altar in your home.** What deities or natural imagery do you feel drawn to? Add these to your altar.

Ritual: Many Paths

Roles: the guide, mountaineers.

Setup: Create your ritual space as you normally would. If you do not have a usual method of setting up your ritual space, or if people from multiple Pagan traditions will be attending the ritual, you can start the ritual with soft drumming, or create a circle opening that combines the openings of different traditions that are represented.

> **Mountaineer 1** *(facing North)*: We approach the sacred mountains, which reach into the heavens, and have their roots in the blessed earth.
>
> **Mountaineer 2** *(facing East)*: We bring the fire in our hearts to greet the dawn.
>
> **Mountaineer 3** *(facing South)*: We stand with feet upon the Earth, our mother.
>
> **Mountaineer 4** *(facing West)*: We seek the waters of infinite joy.

A person from each tradition steps forward and reads a statement of intent for their tradition, describing the gods they honor and the values they hold.

> **The guide:** We come to this place from many different traditions, acknowledging that we hold different things to be sacred but have these core desires: to live in harmony with the Earth and to honor the gods of our ancestors. As our forebear Quintus Aurelius Symmachus wrote, "We look on the same stars, the sky is common, the same

world surrounds us. What difference does it make by what pains each seeks the truth? We cannot attain to so great a secret by one road."

Mountaineer 1: We pledge to work together on the goals that we share.

Mountaineer 2: We promise to uphold each other's freedom to practice our religions in the way that seems best to each of us, provided that this does not infringe upon the rights and freedoms of others.

Mountaineer 3: We pledge to keep each other informed about threats to our communities.

Mountaineer 4: We promise to mourn each other's sorrows and celebrate each other's joys.

Pagan Concepts

The meaning of the old religions will come back
to him. On the high tops once more gathering
he will celebrate with naked dances the glory
of the human form and the great processions of
the stars, or greet the bright horn of the young
moon.

—Edward Carpenter,
Civilisation: its cause and cure (1889)

In this section, I will examine words that are widely used in
Pagan discourse and are foundational to the worldview of many
contemporary Pagans. There are many perspectives and traditions
within the contemporary Pagan community, so these concepts
may be emphasized more in some communities than others. For
example, the concept of sovereignty is important in Druidry, and
mystery is important in Wicca. I have also included concepts such
as immanence, which mean something different to Pagans than
they do to members of other religions.

Apotheosis

In the British Museum, a curious ivory plaque has survived the
ravages of time. It depicts a man being carried from his funeral
pyre into the heavens, and it is known as "The Gherardesca
Diptych" or "The Apotheosis of Symmachus." The Symmachi
family, who commissioned it, were a prominent pagan family in
late antiquity, and Quintus Aurelius Symmachus (345–402 ce),
the man commemorated by the plaque, had defended the ancient
pagan traditions of Rome against the criticisms of the nascent
Christian faith. The other half of the diptych is lost, but it may
have depicted another member of the Symmachi family.

The roots of the word apotheosis are from Greek *apotheoun*,
to change into a god. Its Latin-derived synonym is deification.
Apotheosis is distinct from the concept of theosis, whose Latin-
derived synonym is divinization. Theosis refers to the process of
being filled with God in Christian thought. It is usually preceded
by kenosis, an emptying of self. Apotheosis is the process of
becoming a deity. There are many instances in Pagan mythology
of humans becoming deities and of deities becoming human.

In ancient pagan religions, the concept of apotheosis seems
to have been mainly applied to kings and pharaohs, but it was
sometimes applied to private individuals such as Quintus Aurelius
Symmachus, who defended the ancient Roman religion against the
hegemony of Christianity.

In Hindu and Buddhist thought, becoming a deity is just part
of the endless cycle of reincarnation, as illustrated by the story of
Indra and the Ants, found in the Brahma Vaivarta Purana. In the
story, Indra becomes very concerned with his status and proud
of having slain the serpent Vritra, and he asks Vishwakarma, god

of architecture, to build him a palace. Vishwakarma does so, but Indra keeps on wanting him to make it bigger. One day, Indra is visited by a boy and an old hermit. The boy remarks that this is the biggest palace built by any Indra so far. This confuses Indra. Then the boy sees a column of ants marching across the floor of the palace and starts laughing. Indra asks why he is laughing, and the boy says that each of the ants was previously an Indra. Each of them slew a monster, became very proud, and eventually was reborn as an ant. Next, the boy points to the hairs on the chest of the hermit, which are a bit scraggly. The hermit says that one of his chest hairs falls out every time an incarnation of Indra dies. This is because the existence of the universe depends on Brahma being awake. When Brahma falls asleep, the universe dies and the current version of Indra dies along with it. When Brahma wakes up, the universe is reborn, and a new version of Indra is born too. These revelations humble Indra and he begs the boy and the hermit to stop. The boy reveals himself as Vishnu, and the hermit as Shiva. This story illustrates that the goal of Hindu spirituality is release from the endless cycle of rebirth, rather than apotheosis.

Interestingly, Mahayana Buddhism developed the concept of the Bodhisattva, an enlightened person who is able to reach Nirvana but delays doing so to help other suffering beings. A bodhisattva is a quasi-divine human.

It may be that some ancient pagan mystery religions held a similar view of the journey of the soul to the views of Hinduism and Buddhism, but what has come down to us from antiquity seems to be the opposite: The purpose of the ancient mystery rituals such as the Eleusinian Mysteries seems to have been to help the initiate's soul to survive reincarnation intact (rather than dissolving into the "soul soup") and to enable them to remember their previous lives. This may have been to enable them to escape the cycle of reincarnation, but if so, that knowledge has not survived.

Pagan and animistic religions seem to be more focused on relationships than upon the ultimate fate of the soul. They tend to emphasize reciprocity among the community, which includes animals, land spirits, the ancestors, and the environment.

There is a lot of discussion about reincarnation in contemporary Paganism, but we seem to have lost the concept of an ultimate destination for the soul. Perhaps apotheosis is the missing piece in this puzzle.

Darkness

> The dream is the small hidden door in the
> deepest and most intimate sanctum of the soul,
> which opens to that primeval cosmic night that
> was soul long before there was conscious ego
> and will be soul far beyond what a conscious ego
> could ever reach.
>
> —Carl Jung,
> *The Meaning of Psychology for Modern Man* (1931).

One of the key insights of the Pagan Revival is that darkness is not evil. Darkness often represents the repressed aspects of the psyche. It is also associated with the primeval forest and the divine feminine principle.

Humans emerged from the primeval forests into the open savannah, and began to use fire to keep away larger predators. Hence light became associated with warmth and food and safety, and darkness was where the wild predators lurked. When humanity developed "civilization" (the negative side of which is the impulse to conquer and subjugate other people), people began to associate the feminine, and women, with the primitive and the primeval.

Starhawk examines this process in her excellent book *Truth or Dare* (1989). She shows how, as humans settled down in one place and began to cultivate crops in fields instead of hunting and gathering, notions of property developed. Men wanted to defend their piece of land against outsiders, which gave rise to the concept of warriors. As a result, the male lineage became more important than the female, and men began to repress the aspects of themselves that they associated with women, such as nurturing and empathy. Light was associated with masculinity, warriors, reason, and civilization; darkness was associated with femininity, mothers, intuition, and wildness. In this process, primacy was accorded to the "masculine" values of aggression, dominance, control, and reason, whereas the "feminine" virtues of nurturing, emotion, sexuality, and expression were regarded with suspicion— seen as needing to be controlled, or even treated with downright hostility.

Pagans have realized that people need the darkness and the qualities associated with it, and that an inner marriage of darkness and light must occur for the psyche to be integrated. As Carl Jung said,

> There is no light without shadow and no psychic wholeness without imperfection.[118]

The darkness is necessary for rest, growth, and regeneration. Death is not evil—rather, it is a necessary adjunct to life. If there was no death and dissolution, there could be no change or growth. The cycle of birth, life, death, and rebirth is part of the interaction of the polarities of life and death, heat and cold, darkness and light. Suffering is also part of the process of growth; just as a tree is shaped by the wind, people are shaped by their experiences. In the worldview of many Pagan traditions, the soul goes through cycles of birth, death, and rebirth, but not in an endlessly repeating, always-the-same kind of way. Rather there is change and growth, and the pattern is an ascending spiral, not a treadmill. Everything passes through light (spring and summer) and descends into darkness (autumn and winter). But just as the seasons are not the same each time, nor are the greater cycles.

In the Pagan worldview, humans are not inherently sinful but inherently divine. The rest of the universe is also inherently divine;

---

118   Jung (1944, 2015), *Psychology and Alchemy.*

space-time is curved; the sphere, the circle, and the spiral are the primary geometric forms.

Patriarchal values and the repression of "feminine" values are responsible for many of the problems in society; the balance is only just beginning to be restored, so society is in a period of transition.

Good, in my scheme of things, means balance, and evil means imbalance. Here, balance refers to dynamical balance, not stasis and/or stalemate. Any quality balanced by an opposite quality is not canceled out but creates a third quality. Balance is often assumed to mean canceling out, but if you think about two equal weights in a scale, they do not cancel out each other's weight, they only cancel out each other's impact on the scales. In a complex system, such as climate, high pressure in one area will result in comparatively low pressure in another area, so the flow will be from the high pressure area to the low pressure area. But as it is not a closed system, this will create another flow due to another difference in pressure, so you might say that the system was in dynamical balance, or equilibrium, where it can move in a number of directions or degrees of freedom.

Evil itself can sometimes seem balanced, like the mutually assured destruction of the superpowers in the Cold War. This, however, is not balanced in the sense of possibility to move (dynamical balance), but stalemate. There is nowhere for the opposing superpowers to go—they cannot use their weapons, and it seems to them that they cannot back down. The only way out of the stalemate was to expand the space in which the interaction was taking place, by creating an environment of openness and dialogue where it was possible for them to reduce their nuclear arsenals.

Sometimes a hero or a visionary has to do something radical, taking events in an apparently new direction, but often this is in order to restore true balance (possibility to move, or the dynamical balance between the apparently opposing principles), rather than the stasis (status quo, stalemate) of closed-down possibilities that existed before.

Rather than trying to eradicate darkness and the shadow side of ourselves, Pagans seek to integrate them into the psyche in the alchemical wedding of darkness and light.

Darkness is also the realm of dreams, intuition, and sleep. Sleep is important because it allows us to regenerate damaged areas of the body and process recent events in our lives. In the ancient world, there were healing temples with dream incubation chambers. I have visited two of these: the temple of Asklepios on the island of Kos, Greece, and the temple of Nodens in Lydney, England. Dream incubation was the practice of sleeping in a chamber within the temple in order to receive a dream from the deity of the temple that might provide a solution to a problem or the cure of an illness. In some cultures, people would sleep in a tomb or on a mountaintop to incubate such dreams.

Recently, depth psychologists have revived the practice of dream incubation. The technique involves sleeping somewhere where you will not be disturbed by extraneous light or digital distractions. Before going to sleep, write down the problem you want your dream to provide insights about. Think about the problem for a few minutes, then visualize it as a symbolic image.[119] For example, if the problem is loneliness, visualize yourself alone in a house. Set an intention of dreaming about the issue. Then, when you wake up, lie quietly for a few minutes and wait for any dreams to come to mind. Invite any remaining fragments to surface. You may want to maintain a dream journal and write down your dreams.

---

119   Dale M Kushner (2022), 'Dream Incubation: Solving Problems in Your Sleep.' Psychology Today Canada.

Darkness is not something to be feared. People can do bad deeds under the cover of darkness, but it's those people who are to be feared, not the darkness. Ghosts and spirits may walk abroad at night, but for the most part they are not hostile. Darkness is the realm of the unconscious, which is the source of dreams and creativity.

Some contemporary Pagan traditions have incorporated darkness into their practice by meditating in the dark and performing rituals at night. It is widely believed that the subconscious is more active in the dark, which is useful for magical rituals.

Darkness can be used very effectively in rituals by extinguishing and relighting candles for dramatic effect, and to represent the birth of new light and life. Many Pagan rituals also represent the interaction between darkness and light as a cosmic dance.

Embodiment

In some religions and spiritualities, the spirit is valued more highly than the body. In Pagan religions, the body is cherished: It is not merely a vehicle or a lump of meat, but the meeting place of matter and spirit, where the sacred marriage takes place. We are embodied beings, and being embodied allows us to experience pleasures like eating and making love and looking at beautiful landscapes and seascapes and skyscapes.

In the legend of Baubo and Demeter, Baubo used her body to restore Demeter's joy in life. Demeter was sad because Persephone had vanished from the Earth, and Baubo danced and revealed her vulva. Later Christian writers regarded Baubo's actions as shameful, but in Ancient Greece, they were regarded as beautiful and life-enhancing.

Different people have different physiques, different nutritional needs, energy levels, and body shapes. In diet culture, people are taught to deny the body and regulate what they eat. A more embodied and sensual approach would encourage people to listen to their body and learn to fulfill its needs in a more balanced way.

An important part of embodiment is experiencing yourself as part of the world. A great way to experience yourself as part of nature is to include the sit spot into your practice (see Chapter 4, Connecting with Nature).

Adrian Harris, who writes on embodiment, describes the practice of the sit spot:

> Spending time in your sit spot is a meditation
> that fine-tunes your sensory awareness. . . Such
> subtle embodied communion with one chosen

place can pattern a sacred relationship to the world.[120]

The sit-spot is similar to the ancient Heathen magical practice of "sitting out," known as utiseta.[121] This is a practice for communicating with landwights and should only be used if you specifically need help or answers. The practitioner would sit on a special mat, often divided into quadrants, and practice divination and shamanic drumming. It is important to experience yourself in communion with your surroundings. Feel the position of your body on the ground, take in the sights, sounds, and smells around you: birdsong, the wind in the trees. Then focus your attention inside yourself and find the core of your being. Next, shift your focus outside of yourself, expanding your awareness beyond the boundaries of your body. Practice this expansion and contraction of your attention for several cycles, and it becomes easier to commune with the spirits around you.

Practicing any art, craft, or sport in an embodied way means being aware that you are an embodied being as you do the activity. As Pagan religions celebrate the joys and pleasures of being embodied and alive, we can deepen our connection to Nature and to our Pagan practice by celebrating and taking care of our bodies.

---

120 Adrian Harris (2011, 2018), 'The sit spot.' Body Mind Place.
121 Lydia Helasdottir, 'Utiseta, Breath, and Mound-Sitting.' Northern Tradition Shamanism.

Eudaimonia

It is the exercise of the virtues during one's life
that is held to be at least partially constitutive
of eudaimonia, and this is consistent with
recognising that bad luck may land the virtuous
agent in circumstances that require her to give
up her life. Given the sorts of considerations
that courageous, honest, loyal, charitable people
wholeheartedly recognise as reasons for action,
they may find themselves compelled to face
danger for a worthwhile end, to speak out in
someone's defense, or refuse to reveal the names
of their comrades, even when they know that this
will inevitably lead to their execution, to share
their last crust and face starvation.

—Rosalind Hursthouse and Glen Pettigrove,
Virtue Ethics (2023)

Eudaimonia is the principle of human flourishing. It can
be broken down into six key aspects, according to Charmaine
Sonnex, Chris Roe, and Elizabeth Roxburgh: "personal growth,
self-acceptance, positive relation with others, autonomy,
environmental mastery, and purpose in life." [122]

The idea of eudaimonia was first described in Aristotle's
Nicomachean Ethics. It describes living in a way that leads to the
fulfillment of one's full potential or true self (the *daimon*, the Greek
equivalent of the Roman term genius or indwelling spirit).

---

122   Charmaine Sonnex, Chris A. Roe, and Elizabeth C. Roxburgh (2020) 'Flow, Liminality, and
Eudaimonia: Pagan Ritual Practice as a Gateway to a Life With Meaning.' Journal of Humanistic Psychology,
Vol 62, issue 2.

Eudaimonia can be distinguished from hedonism, because hedonism is about seeking pleasurable experiences and avoiding unpleasant ones, whereas eudaimonia is about living well and actualizing one's full potential, not necessarily about being happy all the time.

Contemporary Pagan religions often emphasize personal growth, the expansion of consciousness, and self-empowerment. Pagan rituals often include opportunities for reflection, change, and transformation, whether through participation in the cathartic enactment of ritual drama, or through a spell.

Our rituals and theologies also emphasize the divinity of the individual, through practices such as invoking deities and working skyclad (in the nude). Contemporary Pagan rituals celebrate the body and have often empowered marginalized groups such as women and LGBTQ+ people. They also seek to integrate the less-accepted parts of the self into consciousness, transforming them into more helpful qualities and energies.

Pagan rituals also include expressions of reciprocity and community, reinforcing positive and healthy relationships between people. They tend to be egalitarian and involve sharing food and drink.

Wicca emphasizes that all initiates are members of the priesthood. In all Pagan traditions, people are encouraged to come to their own understanding of how the world works, what deities are, and what happens to the soul after death. People are encouraged to work magic rather than ask deities for help. Mastery of the practitioner's environment is achieved through magic and is related to the principle of autonomy.

Finding meaning and purpose in life is one of the key functions of religion, and contemporary Pagan religions facilitate this by providing mythology, a seasonal cycle of festivals that reflects the stages of human life, a sense of service to all beings, and the grounding of our life experiences in Pagan mythology and folklore.

Eudaimonia, the cultivation of the inner genius, can be achieved by living a good life. The Stoics defined a good life as one where living virtuously was paramount; virtue was seen as both necessary and sufficient for eudaimonia.[123] Aristotle thought that external factors such as luck were also responsible for eudaimonia. Some cultures regarded a person's luck as an intrinsic quality.

There are several reasons why eudaimonia deserves to be more widely known. Paganism is a life-affirming religion, and the cultivation of virtue in order to maximize human flourishing is a life-affirming practice. Pagans do not believe that humans are inherently sinful, so the cultivation of virtue is a practice that is consistent with the belief that humans can improve themselves, and it is very much akin to the importance placed on personal growth by many contemporary Pagans.

---

123   Rosalind Hursthouse and Glen Pettigrove, 'Virtue Ethics.' The Stanford Encyclopedia of Philosophy (Fall 2023 Edition), Edward N. Zalta & Uri Nodelman, eds., https://plato.stanford.edu/entries/ethics-virtue/

Fertility

The roots of the word fertility are from Latin ferre, to bear or to carry. This developed into the word *fertilis*, "bearing in abundance, fruitful, productive."

I want to reclaim the word fertility from the kind of people who use it as an excuse for being homophobic or transphobic. I also want to reclaim it from the kind of people who claim that Paganism is a fertility religion, because that description is overly reductive.

Fertility magic is a form of sympathetic magic, and the thing about sympathetic magic is that you can do it with any two things or people. It need not involve the literal fertilization of an ovum by a sperm, so anybody can go and do things in the furrows to encourage the crops to grow. You do not need a heterosexual couple to perform the ritual.

In medieval mythology, the stories of King Arthur and the legend of the Holy Grail included the story of the Grail Castle and the Fisher King. In this legend, the knight Parsifal goes wandering about on his quest for the grail. He finds the Grail Castle, but on his first visit, everything goes wrong. He fails to ask the right questions and so the Grail Castle disappears and he has to wander around for another seven years. When he finally finds the Grail Castle once again, he goes into the castle, and he approaches the Fisher King, who is "wounded in the thigh" (probably a euphemism for the genitals). This time, he finally does ask the right question.

In Chrétien de Troyes' version, the question is "Who is served by the grail?" And one possible answer was "The old king, whose heir you are."

211

In Wolfram von Eschenbach's version, the question is: "Sir, why do you suffer so?" And the answer is, "I was wounded by the spear and it alone can heal me."

In composer Richard Wagner's version, Parsifal asks the question of his uncle Gurnemanz when he arrives at the lake in the domain of the Grail. He asks, "Who is the Grail?" His uncle replies, laughing, "That cannot be spoken, but if you are called to its service, the knowledge will not be hidden for long."

It is the asking of the right question that restores fertility to the land. So here you have two men creating fertility, in this case, by asking the right question.

Fertility can be creativity, or it can be spiritual fecundity. It does not have to be literally giving birth or creating life; it can be creating life in the sense of creating more abundant conditions for living.

The blight, or lack of fertility, that was affecting the lands around the Grail Castle, was affecting both "men's minds and women's wombs" (and presumably women's minds and men's reproductive equipment too). The restoration of fertility included both mental and physical fertility.

So let's reclaim the word fertility from any narrow usage of that term and celebrate creativity and joy, especially queer joy. There is no need to take everything literally, since magic is all about metaphor. You can get a pointy thing and a roundish thing and stick them into each other, and that can be a metaphorical magical representation of fertility.

There is also a widespread idea that Paganism is a "fertility religion." The origins of this idea lie in late nineteenth century ideas of what "primitive" religion was about.[124] You cannot reduce the complexity of Pagan religions to a single idea, or a single religion.

The reason ancient pagan religions were labeled "pagan" was that the old religions and customs lingered longest in the countryside, and so they were referred to as rustic and pagan in contrast to the cosmopolitan and urban phenomenon of Christianity. There were several popes who took the regnal name of Urban. The Christian Bible contains a lot of imagery about the heavenly Jerusalem. The imagery of Christianity as urban and urbane—and Paganism as rustic and pagan—persisted for a long time.

Because of the association of Paganism with the countryside, people assumed that the primary reason for the continuation of folk customs was related to fertility: ensuring that the crops would grow. This was certainly an important consideration, but it was not the only reason people continued with these customs and rituals. Sometimes they were a way of dealing with fears of death and otherworldly beings. Sometimes they were about protecting farm animals from disease.

It is also important to recognize that fertility is only one side of the coin. The land must rest and lie fallow for fertility to be restored. Fall and winter are necessary for the rain and snow to water the land and restore its fertility. This is reflected in the story of Demeter and Persephone.

Persephone (or Kore), the spring maiden, was frolicking in the fields with her friends when she was carried off by Hades, the god of the underworld. In the story, she does not go voluntarily, because women are often not given agency in ancient stories.

---

124   Andy Letcher (2009), Paganism and the British Folk Revival.

Her mother, Demeter, deeply distressed by Persephone's disappearance, loses interest in the crops and vegetation, and everything dies back, giving rise to the first winter. She asks the other gods to help her find Persephone, and eventually they discover that Persephone is in the underworld with Hades. The part of the story that often gets forgotten is the encounter between Demeter and Baubo, also known as Iambe. During her wanderings, Demeter goes to the court of the King of Eleusis, where she is quiet and subdued until Baubo appears and makes her laugh by showing her a mystery. Some scholars suggest that Baubo showed Demeter her vulva: the source and origin of life. That would have restored joy to a goddess of life. Martini Fisher suggests that while Demter is the goddess of agriculture and crops, Bauno is an older goddess of a hunter-gatherer culture: the giver of abundance from the wild.[125] Fisher deduces this from the acorn crown that Baubo wears in some depictions of her. The oak is a powerful symbol in Greek mythology, and Fisher reminds us that its roots were believed to reach all the way to the underworld.

When Demeter's joy was restored by Baubo, perhaps a hint of spring returned to the land: the first flush of green along the hedgerows, or a few spring flowers on the hillsides. If so, this could be a story of fertility being restored by two goddesses.

The cycles of birth, life, death, and rebirth are very important in contemporary Pagan thought, and arguably were important to ancient pagans too, as you can see from the story of Demeter and Persephone and the Eleusinian Mysteries that were based upon the story. Fertility is only one part of the cycle, not the whole story.

---

125   Martini Fisher (2023), 'Baubo, the Great and Forgotten.' History Made Beautiful.

Immanence

The immanence of spirit in matter is a key concept in Pagan religions, whether they are polytheist, animist, or pantheist. In my research, I found that 91 percent of my sample agreed that spirit was immanent in matter; the rest were mostly atheist Pagans.[126]

Immanent means "indwelling, remaining within, inherent" and comes from French immanent or directly from late Latin *immanens*, the present participle of *immanere* "to dwell in, remain in."

The concept of immanence in Pagan thought refers to the immanence of deities in Nature. In Christian thought, it refers to the immanence of God in the person of Christ or to the Divine indwelling of the Holy Spirit in people. Because of this, in interfaith contexts, it is sometimes necessary to explain the Pagan understanding of immanence. I was somewhat taken aback when a Christian neighbor asked me if I felt the lack of the concept of immanence in Paganism, and I had to explain that Pagans believe the Divine and/or deities are immanent in Nature, so we see divinity and spirit everywhere.

Every wood, grove, glade, tree, bush, mountain, rock, river, pool, stream, has its indwelling spirit, wight, or genius loci. It is possible to see traces of the movement of the gods in every natural phenomenon: breeze, wind, storm, volcanic eruption, snow, and more. Divinity is immanent in everything and this imbues everything with meaning and enchantment.

Sometimes the immanence of the divine in everything can be misinterpreted, as in the Hindu story of the elephant and the

---

126   Yvonne Aburrow (2008), Do Pagans see their beliefs as compatible with science? Thesis, Bath Spa University.

student. A teacher was sharing with the student his belief in the immanence of the divine. The student became deeply imbued with this concept, and walked home, meditating on the profound truth of immanence. Then an elephant came toward him, and the elephant's rider told him to get out of the way. The student assumed that the divine was immanent in the elephant, and that the divine was love, so he would not be harmed. But the elephant whacked him with its trunk, and he landed in a thorn bush and broke his arm. Next day, he went back to his teacher and complained of the apparent failure of the concept of immanence. The teacher pointed out that the divine was also immanent in the elephant's rider who was telling him to get out of the way.[127]

Many cultures have stories where a deity brings the snow or the rain or the storm. In German folklore, the snow is Mother Holda shaking out her eiderdown.[128] The sound of the storm is the Wild Hunt riding through the sky. In Scotland, the Cailleach brings the storms of winter and freezes the ground with her staff.[129] In medieval times, local saints were petitioned for rain by taking their statue out of the church and dunking it in the river. This suggests a folk belief that deities and saints could control the weather.

Many people see these stories as pseudo-scientific explanations of the origins of winter or storms or snow, but I think it is more accurate to see them as imbuing natural phenomena with enchantment and meaning.

---

127 Dennis Lewis, The Elephant & The Student.
128 Will-Erich Peuckert (1993), Schlesische Sagen, p. 263.
129 F. Marian McNeill (1959), The Silver Bough, Vol.2: A Calendar of Scottish National Festivals, Candlemas to Harvest Home. pp. 20–21.

Land

Closeness to the land is a key aspect of many Pagan traditions. Pagans are inspired by rocks, trees, rivers, hills, and mountains. Many of us love to know the names of landforms. We rejoice when rivers are recognized in law as people. We love to know the mythology and folklore of a landscape and to visit stone circles and burial mounds.

If your ancestors are buried in a specific area of land, and you eat the food produced there, you feel a connection to that land. Many Indigenous people say this. Indigeneity is a specific concept with a precise meaning. To be Indigenous is to have a close relationship with the land, to be a member of a people who have lived on the land for thousands of years, to have historical continuity with pre-colonial societies, distinct languages, culture, and beliefs, and to be the non-dominant group in a society. Examples of Indigenous Peoples include the Sami, several distinct cultural groups in Europe, the Indigenous Peoples of North and South America, the First Nations of Australia and Aotearoa New Zealand, all of whom have strong links to their territories and natural resources.[130]

However, closeness to the land can become problematic when people who feel that closeness embrace right-wing, reactionary politics. Our feelings about our ancestral lands cannot eclipse our humanity and hospitality toward the stranger and the refugee.

If you live on colonized lands, you should learn about the Indigenous Peoples who live there and about their struggle against colonialism. A good place to start is to find out the land acknowledgment for the territory you are on. What treaties cover

---

130   United Nations Permanent Forum on Indigenous Issues, 'Who are indigenous peoples?'

your region? What is the history of the area? What Indigenous languages are spoken there? Are they endangered? You can find out a lot of this information from Native Land Digital, a website with maps of Indigenous territories, languages, and treaties.

If you live in Europe, you could look at the history of colonization of other lands by Europeans, including the Baltic Crusades and the Prussian Crusades when thousands of Pagans (and occasionally Christians) were murdered or forcibly converted by the Teutonic Knights in a huge land grab.

The entire pagan population of Old Prussia was slaughtered and replaced with Teutonic Knights and their vassals in the Prussian Crusade. In some cases, they even claimed that the local Christian population was still pagan and used that as a justification for stealing their land. Similarly, the Northern Crusades, between 1198 and 1290, were the violent overthrow, colonization, and Christianization of the Baltic states.

These crusades in Northern Europe provided the Church with the concept of Terra Nullius, also known as the Doctrine of Discovery—the idea that any land occupied by non-Christians was considered empty and available for colonization. Although the Catholic Church rescinded the papal bull Terra Nullius not long after it was written, it was still cited as a precedent in United States and Canadian colonial law in the nineteenth century. Similarly, Australia, despite 65,000 years of Indigenous habitation, was considered "no man's land" when European settlers arrived in 1788. Indigenous populations in North and South America, Africa, and Australia were forcibly converted to Christianity, and their land was stolen. In North America and Australia, their children were forced to attend residential schools, where thousands of them died of starvation, disease, neglect, and abuse. Huge

numbers of Africans were forcibly transplanted to the Americas
and the Caribbean in the transatlantic slave trade.

While trying to establish a relationship with a new land, it is
a good idea to find out its history. In the British Isles, there is a
history of land grabs by the aristocracy: the Enclosures in England,
the Highland Clearances in Scotland, and the displacement
and death of huge numbers of Irish people caused by the Potato
Famine. In Wales, Welsh-speakers were persecuted in the
nineteenth and early twentieth centuries to force them to speak
English.

I am reminded of a story that someone told me once, which
has also been made into a cartoon.[131] A man was walking across
the moors. Another man stopped him and told him, "Get off this
estate." He asked why, and the man said that the land was his. The
walker asked how he had got the land. The other man answered
that he inherited it from his father. The walker asked, "How did he
get it?" The man replied that his father had inherited it from his
grandfather. The walker asked, "Well, where did he get it?" The
man replied, "He fought for it." The walker said, "Well, I'll fight
you for it, then."

The story highlights the arbitrary and unjust nature of the
acquisition of land by conquest.

It is also good to learn what animals, birds, plants, and fungi live
on the land you inhabit, and what their traditional or Indigenous
names are. What is the underlying geology? How have humans
interacted with the land in your region? Where are the major
watersheds? Is the soil acidic or alkaline? What foods are cultivated
in your region? When are they planted and harvested? What
climate band do you live in? When do the first flowers open in

---

131   'Well, we'll fight you for it.' Imgur.

spring, and what species are they? How has the climate changed in recent decades? Check out the Watershed Commons Department of Bioregions "Bioregional Awareness Quiz," which advocates for gaining deeper knowledge of the area you live in.[132]

Once you have this knowledge of the land around you, you can bring it into your planting plan for your garden, the imagery you use in your rituals, and buying and using local and seasonal foods.

---

132   Tina Fields, 'Bioregional Awareness Quiz.' Department of Bioregion.

Liminality

The concept of liminality was recognized and named by French ethnographer and folklorist Arnold van Gennep in 1909. It comes from the Latin word *limen*, a threshold, and refers to the stage in a rite of passage where the candidate is neither one thing nor the other: They are on the threshold between uninitiated and initiated, unmarried and married, child and adult, and so on (depending on what type of rite of passage they are undergoing). Van Gennep identified three stages in a rite of passage.[133] The first stage is the process of separation from the original group of which the candidate was part. The candidate is sent out into the forest or required to live apart for a period of time. In a wedding ceremony, for example, it is considered bad luck for the bride and groom to see each other immediately before the wedding. The second stage is the liminal phase, when the candidate is passing through the initiatory process. Most initiations have a procedure that must be followed to make them valid. This includes weddings, coming-of-age rituals, divorces, and more. The final stage of an initiation is the integration (or reintegration) of the candidate into the community in their new role, as an initiate, a married person, an adult, or a divorced person. Van Gennep also noted that a rite of passage can move a person from the status of outsider to group membership, or it can change their status within the group (e.g., from child to adult, or from single to married). He also regarded seasonal festivals as being rites of passage: e.g., from one season to another.

In 1974, British cultural anthropologist Victor Turner coined the expression "liminoid experiences."[134] These could

---

133 Arnold van Gennep (1977). The rites of passage, p. 21.
134 Victor Turner (1974), 'Liminal to Liminoid, in Play, Flow, and Ritual: An Essay in Comparative Symbology.' Rice Institute Pamphlet—Rice University Studies. 60 (3). hdl:1911/63159

be encountered or created in any situation that was fluid and changeable, neither one thing nor the other. They could happen in communities or even whole societies where everything was in flux. They can also happen during the process of individuation, where a person makes the transition from identifying with an archetype to becoming a fully rounded individual who has integrated unconscious material into their conscious mind. Turner also identified the concept of communitas: the shared experience and sense of community among people who have undergone the same rites of passage.

Liminality can also refer to the sense of otherness and strangeness that occurs in a ritual, time, or space that is neither one thing nor another. I frequently use it to mean the experience of being at the edge or in both the physical world and the spiritual world at the same time. I think this is why the concept of the hedge-rider (a possible interpretation of *haegtessa*, the origin of the word *Hexe* or witch in modern German) appeals so strongly to people. Witches are people who venture beyond the ordinary mundane world and into liminal zones: the twilight, the boundary between wilderness and civilization, the edges of otherworlds.

In folklore, ghosts and other paranormal phenomena were often observed at the boundaries of spaces, and the ancient ritual of beating the bounds was a way of demarcating territory. Stone circles in Europe are often in places that border two or more ancient tribal territories. People who were between one state and another were hedged about with ritual precautions, for example the bride and groom not being allowed to see each other on the eve of their wedding. Liminal spaces require special ritual and attention to overcome the potential dangers attendant upon being neither one thing nor another.

Pagan rituals pay a lot of attention to boundaries and thresholds. Wiccans cast a circle to contain the magical power they raise. When we are initiated, we cross over the threshold of the circle and of the coven to enter into communion with the coven and the gods. A Wiccan circle is described as being between the worlds, hence it is a liminal space. In the handfasting ceremony, the couple jump over the broom together to symbolize their entry into married life.

Merry

Merry and mirth are related (both etymologically and conceptually). Just seeing the word merry slightly elevates my mood. The word merry originally referred to a fleeting pleasure, and it comes from a Germanic root word meaning short (in the sense of a short time).

The word merry should not be confused with mirrie, which appears in the phrase Mirrie Dancers, and is a Scots word meaning shimmering; it refers to the Northern Lights.[135]

In his book *The Rise and Fall of Merry England* (1994), Ronald Hutton demonstrates that during the period between about 1350 and 1520, the medieval church celebrated a round of festivals in the liturgical year, followed by church ales (when people could buy alcohol from the church). These included the installation of boy bishops, games, pageants, plays, processions, and decorating the churches' rood lofts. In subsequent centuries, people have looked back with nostalgia to the time before the Reformation when jollity seemed to have been the order of the day. In the context of Merrie England, the word merry has an expansive meaning of plenty and relaxation. This is very far from what medieval England was actually like, though people did have some leisure to engage in games, singing, handicrafts, and traditional festivals, and to watch actors, jugglers, minstrels, morris dancers, and mummers.

The Reformation caused massive upheaval in the round of the church's liturgical year, with the abolition of many of the saints' days and holy days of the medieval church. During the interregnum and the Commonwealth, the Puritans abolished even more traditional customs, such as maypoles and dancing.

---

135 'What are the Mirrie Dancers?' Shetland.org. 2021.

Another usage of merry appears in the stories of Robin Hood and his Merry Men. According to the Oxford English Dictionary, a "merry man" was any follower of an outlaw or a knight, and Chaucer used the phrase in *The Canterbury Tales*. A merryman (with no space) was a jester or a buffoon.

The word merry appears in many phrases and compound words, notably merry-begot, which means a child born out of wedlock—possibly as a result of a one-night stand, or a night in the woods on May Eve, which is what happens in the wonderful novel *The Merrybegot* (2011) by Julie Hearn.

In the short story, *The May-Pole of Merry Mount* (1836) by Nathaniel Hawthorne, which is a condensed literary treatment of real events, the battle between Puritanism and merriment is continued in North America. Thomas Morton was an Anglican gentleman and an adherent of Merrie England who started a colony near Boston. He called his settlement Merrymount and was on very friendly terms with the local Indigenous people. In 1628, in defiance of the Puritans of Boston, he erected a large maypole with deer antlers at the top, and he invited the local Indigenous people to celebrate with him and his followers. The Puritans under Myles Standish overran the town of Merrymount the following June and chopped down the maypole. Morton wrote an account of his alternative vision of settlement in North America, entitled **The New English Canaan** (1637), which has been praised as "an important work of early American environmental writing" by author Michael Branch.[136] Thomas Morton is still celebrated today by Indigenous people and by the Morris dancing and folk community of New England and Southern Ontario, but he deserves to be more widely known.

---

136   Michael P. Branch (2004). Reading the Roots: American Nature Writing Before Walden, p. 63.

The concept of merriment is very important in the practice of Wicca, where people say farewell to each other with "Merry meet, merry part, and merry meet again" and where one of the eight Wiccan virtues is mirth, to balance the reverence that it is paired with.[137] Pleasure is an excellent thing. Life is to be enjoyed as much as possible. The Bible tells us to eat, drink, and be merry, not just once but four times.[138]

Pagan spirituality is earthy and pleasure-loving, so merriment and mirth are important components of it. We must be able to laugh at ourselves—and especially at the powerful and the pompous. Traditionally the gift that Prometheus gave humans was fire, but in the novel *Ye Gods!* (1993) by Tom Holt, the gift that he bestowed on humans was humor. I think this rings true, because humor is subversive.

---

137   It seems that I coined the phrase "eight Wiccan virtues," although the high priestess of my original coven referred to them as virtues. They are listed in The Charge of the Goddess by Doreen Valiente: "Therefore, let there be beauty and strength, power and compassion, honor and humility, mirth and reverence within you."
138   'Eat, Drink And Be Merry: Meaning & Context Of Phrase.' No Sweat Shakespeare. (The injunction to eat, drink and be merry appears in: Ecclesiastes 8:15, Isaiah 22:13, Luke 12:19, and 1 Corinthians 15:32.)

Mystery

Mystery religions were a highly significant part of the pagan religions of late antiquity. Thousands of people were initiated into the Eleusinian Mysteries, though none of them ever revealed what was in the rituals. The mysteries of the goddess Isis were hugely important in the classic novel *The Golden Ass* (circa 160 ce) by Lucius Apuleius.

The term mystery is derived from a word meaning to close, shut, or remain silent, which was exactly what the initiates of the mysteries did—they performed their rituals in secret and they remained silent about what was in them. It also comes from a verb meaning "to initiate" or "to reveal a mystery to someone."

The use of the word mystery to denote a detective novel is appropriate in some ways, as detective novels and initiatory mysteries consist of a series of signs and clues designed to reveal the truth at the denouement.

Practitioners of initiatory Wicca describe it as a mystery religion, and it shares many characteristics with the mystery religions of late antiquity: the use of secrets to promote group cohesiveness and to protect the mysteries from the gaze of the profane.

The Ancient Greeks had two words to describe mysteries and secrets: *arrheton*, the ineffable, the mysteries, that which cannot be described because they are purely experiential; and *aporrheton*, secret topics about which it was forbidden to speak to the uninitiated. Although most contemporary Pagans and occultists do not use these words, the concepts to which they refer are well understood and widely referred to when discussing initiatory traditions.

Myth

> He sees no stars who does not see them first
> of living silver made that sudden burst
> to flame like flowers beneath an ancient song,
> whose very echo after-music long
> has since pursued. There is no firmament,
> only a void, unless a jewelled tent
> myth-woven and elf-patterned; and no earth,
> unless the mother's womb whence all have birth.
> — J.R.R. Tolkien, "Mythopoeia" (1931)

Pagans do not tend to take our mythology literally, but it is an important component of our rituals and celebrations. By engaging with these stories, we encounter different archetypes and ways of being, and how the conflicts between different archetypes might be resolved.

In general culture, people often say "it's a myth" to mean that the thing referred to is not true. It is also often the case that Christian stories are referred to as "theology," but Pagan stories are referred to as "mythology." This tends to give Pagan stories a "lesser" status.

Mythology is "true" if it rings true and reflects real life. Mythological stories often contain ethical lessons, even if the ethical lesson is sometimes on how not to behave. They are also meaningful in that they re-enchant the world. This was the point of Tolkien's ideas about mythopoeia. He wanted to see the world as "myth-woven and elf-patterned"—in other words, enchanted.

Mythological or metaphorical truisms are deeply embedded

in cultures, and they constantly influence the way people think. Sometimes these metaphorical constructs can be used cynically to manipulate people; at other times they may be used to great effect to transform the psyche.

Myths and legends and folktales are valuable in that they illuminate the psyche from a different angle, providing a stimulus to stir the depths of the psyche. Events in these stories rarely have a single meaning; instead, different meanings can emerge through further meditation on the material. For instance, the green girdle worn by Gawain and then adopted by the rest of King Arthur's court in *Gawain and the Green Knight* can take on multiple connotations depending on your perspective. Gawain regards it as a badge of shame, indicating that he was not perfectly honorable: He did not disclose to his host Sir Bertilak that he had been given the girdle by Bertilak's wife, because he knew it would be useful when he encountered the Green Knight. But from a magical perspective, it can be seen as the power of the feminine protecting him from harm. It can also be seen as a symbol of pragmatism and cunning, and it involves the reader in a question: If you were given a magical object that prevented you from being killed, wouldn't you accept the gift?

The same story can also be different from one telling to the next. Cliff Eastabrook, a friend of mine who is a storyteller, said that he once told a story where he put in a sound effect of a sword being drawn ("Sching!") and it made the audience laugh, so they ended up laughing throughout the rest of the story. Another time, he told the story, and people did not laugh at the sound effect. Instead the audience received the story as a tale of mystery and wonder.

Stories can change their meanings over time too. In the story of Hades and Persephone, it is debatable whether Persephone wanted to go with Hades, or whether he abducted her against her will, which puts a completely different slant on the story.

The distinction between mythos and logos is important. Mythos is metaphorical truth—something that rings true, that is an accurate symbol for representing something. Logos is literal truth, such as empirical knowledge about how things work. Karen Armstrong explains the difference:

> In most pre-modern cultures, there were two recognised ways of attaining truth. The Greeks called them mythos and logos. Both were crucial and each had its particular sphere of competence. Logos ("reason; science") was the pragmatic mode of thought that enabled us to control our environment and function in the world. It had, therefore, to correspond accurately to external realities. But logos could not assuage human grief or give people intimations that their lives had meaning. For that they turned to mythos, an early form of psychology, which dealt with the more elusive aspects of human experience.[139]

Myth is complex and multifaceted, and it is an essential part of the Pagan Revival. It is not untrue, but rather a different way of expressing truth, as a symbol or metaphorical story to exemplify that truth.

---

139   Karen Armstrong (2009), 'Metaphysical mistake: Confusion by Christians between belief and reason has created bad science and inept religion.' The Guardian.

Nature

The word nature is related to the Latin word for birth. The ancient Greek word that referred to Nature was *phusis* (also the basis of our modern word physics):

> In Greek, the word that later got translated into "nature" is phusis (φύσις), based on the verbal root for "growing, producing," phuein (derived from the Indo-European root bheu, ancestor of the English verb "be"), with a suffix indicating the "objective realization of an abstract concept" 140

Aristotle, in his work *Metaphysics*, offers four different definitions of phusis: the process of generating what grows, the primordial element or principle from which things grow, the spontaneous cause of movement, and the substance from which things are made.

With the arrival of Christianity and rationalism, Nature became seen as a passive creation, organized and moved by divine laws or the laws of physics (which are still seen as somehow governing the universe, even in the absence of a deity to administer them).

During the Middle Ages, the concept of Mother Nature became popular, though more as a personification than as a being in her own right.

The rise of environmentalism and the popularity of the idea of the Gaia principle, first invented by Oberon Zell as the Gaea Thesis in 1970,[141] and then independently reinvented by James Lovelock and Lynn Margulis as the Gaia Principle, has led to a

---

140 Frédéric Ducarme, Denis Couvet (2020), 'What does 'nature' mean?' Nature. 6 (14).
141 Oberon Zell (undated), The Legacy of Oberon Zell.

new understanding of Mother Nature as Gaia, a self-organizing principle of life on Earth. To many Pagans, Gaia, Mother Nature, and the Earth are divine beings.

The first stirrings of the Pagan Revival in the nineteenth century were about a desire to return to Nature after the excesses of the Industrial Revolution. People felt disconnected from Nature by the rise of technology. They also wanted to return to older and simpler forms of religion, stripped of the accretions which had gradually been added to Christianity.

Seeing Nature as a living organism and a divine being (or as inhabited by divine beings) and being in relationship with Nature is a good step toward living sustainably and in harmony with the environment. To truly live in harmony with Nature, humans need to completely restructure our activities to be sustainable.

The focus of our culture on making money and producing endless manufactured objects, and assuming that these will bring us happiness, is completely unsustainable. Hunter-gatherer cultures that lived in harmony with Nature did not accumulate endless possessions or create masses of waste. They lived sustainably and knew how to live off the land and help the land to flourish.

One of the key goals of the Pagan Revival has been to live in harmony with Nature, and many Pagans—especially eco-pagans—seek to live sustainably, reconnect with Nature, and protect ecosystems. Incorporating knowledge of our local ecosystems, flora, and fauna into our rituals helps to resacralize and re-enchant the world, and eating locally and sustainably helps people to live sustainably and understand the ecosystem and bioregion in which they live.

Pagan

Merriam-Webster has updated its dictionary definitions of Pagan. The first meaning given is being a practitioner of a Pagan religion such as Wicca. Then it offers the old-fashioned sense of a person who does not practice a monotheistic religion and points out that this usage is often offensive. Next it offers the historical meaning, a practitioner of an ancient polytheistic religion, and finally the sense (now rarely used except in Papal encyclicals) of "a nonreligious hedonistic person." The Cambridge Dictionary gives the ancient meaning first, and the meaning of being a practitioner of contemporary Paganism second. Oxford Languages offers the same three meanings as Merriam-Webster, but with the historical meaning first, the old-fashioned and derogatory meaning second, and the meaning of a practitioner of contemporary Pagan religion third.

Early Christians applied the term Pagan to followers of ancient polytheistic religions as a derogatory term. It meant rustic or villager, and was derived from the Latin word *pagus*, a country district. A similar process gave rise to the word Heathen:

> In translating the Gospel of Mark from
> Greek into Gothic during the 4th century,
> the Christian bishop Ulfilas (c. 311–82)
> developed the term haiþno as a counterpart for
> Hellēnis, "gentile woman." Variants of haiþno
> subsequently came to be widely used in other
> Germanic languages, notably including the Old
> English hǣþen, from which derives the Modern
> English term heathen. An often repeated
> argument is that this term pertains to things
> being "of the heath"—it is possible that Ulfilas

was deliberately evoking the sense of rurality
that he believed was embodied in the Latin
term pagan.[142]

Reclaiming the concept of Pagan from pejorative meanings of
the term has been an important part of the contemporary Pagan
Revival.

In his magnum opus *The Triumph of the Moon* (1999), Ronald
Hutton identified four languages or discourses about Paganism
that were prevalent in earlier centuries.

The first is that of evangelists and missionaries, who called
anything that wasn't Christianity "pagan" (including Indigenous
religions and Hinduism). They regarded other religions as
primitive and erroneous, sometimes even inspired by their devil.
A possible name for this discourse is the "primitive" discourse.

The second discourse is that of the enlightenment scholars
who defended ancient paganisms as having paved the way for
Christianity, though they still believed that they lacked morality.
A possible name for this discourse is the "precursor" discourse.

The third discourse is that of the Theosophists who regarded
ancient paganisms as alternative belief systems. It tended toward
the perennial philosophy, viewing all religions as variations
on a single theme. A possible name for this discourse is the
"perennial" discourse.

And the fourth discourse is the one that regarded ancient
paganisms as Nature religions, and expressed a longing for an
ancient past when people were closer to Nature. A possible name
for this discourse is the "Nature Religion" discourse.

---

142   Ethan Doyle White, "Paganism." Encyclopedia Britannica, October 10, 2023.

None of these discourses presented an accurate picture of ancient paganisms, but the "nature religion" one was very popular with people reviving Paganisms.

Since it is possible to be a member of more than one revived Pagan religion, it makes sense to have an umbrella term to refer to revived Pagan religions collectively. It is unnecessary to add the prefix "neo"— no one refers to charismatic forms of Christianity as "neo-Christianity," or to the Hare Krishna movement as "neo-Hinduism." If you are trying to distinguish between ancient pagans and contemporary Pagans, just use the terms "contemporary Pagans" and "ancient pagans." (I avoid writing "modern Pagans" because the current era is often referred to as postmodern, so modern is now retro.) If you want to distinguish between reconstructionists, polytheists and other types of Pagans, just use the term "eclectic Pagan" to refer to people who do not belong to any specific tradition, and refer to Wiccans and Druids as such.

It is important to note that many witches, druids, polytheists, Heathens, and occult practitioners do not identify as Pagan for various reasons, but their practices have a lot in common with those of the people who do identify as Pagan. I once attempted to create a Venn diagram to describe all these intersecting groups and it became quite complex.

There have been endless online discussions where people have sought to define or describe Paganism. Because it is not a creedal religion, but rather a loose association of different Pagan traditions, it is hard to come up with a definition without introducing a number of caveats and exceptions.

For example, you might say that Pagans worship the gods of ancient polytheistic religions—but what about atheist Pagans and worshippers of the Great Goddess, who is largely a twentieth century construction,[143] albeit one with elements of older goddesses?

You might say that Pagans are followers of a nature religion, but this is problematic as not all Pagan and polytheist traditions are focused on Nature.

You might say that Pagans worship deities that are immanent, but not all Pagans do that either.

The best way to describe being Pagan is to list characteristics and say that most Pagans do many of the items on the list. Even then, the list will probably exclude someone, or inadvertently also function as a description of a religion that does not call itself Pagan. So it is the combination of a cluster of these characteristics, plus identifying as a Pagan, that makes someone a Pagan.

Most Pagans worship or honor ancient Pagan deities or deities that are based on ancient Pagan deities. These deities include goddesses, and tend to be seen as immanent. They are not usually regarded as omnipotent.

Most Pagans honor and revere Nature. This can take the form of environmental campaigning, and/or performing rituals outdoors.

Most Pagans celebrate being alive and have a liberal and progressive attitude about human sexuality and consensual sexual activity.

Pagan religions are joyful and world-affirming, mostly optimistic about human nature, and tend to emphasize the autonomy of their practitioners.

---

143   Jack Chanek (2023), *Queen of All Witcheries: A Biography of the Goddess.*

A description of Paganism offered by a National Health Service Trust in the UK captures most of the main points:

> Pagans understand deity to be manifest within nature and recognise divinity as taking many forms, finding expression in goddesses as well as gods. Goddess worship is central in paganism. Pagans believe that nature is sacred and that the natural cycles of birth, growth and death observed in the world around us carry profoundly spiritual meanings. Human beings are seen as part of nature, along with other animals, trees, stones, plants and everything else that is of this earth. Most pagans believe in some form of reincarnation, viewing death as a transition within a continuing process of existence.[144]

A good exercise is to write your own statement of beliefs and values. What do you believe about deities or the divine, spirits, human sexuality, Nature, ethics, death and the afterlife, and so on? It is interesting to compare this with other people's statements and see how they align. Everyone's list will be slightly different, but this diversity and freedom to explore is at the heart of contemporary Paganism.

---

144   Weston Area Health NHS Trust (2020), Paganism.

Polarity

POLARITY, or action and reaction, we meet
in every part of nature; in darkness and light;
in heat and cold; in the ebb and flow of waters;
in male and female; in the inspiration and
expiration of plants and animals; in the equation
of quantity and quality in the fluids of the animal
body; in the systole and diastole of the heart; in
the undulations of fluids, and of sound; in the
centrifugal and centripetal gravity; in electricity,
galvanism, and chemical affinity. Superinduce
magnetism at one end of a needle; the opposite
magnetism takes place at the other end. If
the south attracts, the north repels. To empty
here, you must condense there. An inevitable
dualism bisects nature, so that each thing is
a half, and suggests another thing to make it
whole; as, spirit, matter; man, woman; odd,
even; subjective, objective; in, out; upper, under;
motion, rest; yea, nay.

—Ralph Waldo Emerson, *Compensation* (1841)

Polarity means having two opposite qualities or poles or any
contrasting pair of opposites. In the Ralph Waldo Emerson quote
above, which comes from an essay called *Compensation*, he writes
that polarity is light and darkness, spirit and matter, upper and
under, yea and nay, the systole and diastole of the heart, and other
opposite things. He also lists man and woman as two halves of a
whole, but among a host of other complementary phenomena.

I would say that the ultimate polarity from the personal point of view is that of the self and the other, and from a universal point of view, that of spirit and matter.

In magical discourse, polarity is the idea that magical energy can be created by bringing together two things that are opposite in nature. In my experience, magical polarity can be created by any pair of complementary qualities. Inner and outer, up and down, spirit and matter, lover and beloved, dark and light, masculine and feminine, camp and butch, air and earth, water and fire, and so on. And each pair of opposites is unique and cannot be mapped to other pairs of opposites.

As a nonbinary (not identifying with any particular gender) and bisexual person (which I define as attracted to multiple faces and body types), I have always known that I could create magical polarity with a person of any gender. And I have experienced times when I could not create polarity with another person, which seemed to me to be caused by a lack of erotic or sympathetic connection with that person. However, if we do experience erotic connection with someone in a magical context, we do not act on it, but rather sublimate it (transform it alchemically) to produce magical energy.

Polarity exists on a spectrum too. It is not the same as duality, where two absolute qualities are seen as opposites. A person can be more yang than another person, but can be yin in relation to a different person. People become a different polarity in relation to different people. Polarity is not immutable; it can shift and change depending on your mood, on the situation, and on who or what you are interacting with.

Polarity can be any pair of complementary opposites and that is how it has been used for most of its history as a term. It also refers to the positive and negative ends of a magnetic field.

Some people are convinced that in Wicca, polarity only represents the interaction of male and female, whereas it can involve any pair of complementary opposites.

Polarity is a much more complex concept than reducing it to male and female would allow for. I would argue that male and female are not in fact opposites; they are social constructs of gender and biology. If there are two people working together, trying to make polarity, in my experience, polarity emerges between them because of some other quality in those people. I have tried to create polarity with people of various genders, and whether or not you can make polarity with someone tends to vary according to whether you can create a personal connection with them. There needs to be some sort of mutual attraction or sympathy between you (not necessarily erotic, although it can be). If the concept of polarity is restricted to just male and female, it is unhelpful. It is also a mistake to conflate male and female with other qualities like darkness and light or day and night.

Polarity is usually between two points on a range of values, and not usually a standalone quality. For example, darkness and light are opposites, but clearly there are shades in between: twilight and daylight and shadow. The same applies to heat and cold. Between absolute zero and the heat of the sun, there's a huge range of temperatures. Usually, these pairs of opposites are complementary, and they can interact in the environment. For example, darkness and light interact through the fact that the sun comes up and the darkness recedes; as the sun goes down, the darkness returns. Darkness is the absence of light, not a thing in its own right. Light exists as a particle or a wave, but there is no corresponding particle or wave of darkness. Similarly, with hot and cold: heat is the increased agitation of the molecules of the heated object; but cold is the absence of agitation.

It is also interesting that on planet Earth, you are more likely to see a mixture of qualities, rather than an extreme such as absolute zero, because Earth is hospitable to life.

The original use of yin and yang referred to the shady side of a hill (yin) and the sunny side of a hill (yang). They have come to be associated with gender, but they were not associated with it originally.

The Kybalion has this to say about polarity:

> "Everything is dual; everything has poles;
> everything has its pair of opposites; like and
> unlike are the same; opposites are identical in
> nature, but different in degree; extremes meet;
> all truths are but half-truths; all paradoxes may
> be reconciled."[145]

Although *The Kybalion* originated from the New Thought movement, what strikes me about this is that, even in 1912, the authors of this text knew that seeming opposites are always of the same substance. They seem to be hinting at the idea that the opposites that are made manifest on the physical plane are reconciled on some other level, as Jung made clear in his visionary text, *The Seven Sermons to the Dead*,[146] where he says that pairs of opposites are reconciled in the pleroma (the ineffable unmanifest), and only become differentiated when they are manifest in the apparent world.

---

145   Three Initiates (1912), The Kybalion. https://sacred-texts.com/eso/kyb/kyb12.htm
146   Carl Gustav Jung (1916), Seven Sermons to the Dead. http://gnosis.org/library/7Sermons.htm

The Kybalion has a section about polarity and a separate
section about gender. Although it links gender to generation, the
significant thing about the fact that it has two separate sections for
polarity and gender is that its authors did not make the mistake of
conflating polarity with gender—and neither should we.

Reciprocity

A man should be loyal through life to friends,
And return gift for gift,
Laugh when they laugh. . .
If you find a friend you fully trust
And wish for his good-will,
exchange thoughts,
exchange gifts,
Go often to his hous…

—The Hávamál

In ancient times, hospitality and reciprocity were regarded as sacred. In English, the words "guest" and "host" are very closely related. In German, the words are *Gast* (guest) and *Gastgeber* (host, or literally, guest-giver). There were rituals of giving and accepting hospitality, and it was regarded as a sacred exchange. A guest under your roof was to be protected. That is why stories where the relationship of hospitality is betrayed are so powerful and shocking. In Germany and in Pakistan, it is still the custom for a guest to bring a gift for the host on their first visit to a house (even if they are not staying the night). This is the custom in other countries too. Hospitality was regarded as a sacred obligation in ancient Greece; it is mentioned several times in Homer's Odyssey. When Odysseus is shipwrecked, it is because of the obligations of the host toward the stranger that Nausicaa comes to his aid; and when he returns home to Ithaca disguised as a beggar, the shepherd Eumaios welcomes him as a guest. In India, the guest is regarded as a manifestation of the Divine, and hospitality is based on the principle Atithi Devo Bhava, meaning "the guest is God."

The exchange of gifts is a way of establishing a relationship. In gift economies, gifts are given without any formal agreement as to when the favor will be returned; however, the ethic of reciprocity is so strong that the gift creates an obligation to return the gift or favor, and in this way, an ongoing relationship is created, especially if the gift given in return is not an exact match in value for the gift that was given. You can see this ethic at work in the giving of gifts for Yule and birthdays. If a friend gives me a gift, I feel an urge to get them a gift in return—not in a transactional way, but because the friendship has now developed to the level of gift-giving. If you visit someone's house for dinner, that suggests that you are now on a dinner footing, and at some point you will probably reciprocate. You don't keep track of exactly how many times each person has hosted a dinner, but eating dinner together becomes part of the friendship. If someone looks after your cat while you are on holiday, you get them a gift while you are away. The gift is a token to say that you are grateful for the time they spent looking after your cat, and it shows that you were thinking of them; it is not a repayment of the time expended in cat-sitting.

Sadly, the giving of gifts has become bound up with monetary considerations, as people often feel the need to buy something of equal value to the gift they were given. However, the point of a gift is the amount of effort that went into it. Perhaps your friend went to a lot of effort to find something that they knew you would like; perhaps they went to a lot of effort to make something beautiful. Either way, it is the effort that counts, not the money. It is the idea that the friend cares enough about you to spend time making something for you, or finding a gift that expresses something about who you are. The gift then becomes an outward and visible symbol of your relationship with the giver. This is why I disagree with the idea that people should give up on all material things and get rid of stuff; quite often the stuff that you have around your home represents friendships and relationships.

The giving of money in exchange for something does not create a relationship, it ends it. If I pay in full for a service or a commodity, my obligation is discharged, and that ends the relationship. If I pay for a massage, a Tarot reading, or a workshop, that is because the masseur, Tarot reader, or workshop leader is not going to receive from me (at some unspecified future date) a massage, a Tarot reading, or a workshop. The relationship is ended by the payment. There is an exception to this, which is that people sometimes develop an ongoing relationship with a business that offers a good product or service, but this is not the same as a friendship. It may eventually develop into one, or it may not.

The way in which payment generally ends any ongoing relationship is, I think, why Wiccans believe strongly that we should not charge trainees for training. Members of a coven are in a relationship, and payment for training would end that relationship. What you gain in return for teaching is an opportunity to formulate, clarify, and refine your own views in the process of transmitting them to others. You can also learn from your trainees. And in due course, you will have a coven to work with who can write rituals for you to take part in. All members of a coven are expected to contribute food for the feast and candles and incense for rituals, and to help with clearing up after the ritual, however.

A similar situation exists in the development of friendships. A friend is someone you can open up to, who will not judge you for your actions; they may offer constructive criticism, but they do not reject you for your oddities and quirks. However, the process of opening up to each other is gradual and reciprocal. One person will reveal something about themselves, and the other will reciprocate. Revealing your innermost thoughts and feelings is to make yourself vulnerable, to give the gift of yourself. If the other person does not reciprocate with a revelation of similar import, it feels as if there is a major imbalance in the relationship: You have made yourself vulnerable, giving the other person power over you, so you need them to reciprocate. The gradual peeling away of layers of the onion applies to thoughts, to feelings, and to social space. First you meet a new or potential friend outside the home, in a pub or other neutral space; only later do you invite them to your house. At first you talk about current affairs and other relatively impersonal topics; only later do you reveal your more inward feelings and experiences.

This ethic of reciprocity appears in many cultures, but it is grounded in the idea of creating relationships. Humans are social animals and like to form bonds and associations—friendship groups, clans, tribes, families. These groups gradually form their own traditions, rituals, and symbols, but they are grounded in the mutual relationships of the members, who help each other, forgive each other, and form bonds of obligation through the exchange of gifts and hospitality.

It can be a good thing that the money economy has developed; sometimes people do not want to enter into a relationship with a person who has done something for them, because they are not part of the same social group. But it is important not to confuse the practice of gift exchange with the money economy. The two "systems" work differently, and they have different rules.

Traditional Pagan and other cultures had a strong ethic of reciprocity, hospitality, and gift exchange, and it is worth investigating these ideas. They can help us to understand the dynamics of gift-giving (always fraught with social minefields, especially around Yuletide), to learn to value what is of real worth (the emotional associations of a thing, rather than its monetary value), and not to feel guilty about having possessions. They can also make us more aware of the underlying currents of social intercourse—always a valuable insight for a magical practitioner who aims to be effective in all the realms (physical, spiritual, astral, social, and mental).

Reciprocity also exists in nature, in the form of symbiotic relationships: birds that pick insects out of buffaloes' fur, or cleaner wrasse that eat the parasites on sharks and clean bits of food out of their teeth. This natural reciprocity is found in ancient myths too. To gain wisdom from Mimir's Well, Oðinn had to sacrifice an eye. He gave up part of his physical sight in order to gain inner sight or wisdom. To gain the knowledge of the runes, Oðinn hung nine days and nights on the World Tree. The gain of one thing entails the loss of another; that is how equilibrium is maintained.

Sacred

Interestingly, many Pagans (myself included) seem to prefer the word "sacred" to the word "holy." To me, "sacred" implies something that celebrates the sanctity of being alive, and it can include the erotic and the wild.

"Holy," on the other hand, can imply abstinence from the erotic and embracing "civilization."

Interestingly, the first sense of "sacred" offered by the Merriam-Webster dictionary uses a Pagan-sounding example, that of a tree sacred to the gods, but their definition of "holy" is defined using Christian and monotheistic examples, including a quote from the Psalms.

Some Pagans do use the word "holy" occasionally, but the word "sacred" is much more frequently used in contemporary Pagan discourse. (Google for Pagan + sacred versus Pagan + holy if you don't believe me!)

Interestingly, when an Anglo-Saxon Heathen set out to create sacred space, it was a space set apart from the surrounding land, which was inhabited by spirits regarded as malevolent.

The etymology of sacred comes from Middle English, but ultimately from the Latin verb sacrare, "to make sacred, consecrate; hold sacred; immortalize; set apart, dedicate."

Etymology Online defines "holy" as associated with the Divine, whereas "sacred" is associated with something more generally consecrated for ritual use.

So "sacred" is used as a more general term without reference to the Divine.

Pagans use the term "sacred" to refer to sacred space (usually a place consecrated for ritual), sacred sites (usually places that feel special and numinous, often because they were used for ritual in the past, such as stone circles, burial mounds, and holy wells), and sacred sexuality (consensual sexual activity for a spiritual purpose).

Perhaps Pagans prefer the term sacred because we believe everything is sacred in its own right, and so it does not depend on divinity to sanctify it.

In Pagan usage, the sacredness of a thing or place can be either an inherent quality or something conferred on it by using it in a ritual, or consecrating it.

Sovereignty

Sovereignty is an ancient concept relating to bodily autonomy, and connection with the land, which is illustrated by the story of Goewin in *The Mabinogion*, and Chaucer's *The Wife of Bath's Tale*, ostensibly a retelling of *The Wedding of Sir Gawain and Dame Ragnell*, but with added commentary from Chaucer.[147]

Sovereignty is a word that people don't tend to use in spiritual contexts, but it has been reclaimed by Druids as meaning personal autonomy. It has ancient roots in a sense of connection with the land. For example, in ancient pagan kingship, a man became the King by virtue of marrying the goddess of the land or the goddess of sovereignty; so he could not rule if he had lost the favor of the Goddess. That's why, in the epic series of tales known as *The Mabinogion*, King Math has a sacred foot-holder called Goewin. Unfortunately, she gets raped by two of the other characters, Gwydion and Gilfaethwy. They are suitably punished by getting turned into various creatures and impregnating each other and giving birth. As a foot-holder, Goewin has to be a virgin (an independent woman) because she represents the goddess of sovereignty. There is an excellent analysis of the whole story of Goewin, Math, Arianrhod, Gwydion, Gilfaethwy, Lleu Llaw Gyffes, Blodeuwedd, and Gronw by Jhenah Telyndru in her book, *Blodeuwedd: Welsh Goddess of Seasonal Sovereignty* (2021).

Later on, the concept of sovereignty is discussed by Chaucer in *The Wife of Bath's Tale*, and the moral of this story is that women desire sovereignty. Chaucer appears to interpret sovereignty as the ability for women to have control over their own destiny (something that was sadly lacking in the medieval period). The

---

147   Denise Canning (2013), The Wife of Bath's True Quest for Sovereignty. Thesis submitted to the Department English at California State University, Bakersfield.

story begins with a knight who has raped a maiden. He is brought before the court and sentenced to death, but the ladies of King Arthur's court plead for clemency, which King Arthur grants. The knight is given one year to find out what it is that women most desire. He goes around asking many women and gets different answers from each of them. Finally he meets an old hag in the forest, and she tells him that what women desire most is sovereignty. She returns with him to the court and demands that he marry her, since she has saved his life by telling him the answer. He does not want to marry her, but she offers him a choice, that she will either be young and lovely and therefore a temptation to other men, or a hag who is faithful to him. He says that he will trust her with the choice, and thereby restores her sovereignty to her.

So again the subject of rape is linked to sovereignty, and it is possible to see that the concept of sovereignty is linked to bodily autonomy and bodily inviolability. Sovereignty is closely linked with feminist ideas of consent and the sacredness and inviolability of the body. It is also linked to land, and to goddesses of sovereignty as personifications of the land.

Sovereignty is important. It doesn't just mean ruling over others, but also having sovereignty of your own body. It's in this sense that modern Druids have reclaimed the word sovereignty to mean a connection with the land, bodily autonomy and self-determination.

Sovereignty is not just a word that's reserved for royalty; it is for all of us to assert our inviolable, sacred self.

Spirituality

Spirituality, once described by Lucy Bregman as "a glowing and useful word in search of a meaning" is one of those terms that can mean different things to different people.[148]

I use it to mean the sense of awe, wonder, and delight that I experience in contemplating beauty: the beauty of Nature, the beauty of relationships and connectedness; the joy of being truly connected and supported; and the experience of feeling part of something greater than myself.

Many people use the term spirituality to denote private or personal feelings of connectedness or transcendence, in contrast to collective experiences provided by a religious tradition.

However, it is clearly possible to have mystical experiences in a group setting or within a religious tradition, so the dichotomy implied by the phrase "spiritual but not religious" does not seem very helpful to me.

Another implication of the word spirituality is that it is about the spirit and not about the body. However, I think that much is lost in trying to divorce spirituality from embodied experience. It is possible to have a spiritual experience while making love, or swimming in the sea, or walking in Nature. I like to talk about embodied spirituality to emphasize that the body is integral to spiritual experience.

In essence, spirituality refers to the inner experiences of awe, wonder, and joy that people have while connecting with the numinous (the mysterious referent of our spiritual and religious lives).

---

148   Lucy Bregman (2006), 'Spirituality: A Glowing and Useful Term in Search of a Meaning.' OMEGA--Journal of Death and Dying 53(1).

Because of the vagueness and ambivalence of the word spirituality, I like to talk about the inner work. Spirituality can often involve spiritual bypassing (avoiding "unpleasant" subjects and feelings like anger, grief, and despair, which are often caused by violence, climate change, and other pressing social justice issues). It is necessary to develop both compassion and resilience in your spirituality, so that you can help others. It is all very well being super spiritual and magical and mystical, but if you do not have compassion for others, it is of no practical use, as Paul of Tarsus reminds us: "If I speak in the tongues of men or of angels, but do not have love, I am only a resounding gong or a clanging cymbal." [149] This insight is not restricted to Christian discourse. There is a traditional story from the East where a guru sends his disciples out into the world. After a few years, one reports back that after much practice, he can now walk on water. Another tells the guru that he can levitate. And the third disciple tells the guru that he can heal people. Only the third disciple has passed the test, because he is exercising compassion.

Spirituality does not have to be entirely devoted to the service of other people, but neither should it be entirely self-centered. It is necessary to develop your own gifts so you can be resilient and self-reliant—otherwise you could not help other people anyway. As with anything else, balance is the key to a healthy spiritual life.

I have written extensively about spirituality and the inner work in my previous books, *Dark Mirror: The Inner Work of Witchcraft* and *The Night Journey: Witchcraft as Transformation*.

---

149   1 Corinthians 13:1, New International Version.

Wild

The last people to continue ancient pagan practices and traditions were those who lived in the countryside. This is perhaps why people tend to associate Paganism with wildness. On the other hand, ancient pagan religions tended to have a dialogue with the wild. For example, the festival of Lupercalia (and many other ancient festivals) included wild behavior and was arguably a dialogue between the wild and civilization. By contrast, Christianity tended to see itself as the religion of civilization and cities and to regard the wilderness as the abode of demons. However, a daemon (from which the word demon is derived) was not an evil spirit, but a spirit of place.

For most of the Middle Ages, the wilderness was seen as desolate, scary, and inhospitable. Anne Warner writes:

> European culture perceived wilderness as dangerous, ungodly, and a place in which one risked getting lost. Indeed, European folktales and fairytales portrayed forests as evil places where the hero or heroine could be abducted and led into temptation. In addition, Satanic rituals and witches gatherings were assumed to happen in the deep forest, where Satan was thought to be. Thus, in its earliest construction wilderness was viewed as unsafe and threatening and this perception was brought over to the New World.[150]

---

150 Anne Warner (2008), 'The construction of "wilderness": an historical perspective.' Contributed paper for the Canadian Parks for Tomorrow: 40th Anniversary Conference, May 8–11, 2008, University of Calgary, Calgary, AB. PRISM Repository, University of Calgary.

Warner points out that wilderness is always a socially constructed concept in relation to civilization, and how it was seen at any period in history depended on socio-political discourse at the time.

With increasing industrialization and domination of the natural world, the Romantic movement emerged as a response to the subjugation of Nature, and people began to see the wilderness as pristine and untouched, majestic and sublime (inspiring awe and terror). Cities were overcrowded and technology began to take over—which led to people yearning for the bucolic, the rural, and the wild. Warner further explains:

> The popularization of the sublime meant that wild, harsh, and barren landscapes gained aesthetic value, and were less threatening. One could feel God's omnipotence surrounded by natural wonders like waterfalls, mountains and canyons. By the nineteenth century, modernism was intact in the Western world meaning society was increasingly urban, industrial, and technological. With the help of the Romantic Movement, the perception of wilderness had changed from wasteland to temple, and as a result, wilderness became something of value to be protected and appreciated.

The desire to return to the wild gave rise to camping, hiking, and outdoor appreciation movements in the late nineteenth century. Unfortunately, the Indigenous Peoples who had lived in the "wilderness" of North America were not seen as part of it, and people wanted their wilderness uninhabited. When Yellowstone National Park was created, the Indigenous Peoples who hunted and gathered and camped there were forcibly expelled from the area, and the park's boundaries were patrolled to keep them out.[151]

The notion that nature would be better off without humans was persistently peddled by conservationists drawing on the ideas of John Muir (co-founder of the Sierra Club), who wanted the Miwok and Mono people expelled from Yosemite National Park.[152] Similarly, the World Wildlife Fund expelled the Maasai people from their traditional hunting grounds in the 1950s and 1960s. It has frequently promoted the idea that Indigenous Peoples do not have the right to hunt, despite the fact that Indigenous hunting practices are sustainable, and the scarcity of wildlife is due to white "big game" hunters and encroaching industrialization. The earliest form of conservation was the preservation of wilderness areas as a playground for rich white people who wanted to hunt the game there. The idea that humans are harmful to Nature is racist. Indigenous Peoples who hunt and gather in a sustainable way are working in partnership with Nature.

In fact, 80 percent of the world's biodiversity is in lands protected by Indigenous Peoples, and Indigenous knowledge is a key part of working with Nature.[153] Indigenous Peoples' lands include around 36 percent of the world's remaining forests. Indigenous controlled burning practices prevent forest fires by removing underbrush from the forests. Indigenous people know how to live sustainably on the land because this knowledge is transmitted through their culture and language. As Nature for Justice's manager for Canada Steve Nitah explains:

151   Richard Grant (2021), 'The Lost History of Yellowstone.' Smithsonian Magazine.
152   Michelle Nijhuis (2021), 'Don't cancel John Muir. But don't excuse him either.' The Atlantic. (Despite the title of this article, I think knocking John Muir off his pedestal would be an excellent idea.)
153   Steve Nitah (2021), 'Indigenous peoples proven to sustain biodiversity and address climate change: Now it's time to recognize and support this leadership.' One Earth, Volume 4, Issue 7, 23 July 2021, Pages 907-909. ScienceDirect.

Indigenous peoples sustain nature because we know we are a part of nature. We realize that trying to bend nature to our will would harm us as well as the animals, plants, and ecosystems we all depend on. Instead, Indigenous peoples have a reciprocal relationship with our territories. We know that if we take care of the land, the land will take care of us. And so, we honor our cultural responsibility to be careful stewards. When these relationships are respected and when the rights and responsibilities of Indigenous peoples are recognized and supported, the entire planet will benefit. Our territories span massive, vibrant areas that serve as sanctuaries for humans, animals, and plants; hold massive amounts of carbon; and ensure the health of our water and air. These lands—and the Indigenous relationship to them—have global significance, especially as governments seek ways to achieve increasingly urgent biodiversity and climate goals.[154]

Previously, Indigenous knowledge was not respected, and Indigenous people were driven off their ancestral lands and prevented from engaging in their traditional sustainable practices. This decreased the biodiversity of these lands; it did not improve it.

The concepts of Nature and wilderness are also heavily gendered. People talk about Mother Earth and Mother Nature, but this is tangled up in Western discourse with patriarchal concepts of the subjugation of women. This is one of the key

---

154   Ibid.

premises of ecofeminism.[155] Ecofeminists have pointed out that setting aside areas of wilderness for protection removes the possibility of traditional means of subsistence, often those carried out by women and assisting them to be economically independent, and that setting some areas of wilderness aside as places where humans don't belong is used to justify the ruthless exploitation of the rest of Nature for economic gain through resource extraction and industry. The separation of nature and culture, ecofeminists argue, is part of the dualistic division in Western culture between ruler and ruled, rational and irrational, "higher" and "lower," which is used to justify genocidal policies toward Indigenous Peoples.

I have seen notions of "pristine wilderness" and the idea that humans are always harmful to the environment peddled in Pagan online spaces. These ideas are simply untrue. It is capitalism, colonialism, and industrialization that are harmful to the wilderness. If you want to protect the wilderness, standing up for the rights of Indigenous Peoples to live on their ancestral lands is the best place to start.

Contemporary Pagan ideas of the wild and wilderness tend to be more about living in harmony with Nature, but there is also a tendency to romanticize Indigenous Peoples and want them to live in a certain way so as to fulfill these romantic notions. Romanticizing them is not helpful; they are real, complex people, not archetypes.

Is it possible to disentangle notions of the wild from this complex and troubling history? I am not sure if it is, but at the very least, it is necessary to become aware of it. Contemporary people's fascination with the wild and the wilderness stems more from the

---

155   Linda Vance (1997), 'Ecofeminism and Wilderness.' NWSA Journal, Vol. 9, No. 3, Women, Ecology, and the Environment (Autumn, 1997), pp. 60–76. The Johns Hopkins University Press.

Romantic Movement than from ancient pagan attitudes to Nature. That said, recovering the worldview of our animist ancestors would be a good start. It is also a good idea to see the world through a less anthropocentric lens. Humans are in partnership with Nature, not rulers of it. In this context, contemporary Pagans' veneration of the Earth as a Goddess is helpful (except when people talk about humans as parasites on the Earth). Pagans value the qualities of wildness, nurturing, and abundance associated with Nature, but at the same time, we are influenced by Western discourse about Nature, "pristine" wilderness, and the racist ideas of many conservationists.

By looking back at ancient pagan cultures, it may be possible to recover a more balanced appreciation of Nature and the wild.

Pagans could also examine archetypes of Nature and the wild that are not survivals of ancient pagan traditions but new personifications that have developed in popular folklore, such as those investigated by Ronald Hutton in his book *Queens of the Wild*.[156] These are Mother Earth, the Fairy Queen, The Mistress of the Night, the Cailleach, and the Green Man. They are a glimpse of what might have emerged if ancient paganism had survived as a cohesive religion, and they are arguably continuations of ancient pagan ideas and symbols into medieval and Renaissance culture.

Mother Earth was originally an allegorical literary trope, but she is now an archetype of the Earth, popularized by Oberon Zell's Gaea Theology and James Lovelock's Gaia Hypothesis. The Fairy Queen, also known as the Queen of Elfhame, appears in folk songs such as "Thomas the Rhymer" and "Tam Lin," but also in literary poetry such as Edmund Spenser's "The Faerie Queene." The Mistress of the Night (an embodiment of nocturnal wildness) and

---

156   Ronald Hutton (2022), Queens of the Wild: Pagan Goddesses in Christian Europe: An Investigation. Yale.

the Cailleach (the Scots Gaelic personification of winter) emerged from folklore. Similar figures in other cultures, such as Frau Holle, are equally important. The Green Man, an archetype created and popularized by amateur folklorist Lady Raglan in the 1930s from the carvings of green men found in churches (which originally represented the sinful nature of wild and untamed human nature), has become a personification of Nature that is popular with Pagans and non-Pagans alike.

Another important motif associated with the wild is the Wild Hunt. In this context, wild has connotations of untamed, uncontrolled, and roving free, which were the original meanings of wild. The Wild Hunt is a very widespread motif in Indo-European folklore and mythology, appearing in Indian, Greek, Czech, Polish, Slovenian, Swedish, Dutch, Danish, German, Italian, Spanish, English, and Welsh legends. The deity who leads it varies from one culture to another, and it has different names in different places, but there are enough shared characteristics to be fairly certain that it is the same folklore motif. It even has its own classification number, ATU E501, in the Aarne–Thompson–Uther Index, a system of classifying folk tales and motifs used by folklorists.

The hunt is often seen as a cavalcade of dead warriors or other spirits. In many legends, it is Odin or Woden who leads the hunt, and the Einherjar (his army) who ride with him; in German they are called the Totenheer, the army of the dead. In this guise, his by-name is Herian, and this may be the origin of the name Herne, who was also associated with the Wild Hunt. The goddesses Berchta and Holda are also associated with the Wild Hunt, and with geese. The whirring sound made by the wings of geese in flight was associated with the Wild Hunt, and it is sometimes called Gabriel Hounds or Ratchet Hounds. Sometimes a lame goose that has trouble keeping up follows the Hunt.

In Southern Europe, the hunt is associated with Hecate and her hounds. In India, it is led by the storm god Rudra, and the Maruts ride with him. In the Vedic period, Rudra's epithet was Pashupati, Lord of the Animals (also a title given to Merlin and Cernunnos in Europe). This epithet now belongs to Shiva. (Shiva, meaning the kind one, was originally an epithet of Rudra, and they are often seen as the same deity.)

Several legendary leaders of the Wild Hunt were knights or kings who committed some crime or who had not completed their task on Earth. In Christian folklore, those who were too good for hell but not good enough for heaven would often be consigned to ride in the Wild Hunt.

One of my favorite legends associated with the Wild Hunt is that of Wild Edric, who was an Anglo-Saxon nobleman who put up a valiant resistance but surrendered too soon to the conquering Normans. Because of this, he was condemned to wander with the Wild Hunt, where his job is to warn of imminent invasion or war. Seeing the Wild Hunt is often said to be an omen of war. Wild Edric was last seen shortly before the Crimean War by a miner's daughter. He was riding with his faery wife, Lady Godda, who was dressed in green. Wild Edric's sword is said to be in Bomere Pool, worn by a fish that cannot be caught with any net.

There was a sighting of the Wild Hunt in Sweden in the nineteenth century, where it was pursuing a white hind and a naked woman with a distended stomach. In other parts of Sweden, the hunt pursues Saint Walpurga for nine nights culminating on Walpurgisnacht. Walpurga wears a golden crown and carries a distaff, a wheatsheaf, and a three-cornered mirror that gives glimpses of the future. Bonfires are lit on May Eve to protect her from the hunters.

The Hunt is generally sighted at the solstices, particularly the winter solstice, and on spirit roads across the landscape. It is heralded by a clap of thunder, the noise of wind in the trees, ghostly music, the rattle of chains, the baying of hounds, the clash of swords, the whinnying of horses, or the sound of a hunting horn. Just before it disappears, there is an increase in its loudness, followed by an eerie silence.

German author and linguist Jacob Grimm believed that the hunt was originally a cavalcade of gods riding out in solemn and stately procession (rather like the faery rade or Sluagh Sidhe). It could also be a procession of spirits riding on the host-paths of the dead, which often align with old trackways across the landscape.

Summer thunderstorms are often very evocative of the Wild Hunt, and can easily provoke images of horses thundering across the sky—especially when the storm seems to circle overhead.

The concepts of wildness, the wild, and wilderness are complex and contradictory. The wild is a place people want to visit to feel connected to Nature, but they do not necessarily want to live there—preferring the comforts of a warm bed and an absence of large predatory animals that might eat them. At the same time, humanity needs to recognize that our survival as a species depends on living in harmony with Nature, so a return to an animist worldview in which we see lands, rivers, and other natural features as people, and ourselves as partners with them, is not only desirable but necessary.

Wyrd

It is a mistake to assume that events far apart
in time are thereby separate. All things are
connected as in the finest web of a spider.
The slightest movement on any thread can be
discerned from all points in the web. . . The
pattern of wyrd is like the grain in wood, or the
flow of a stream; it is never repeated in exactly
the same way. But the threads of wyrd pass
through all things and we can open ourselves to
its pattern by observing the ripples as it passes
by. When you see ripples in a pool, you know
that something has dropped into the water.
— Brian Bates, *The Way of Wyrd* (2005)

Wyrd is an ancient word that describes the web of destiny woven
by the Three Norns. It is related to the Old English verb weorðan,
to become, and is often translated as doom, fate, or destiny. Wyrd
is not set in stone, however; people's actions and their character
can influence their wyrd. It is worth contrasting wyrd with the
concept of *orlog*, which is the accumulation of previous actions and
outcomes that shapes events in the present. It could be thought of
as the threads in the web of wyrd.[157] Another way of looking at it is
that it is the layers of leaves that fall from the world tree, Yggdrasil,
into the Well of Wyrd, forming layer upon layer of past events.[158]

The web of wyrd—the interwoven strands of destiny—is woven
by the Three Norns: Urðr, Skuld, and Verthanði, whose names are
often translated as past, present, and future.

---

157 'Wyrd & Orlog.' Skald's Keep.
158 'Wyrd and Orlog.' The Modern Heathen.

Wyrd and *orlog* are not the same as karma. Karma is the Hindu word for action, and denotes how your actions affect your future incarnations. There is no moral element to the concept of wyrd; it denotes how your actions are woven into the web of fate.

Destiny is not completely fixed or predetermined, but once a certain course of action has been followed, some consequences are more likely than others. If you drink excess alcohol, it will very likely result in a hangover—just because that's how our bodies work, not because you are being "punished" for drinking (though some hangovers can feel like that).

By using divination to examine our subconscious motivations and the likely outcomes of a given action, you can discern the patterns of wyrd and choose your actions with some foreknowledge of the consequences.

Reclaimed Concepts

> What paganism most broadly imagines is a
> particular relationship between immanence
> and transcendence within nature, and this
> relationship generates a certain enchanted
> meaning of which there is a deficit in the
> contemporary world…
>
> —Ed Simon, *A new paganism* (2023)

Many concepts are so strongly associated with non-Pagan religions that people do not see them as part of Pagan discourse. But to have a revived form of Paganism that can address all situations in life, I believe that it needs to include these concepts. It can reclaim them to mean something like what they meant to our ancient pagan ancestors, or at the very least it can de-fang them so they cannot be used to hurt us. If a worldview that treats Nature, bioregions, trees, and rivers as beings in their own right is ever to take hold and quicken the imaginations of more than a minority, the collective understanding of some of these concepts will need to be transformed. This is already happening with the process of re-enchantment and the rise of occulture, animism, pantheism, and increasing concern for the environment and the climate.

Belief

Many Pagans will tell you that they do not have a belief, because they know by experience that the gods exist. Here they are using the word belief in its modern sense of "assent to a creed." Other Pagans will quite happily use the word belief, because they mean something different by it.

The word belief has been twisted out of all recognition from its original meaning, which is related to beloved. It was originally *geleafe* which was a modification of the root word *lief* (as in "I would as lief do something or other," meaning "I would just as much like to do that as the other thing," or "I would liefer do something than something else," meaning "I would rather do…"). In the twelfth century, it became *bileaven* ("to prize; to value; to hold dear").

When people think about the word belief in its modern usage, they tend to think of blind belief in something impossible: e.g., believing in the creation of the universe by a deity, which seems a bit unlikely to me. I believe that gods emerged from the universe and not the other way around. People tend to think of belief as accepting a number of orthodox propositions from a religion without thinking about them and trusting in somebody else's view of how the world works. I have always said that I don't have a fixed belief (in the sense of assenting to a creed); instead, I have working hypotheses to explain my experiences.

I prefer the older meaning of belief that is about loving the divine. I believe in the gods. I believe that I'm in partnership with the universe, not subservient to it. You can love your religious practice, your deities, Nature, the universe, other people. To me, belief should be about trust, community, and creating connections.

To believe in something in the original sense is to prize it, to value it, to hold it dear. Do you prize your Pagan practice, your relationship with the gods? Do you hold dear the culture and values of Paganism? Then you believe in them. If you value something, you trust it, you invest your time and energy in it— you believe in it. People still use this sense of "belief" in everyday speech—"I believe in you" means "I value you and trust you."

You can also believe in values, such as love, equality, trust, mirth and reverence, honor and humility, power and compassion, strength and beauty, and being kind to other people.

Belief is reinforced by belonging—the more you feel part of something, the more you place your trust in it; and the two are mutually reinforcing: the more you believe and trust in something, the more you feel that you belong. This process, however, is contingent on experience; if your community lets you down, it is hard to continue with that same level of trust. Trust and belonging and belief are created by practice, which is why most religions place much more emphasis on practice than they do on assent to creeds.

British author and commentator Karen Armstrong explains how religion is about practice:

> Religious truth is, therefore, a species of practical knowledge. Like swimming, we cannot learn it in the abstract; we have to plunge into the pool and acquire the knack by dedicated practice. Religious doctrines are a product of ritual and ethical observance, and make no sense unless they are accompanied by such spiritual exercises as yoga, prayer, liturgy and a consistently compassionate lifestyle. Skilled practice in

these disciplines can lead to intimations of the transcendence we call God, Nirvana, Brahman or Dao. Without such dedicated practice, these concepts remain incoherent, incredible and even absurd. [159]

Being open to the experience of the numinous (without trying to come up with a theory to explain it) can lead to more experiences of the same kind. American anthropologist Tanya Luhrmann referred to this phenomenon as "interpretive drift." [160] I would prefer a more neutral term, such as openness, as her terminology (and indeed her study of magic users) was based on the premise that everyone starts out rational and then shifts, or drifts, toward a belief in magic. I do not think that a belief in magic is irrational, or incompatible with science, however. Pagans have a variety of ways whereby we reconcile our theories of magic with the materialistic worldview of science.

Let's reclaim the word belief to mean what it originally meant, and not use it to mean "assent to a creed." It means far more than that; it is about creating relationships with the gods and/or Nature, reconnecting with the sacred, and re-enchanting the world. Pagans believe in the gods and spirits, Nature and the Earth and the land, because we hold them dear and value our relationships with them; we have opened our hearts to them. We have faith in them because we are relaxed in their presence and have let go of our assumptions, and we trust them.

---

159   Brian McGrath Davis (2009), 'Religion is not about belief: Karen Armstrong's The Case for God.' Religion Dispatches.
160   Tanya M. Luhrmann (1989, 1991), Persuasions of the Witch's Craft: Ritual Magic in Contemporary England. Harvard University Press.

Charity

Homer's *Odyssey* (A.S. Kline translation, 2004) recounts the correct way to welcome a stranger who has been washed ashore: with food and drink, fresh clothing, and fragrant oil to clean the salt from the skin. Odysseus has been washed ashore after a shipwreck and encounters Nausicaa, a princess of Phaeacia, who tells her maids:

> We must care for him, since all strangers and
> beggars come from Zeus, and even a little gift is
> welcome. So bring him food and drink, girls, and
> bathe him in the river wherever there's shelter
> from the wind. [161]

Similarly, the story of Baucis and Philemon from Ovid's *Metamorphoses* (VIII:621–696) recounts how the old couple were the only ones to welcome Jupiter and Mercury when they visited in disguise.[162]

And in northern Europe, *The Hávamál* and the sagas recount instances of hospitality and praise the generosity of the host:

> Fire he needs   who with frozen knees
> Has come from the cold without;
> Food and clothes   must the farer have,
> The man from the mountains come.
> Water and towels   and welcoming speech
> Should he find who comes to the feast. . . [163]

The virtue of hospitality is one of the most ancient and sacred of Pagan virtues, and it is also praised in Judaism, Christianity, and Islam.

---

161 A S Kline (2004), 'Homer: The Odyssey. Book VI.' Poetry in Translation.
162 A S Kline (2000) 'Ovid: The Metamorphoses. Book VIII.' Poetry in Translation.
163 Henry A. Bellows' translation of The Hávamál.

At the same time, the miser, who accumulates wealth and then refuses to share it, was regarded as repugnant in every ancient culture.

The word charity is derived from the Greek name for the Three Graces, the Kharites, which refers to the lovely appearance of a garden or a fertile field. Different legends listed varying numbers of Graces, but the most frequently mentioned are Aglaea (splendor, brilliant, shining one), Euphrosyne (joy, merriment, mirth), and Thalia (blooming, abundant, good cheer).

In Religio Romana, generosity and charity are part of the virtue of *innocentia*, which can be described as innocence in motivation when pursuing a course of action. According to the Roman Republic website,

To demonstrate *innocentia* requires a desire to strive towards the greater good over self-enrichment or aggrandization. The individual who demonstrates innocentia is altruistic and benevolent. Such kindness may include financial generosity, but is not limited to only monetary donations. Charity of action and thought are essential attributes of this virtue…An individual with *innocentia* should not flaunt charity or generosity in carrying out the act. Such demonstrations demean the virtue and refocus attention on the act of giving rather than the beneficial action that is the virtuous purpose of the act. Generosity, charity, and other selfless acts should not be performed with the expectation of recognition or personal gain.[164]

Charity was not only giving money to causes, but also putting a charitable interpretation on awkward social situations. It formed part of *innocentia*; and in the form of hospitality, it was a sacred

---

[164] 'Roman Virtues.' Roman Republic | Res publica Romana. https://romanrepublic.org/roma/bibliotheca/roman-virtues/

duty to welcome the stranger. Hospitality is a key concept in most traditional cultures—and so is taking care of the needy and the vulnerable.

One of the criticisms of contemporary Paganism frequently put forward by other religions is that Pagans do not have charitable organizations. That is because we donate to charity because we believe in the importance of the work of the charity, not because we wish to demonstrate how virtuous we are to attract converts. It is probably also because the Pagan movement is not big enough to have its own charitable organizations, although there are one or two Pagan charities.

I see volunteering for and donating to charities as compassion in action, and a way of working toward a more just and sustainable future, and therefore a key aspect of Pagan spirituality.

Devil

Some folkloric Craft practitioners have always honored Lucifer and Jesus, regarding them as brothers (from the reference in the book of Job about Samael being among the Sons of God). Cain is also an important figure in folkloric witchcraft mysteries. He is viewed as the son of Samael and Lilith, while Tubal-Cain is viewed as the earthly vessel of Azazel. They place a lot of importance on the smith-gods such as Prometheus, Tubal-Cain, Hephaestos, Wayland, and Vulcan.

I can understand why many Wiccans completely denied that they even believed in the Devil, as I vividly remember the fear instilled in us by the Satanic Panic of the late 1980s. It is much easier to say that Pagans do not believe in Christian mythology at all than it is to say something more complicated, such as explaining that we do not accept a dualistic cosmology, but we do believe there is a place for acknowledging the darker aspects of the psyche, and deities associated with them. We believe that rather than demonizing them, it would be better to integrate those forces into consciousness and work with their energies. Some Wiccan and Pagan writers did attempt to convey this more complicated message.

Various concepts and images of these entities are lurking about in the basement of the Western psyche but it is possible to change them. Some people will prefer to ignore them altogether; others feel the need to change these images by working with them. That is their prerogative.

However, there is no need to throw Satanists under the bus when stating that Wiccans do not worship the Devil. There are at least three flavors of Satanism: the philosophical and anarchist variety allegedly espoused by Mikhail Bakunin, the inversion-of-Christianity variety, and the people who worship the Egyptian god Set. Therefore, claiming that Satanism is merely an inversion of Christianity is an inadequate explanation.

I think that Wicca and Satanism are two separate and distinct traditions, but Pagans are not being fair and reasonable if we demonize Satanism in the same way that some Christians have demonized Pagans.

From a polytheist point of view, I would argue that Lucifer, Satan, Samael, Asmodeus, Beelzebub, and various other entities are different beings. One of the Pagan deities whose image fed into the Christian concept of the Devil was Pan, and it is thought that that is how the Devil acquired his cloven hooves (unless it was from the image of Azazel as the scapegoat).

Some people have argued that neither Jesus nor Satan has a place in contemporary Paganisms, because Pagans do not accept the dualistic and antagonistic world-view of Christianity. However, I do not have to accept that monotheism's assessment of the stature or nature of a being is true in order to accept that the being (or at least, its archetype) exists. I do not accept the philosophy of Buddhism, but I am happy to honor Kwan Yin. I think Jesus probably existed, but I certainly don't accept monotheism's view of who he was. So why do we avoid his alleged brother Lucifer? Pagans obviously do not accept Christianity's assessment that all our deities are the devil in disguise—so why should we accept their view of Lucifer?

In ancient religions, there were various deities that were some form of adversary—and a necessary source of creative conflict. Examples include Loki, Angra Mainyu, and Set. The Jewish concept of Samael or Satan was quite different from the Christian concept, and he existed alongside other figures such as Lilith as necessary aspects of the cosmic order.

I think the Christian view was probably influenced either by the two gods of Zoroastrianism (Ahura Mazda and Angra Mainyu), or by the good and evil entities of Manichaeism. Manichaeism was essentially a Gnostic view of the world that held that matter was created by an evil demiurge, and that the source of all good was the creator, to whom light and spirit seek to return by escaping from matter. Zoroastrians, on the other hand, say that the world was created by Ahura Mazda, the good god. However, both systems have an ultimate force of good pitted against an ultimate force of evil. Contrast this with Judaism, where Samael was essentially under the control of YHWH—in this view, Samael existed to punish transgressors. If you look at the history of Jewish mythologization of Satan, Samael, Azazel, Asmodeus, and other characters, they are much more nuanced than the Christian versions. I wish people would not conflate Judaism and Christianity, or back-project Christian attitudes onto Judaism, which is a completely different religion than Christianity. And as far as I know, it is a heresy in Christianity to regard the Devil as being of equal power with God.

As I do not accept monotheism's view that there is only one god and one adversary, I have room in my concept of deities for some that like to promote conflict for whatever reason they think it necessary (even if they do not happen to be among the deities with whom I have a personal relationship, because I do not like conflict). If I acknowledge the existence of Lilith and Loki and Set and YHWH and Asherah, then I am prepared to accept that Lucifer, Samael, Baphomet, and Asmodeus also exist.

As to whether the Wiccan Horned God contains a bit of the Devil in his DNA. . . I think he probably does. If the Devil is equated in the Christian world-view with prancing about naked by moonlight, joyous lovemaking, and wild shenanigans—then the God of the Witches does indeed represent these things.

Pan is one of the few beings who may have informed some of the Christian idea of the Devil (because he represents wildness and wilderness and unbridled sexuality) that was not an adversary figure in ancient mythology.

In Charles Godfrey Leland's *Aradia, or the gospel of the witches*, Aradia is presented as the consort of Lucifer, and it appears that Gerald Gardner and Doreen Valiente replaced Lucifer with Cernunnos when they were forming Wicca—in part because they believed Margaret Murray's theory that the being worshiped by witches was an ancient pagan Horned God (but also because they were well aware of the media furor that would result if they admitted to devil-worship). However, it appears from some research by Sabina Magliocco that the legend of Aradia is older than the association of witchcraft with devil-worship.[165]

Horned deities in India were possibly associated with shamanism and animism, both of which have been viewed as transgressive by monotheistic religions.

It is also worth noting that the word demon (daimon in Greek) originally meant a spirit of place, or the genius of a gifted person, and it had no negative connotation in ancient paganism.

My personal theology celebrates the marriage of spirit and matter, and not their separation. I celebrate wildness, chaos, and the joys of physical pleasure. I do not think that blind obedience is

---

165 Sabina Magliocco (2019), 'Aradia in Sardinia: the Archaeology of a Legend.' Academia.edu.

a virtue. So I think a deity that represents anarchy and rebellion against absolute authority is worth looking into.

Some ancient paganisms had the concept of a struggle between two groups of deities (in Greek mythology, the clash of the Olympian gods with their rivals, the Titans; and in Norse mythology, the clash of the Aesir and Vanir with the giants) but these were not so much conceived of as a struggle of good and evil as they were a struggle between natural forces such as fire and ice—some of which were more inimical to humans than others. But things were complicated in the Greek myths because Prometheus stole fire from the gods to give to humanity (allegedly an impious act, but one for which humans can be grateful). And in the Norse myths, the gods were born from the primal giant, Ymir, and then slew him to make the heavens and the Earth.

Some ancient religions of the Near East had powerful beings who were slain by the creator god (for example in Sumerian mythology, Tiamat the serpent goddess was slain by Marduk, who formed the Earth from her body—probably the original of many dragon-slayer stories). It is possible to trace some of the motifs that went into the making of the archetype of the Devil back to some of these figures.

Given the enormous weight of negativity attached to the archetype of the Devil, anyone invoking these entities needs to be careful to invoke the aspects of the complex that they want (the freedom, anarchy, hedonism, and sex-positive aspects) and avoid the negative associations with it (selfishness, greed, destructive impulses, and so on). I find it very interesting that most people work with lesser-known names and beings such as Samael and Lucifer (arguably the bright side of this archetype, since his name means "light-bearer") and avoid the more negative aspects. So much negativity has been loaded onto the archetype that it may be difficult to recover the bright aspects of it. If you do invoke or evoke such a being, are you a powerful enough magician to handle it?

It is fairly easy to see how gods of the wildwood (symbols of the wilderness and therefore opposed to civilization, with which Christianity strongly identifies itself) may have fed into the Christian archetype of the Devil. In *Lolly Willowes, or the Loving Huntsman* (1926) by Sylvia Townsend Warner, the god of the witches is unequivocally represented—with considerable glee—as Satan. He is quite kindly, and the freedom of the countryside where he holds sway is contrasted with the stifling atmosphere of middle-class respectability from which the heroine escapes.

Many myths and legends (from ancient times until very recently) are about the struggle to establish civilization and order, set against the urge to return to a state of nature and chaos. It has not been universally agreed that the imposition of law and order and civilisation is all good.

If someone was to draw a mindmap or a family tree describing all these entities and their mythological relationship with each other, it would get quite complicated. The massive number of references to the Devil in popular culture add an extra layer of complexity.

So—when you mention the Devil, you might need to be a bit more specific. Do you mean Old Nick, Satan, Asmodeus, Azazel, Beelzebub, Baphomet, Samael, Lucifer, Mephistopheles, Angra Mainyu, Iblis, Loki, Set, Apep, Prometheus, or some other adversarial figure? The Devil really is in the details.

Faith

Faith is an interesting word that has gone through a number of evolutions in its long history. It comes from an Indo-European root that means to trust, confide, or persuade. People tend to think of faith as "blind faith," a creed embraced by a person who is rather rigid in their religion. This is essentially a modern meaning that emerged in the wake of the development of fundamentalism.

Having faith originally meant trusting in something. To keep faith with someone means to maintain trust with them; to be faithful in a marriage means to maintain that trust by not sleeping with someone else without telling your spouse (because there's a difference between negotiating an open relationship and actually cheating on someone).

To speak of faith in the gods is to talk about trusting in the gods or trusting in the universe or the divine or whatever it is you believe in.

According to Karen Armstrong:

> "Faith" has its etymological roots in the Greek pistis, "trust; commitment; loyalty; engagement." Jerome translated pistis into the Latin fides ("loyalty") and credo (which was from cor do, "I give my heart"). . . . Faith in God, therefore, was a trust in and loyal commitment to God. [166]

Similarly, Alan Watts, who popularized Zen in the West, regarded faith as an attitude of openness to mystery and uncertainty:

---

[166]   Karen Armstrong (2010), The Case for God. Anchor.

"Faith is a state of openness or trust. To have faith is to trust yourself to the water. When you swim you don't grab hold of the water, because if you do you will sink and drown. Instead you relax, and float. And the attitude of faith is the very opposite of clinging to belief, of holding on. In other words, a person who is fanatic in matters of religion, and clings to certain ideas about the nature of God and the universe, becomes a person who has no faith at all. Instead they are holding tight. But the attitude of faith is to let go, and become open to truth, whatever it might turn out to be."[167]

When you view faith as meaning trust, commitment, and opening yourself to experience, it is a much more attractive idea. Being open to whatever truth emerges from our experience is beautiful to me.

The concept of trusting the sea reminds me of the story of Arion and the dolphin, told by the fifth century bce Greek historian Herodotus. Arion was said to be the world's greatest lyre-player. He had spent most of his time in Corinth, but he also went to Italy and Sicily, where he made a lot of money. He booked passage on a Corinthian vessel in Tarentum in Southern Italy to take him home to Corinth.

Once the ship was out at sea, the sailors stole his wealth and said that he should either kill himself so that he could be buried on land, or else jump into the sea. It was considered preferable to be buried on land, as then the proper funeral rites could be observed and the spirit of the deceased would not wander.

Arion asked the sailors to let him sing before he jumped into the sea. He sang and played his lyre, and then he jumped into the sea.

---

167   Alan Watts (1977), The Essence of Alan Watts.

A dolphin appeared and carried Arion on his back to Taenarus, at the southern tip of the Peloponnese.

Arion traveled from Taenarus to Corinth, and told his story to Periander, the ruler of Corinth. Periander was skeptical of the story, and confined Arion while waiting for the ship to arrive. When it did, Periander summoned the sailors and asked them about Arion. The sailors claimed that Arion was back in Italy, so they were stunned and amazed when Arion appeared before them. Arion must have had considerable faith in the gods, or at least a hope that he would survive if he jumped into the sea.

If you have faith in the gods, it means you trust them. What are the implications of that? Well, if you trust your friend, it means you believe they have your best interests at heart; that you can confide in them; that they will not let you down in a crisis. So maybe you don't have that kind of faith in all the gods, but rather in the ones you have a special devotion to or a special relationship with. Or maybe you place your faith in Nature and your relationship with it.

This faith—this relationship—is what sustains you when you feel doubtful, depressed, or otherwise wobbly. It doesn't mean you never have doubts; it means that you keep on keeping on, even when you do have doubts. You lean back into the water, and trust that it will hold you up, even when you don't know how deep it is.

Even when people have direct experience of the gods, or of magic, we still don't really know how it works or what the gods really are. The face of the gods that humans see is only one facet of their nature, whatever that may be. The gods are vast ancient cosmic forces, and our personifications of them are their reflections in human culture. As author and mage Sam Webster wrote:

> Let us start with the Gods as we experience
> them. Much to my surprise, I am no longer
> convinced that the Beings we experience are the
> Gods Themselves. What we are experiencing is
> a projection of Those who are Gods refracted
> through our souls and the cultures we are a part
> of. [168]

No-one really knows the full nature of the gods, so people are often open and trusting toward them so they can experience more of their nature. They do not cling to limited ideas about them, but are ready to open themselves to more experience and insight.

It is possible to use the term faith in a Pagan context. We can talk about faith in the gods, faith in the universe. We could talk about Paganism as a faith. Pagans trust in the gods and Nature, have faith in the gods and spirits, Nature and the Earth and the land, because we hold them dear and value our relationships with them; we have opened our hearts to them, we are relaxed in their presence, we have let go of our assumptions, and we trust them.

---

168   Sam Webster (2015), 'Genus before species: What are the Gods?' At the Herm.

God, Goddess, Deity

What is a deity? The word god is of uncertain etymology and may relate to the concept of pouring a libation, or refer to that which is invoked. The Old English word god was originally gender-neutral, but it changed to masculine on the arrival of Christianity in England. Because of this, it was necessary to invent the word goddess (coined in the mid-fourteenth century to refer to female deities in polytheistic religions), and to use deity as a gender neutral term. What's more, god did not always mean a person; it could mean a manifestation of the numinous (the mysterious referent of religions), that which is invoked, that which Pagans pour libations to, or even a spirit that is immanent in a burial mound:

> Old English god probably was closer in sense to
> Latin numen. A better word to translate deus
> might have been Proto-Germanic *ansuz, but
> this was used only of the highest deities in the
> Germanic religion, and not of foreign gods, and
> it was never used of the Christian God.[169]

Pagan deities are not omniscient, omnipotent, or omnipresent. They are entities or identities that emerge from a particular place, context, or concept—or from people's interactions with it.

There are many different views of how deities relate to each other and to the universe. My personal view (which I offer as one possible view, and not as normative in any way), is that there is an underlying divine energy that emanates from the divine source. In my view, neither the underlying energy nor the divine source has a personality. From the underlying energy, all beings

---

169   'Etymology of god by etymonline.'

emerge—humans, spirits, deities, and animals. However, none of these beings are discrete entities—humans have fuzzy boundaries and exchange food, energy, and breath with the world around us. Rather, humans are distinct entities, and so are the deities. They are affected by our attention, gifts, and communing with them (or lack of it). Deities can also change over time, because they are manifest entities and therefore subject to change. I am a big fan of process theology, which suggests that the divine changes in response to the world, and I am also a polytheist, so I do not see why deities wouldn't change too.

The Hindu and Buddhist traditions have deities reincarnating in different avatars. In Buddhism, becoming a deity is not the ultimate aim, as you can always slip down the great chain of being if you transgress as a deity; the ultimate aim is to cease to exist, to rest in Nirvana (which literally means 'no flame').

I do not think that Thor is the same as Jupiter or Perkunas or Indra or YHWH the thunder god. They are all thunder gods (that's their job) and so they are local manifestations of the thunder principle—but they are distinct from each other, just as all web developers share certain characteristics, and may be expressing an archetype when they are doing web development, but are still distinct individuals, similar to the many avatars of Indra in the story of *Indra and the Ants* (see the section on Apotheosis for the full story).

It is important to understand the distinction between monism (the belief that the whole universe is composed of the same energy) and monotheism (the belief that it was created by a single deity). Monism is compatible with polytheism; monotheism isn't.

I think deities emerge from the underlying energy in various different ways. They can be deified humans (such as Quintus

Aurelius Symmachus or Antinous); they can be personifications of natural forces (such as thunder gods, rain gods, and so on); they can be a combination of these (such as Oðinn, who was a human king and the god of the winds); or they can be spirits of place who become particularly powerful (such as Athena, goddess of Athens).

In his novel *Small Gods*, Terry Pratchett describes how a small particle of consciousness floating around in the desert lodges in the brain of a young man, who then becomes its prophet and founds the religion of Omnianism, with disastrous and hilarious consequences (hilarious because of the resemblance between Omnianism and fundamentalist Christianity, and disastrous for exactly the same reason).

Pratchett has rightly been hailed as Britain's foremost Pagan theologian, although he was an atheist. If you haven't read his novels, you're in for a treat. I especially recommend *Small Gods, Pyramids, Equal Rites, Wyrd Sisters, Witches Abroad, Lords and Ladies, Maskerade, Carpe Jugulum, The Wee Free Men, A Hat Full of Sky, Wintersmith,* and *I Shall Wear Midnight*—that should keep you busy for a bit! These are the ones about witches, deities, and faeries. (Pratchett's faeries are not nice—on the Discworld, stone circles were built to keep them out.)

Anyway, back to deities and on to the thorny question of gender. In Buddhism, Kwan Yin has two avatars—Avalokitesvara, a male avatar, and Kwan Yin, a female avatar. In Roman religion, the Parilia was a festival celebrating Pales, a deity of uncertain gender, who may be male, female, or a couple. There are numerous transgender, gay, lesbian, and bisexual deities, although unfortunately much of this mythology was suppressed in the past. An excellent source for LGBTQ+ deities is *Cassell's Encyclopedia of Queer Myth, Symbol and Spirit.*

The underlying divine energy has no gender, in my view, though I do tend to regard it as giving birth to the universe. I think it includes all genders, and also transcends gender. There are more than two genders; Indigenous cultures from around the world attest to this. So the underlying energy of the universe is not, in my view, divided into "the God" and "the Goddess." I do tend to have a male and female patron deity when working in a Wiccan coven, but they are not invoked exclusively, they are asked to be the protectors of the coven, and I do not regard them as manifestations of the ultimate polarity.

I also think that deities exist on different scales. There are spirits of place, deities of cities and rivers (usually goddesses), deities of countries, deities of planets, deities of galaxies, and the emerging universal mind (which may or may not have a personality). Just as all beings exist within the universe, so the deity or spirit of a place exists within the deity of that country (but it still has a distinct identity within that). For example, the ancient Greeks had Gaea, goddess of Earth, and Rhea, goddess of the universe. Clearly Gaea exists within Rhea.

In my view, deities are emergent properties of the complexity of the universe. They are products of the interaction between mind and matter. There was no Creator God, rather the universe and its inhabitants are becoming more conscious, more compassionate, more empathic, with the arising of the universal mind (which proceeds from the unfolding of the Tao, the mysterious Way or emergent pattern). As humans interact socially with the natural world, we increase its consciousness, just as we do for each other. First we awakened spirits of place, then we gradually began to perceive the totality of the universe and wonder at the glories of Nature. We are part of the arising of the universal mind, as we become more conscious and more empathic. As we become more empathically connected to the universe, when we die we contribute part of our consciousness to the All (part is probably reincarnated), and it is in this process of interconnection that the universal mind arises. Those who connect with the world around them contribute to the process of expanding awareness and continuing the process of making everything more conscious. The process of individuation and self-development is part of the process of awakening. But the awakening will not be from the "illusion" of matter, but rather matter itself is becoming ever more conscious or ensouled.

Paganisms seek to reclaim the concept of divinity from people who want it to mean an all-powerful creator deity, which is an extremely improbable concept. By contrast, the idea of mind arising from the complexity of matter seems quite reasonable. The Divine did not create the universe; rather, the universe birthed deities and spirits.

Grace

The quality of grace is related to the three Classical Pagan goddesses known as the Three Graces, and it comes from a root word meaning "favorable" or "favored."

One night I went for a walk with my beloved in the beautiful evening light. The rain had cleared, and the low summer sun was illuminating everything in a lovely dreamy gold—the sort of light that makes everything look as if it is lit from within. And because everything was freshly washed, it all looked brighter. The scent of roses and mock orange filled the air, and the birds were singing. The trees hung over the path and formed a tunnel of green leaves.

At moments like that, when divinity shines within all things, I feel reconnected, refreshed, renewed. You might call it a moment of grace.

Grace means something to be thankful for—something that is praiseworthy, desirable, elegant, right, and fitting.

In Greek mythology, a Charis or Grace is one of three or more minor goddesses of charm, beauty, nature, human creativity, and fertility, together known as the Kharites or Graces. The usual list is Aglaea (splendor, brilliant, shining one), Euphrosyne (joy, merriment, mirth), and Thalia (blooming, abundant, good cheer). They are said to be daughters of Zeus and Hera (or Eurynome, daughter of Oceanus) or of Helios and Aegle, a daughter of Zeus. Frequently, the Graces were taken as goddesses of charm or beauty in general and hence were associated with Aphrodite, the goddess of love; Peitho, her attendant; and Hermes, a fertility and messenger god.[170]

---

170   Amy Tikkanen, 'Grace.' Encyclopedia Britannica.

In Roman mythology they were known as the Gratiae, the "Graces." In some variants, Charis was one of the Graces and was not the singular form of their name.

Grace is also related to renewal and a sense of being right with the world and the divine. It isn't on a list of ancient Roman virtues—the nearest concept is Laetitia, meaning joy, gladness, the celebration of thanksgiving, often of the resolution of crisis.

Among the Lacedaemonians, there were two Graces, Cleta ("sound" or "renowned") and Phaenna ("light" or "bright"). The fact that a feeling of grace can be created by harmonious sounds and soothing light makes these names seem particularly apt. Splendor, good cheer, and mirth also seem apt descriptors. And the more modern meaning of elegance and harmony also fits in with these ancient concepts of grace. I can think of several people whom I think of as being graceful in the way they interact with others.

So I think the word grace can be reclaimed to mean the beauty and harmony and radiance of Nature, the gift of being aware of the glories of Nature, and the feelings of awe and gratitude, wonder and joy and healing evoked by that beauty.

And humans need these moments of blessing and grace to rest and renew when the magic runs out, or when we are heartbroken by the state of the world.

Heresy

The word heresy is interesting because it came to mean a deviation from orthodoxy sometime around the twelfth century, which was just slightly before the emergence of Middle English. Before that, it was the Latin word *hæresis*, meaning a school of thought or a philosophical sect, from Greek *hairesis*, which meant "a taking or choosing for oneself, a choice, a means of taking; a deliberate plan, purpose; philosophical sect, school," from *haireisthai* "to take, to seize."

If you look at various polytheistic traditions, they all have multiple schools of thought. For example, the Ancient Greeks had the Stoics, the Epicureans, the followers of Plato, Aristotle, Socrates, and many other philosophical schools of thought, as well as religious schools of thought. Some of them were what might be called hard polytheists and some of them were Neoplatonists (a school of thought in religion and magic, derived from earlier schools of thought, that believed that all the gods emerged from one single divine source).

There were many schools of thought in ancient paganism and there are many schools of thought in Hinduism (for example Bhaktivedanta and Shaivism and people who worship Vishnu, and so on).

Similarly, in contemporary Paganism, there are many different schools of thought, for example polytheists, duotheists, monists, pantheists, and Atheopagans.

These different schools of thought are all regarded as different pathways to the truth. The late Roman orator, Quintus Aurelius Symmachus, wrote:

> We ask, then, for peace for the gods of our
> fathers and of our country. It is just that all
> worship should be considered as one. We look
> on the same stars, the sky is common, the same
> world surrounds us. What difference does it
> make by what pains each seeks the truth? We
> cannot attain to so great a secret by one road.[171]

I think that liberal religions should reclaim the word heretic to mean somebody who follows a different school of thought from another person.

There's a great poem, "Outwitted," written by Edwin Markham:

> He drew a circle that shut me out—
> Heretic, rebel, a thing to flout.
> But love and I had the wit to win:
> We drew a circle and took him in! [172]

So if anybody calls you a heretic, just recite that poem to them and draw a circle around them muttering darkly—it usually puts the wind up people.

---

171   Quintus Aurelius Symmachus (384), The Memorial of Symmachus, Prefect of the City. 415: 10.
172   Edwin Markham (1913), The Shoes of Happiness, and Other Poems.

Holy

The etymology of "holy" comes from Old English *hālig, hāleġ* ("holy, consecrated, sacred; godly; ecclesiastical"), from Proto-Germanic **hailagaz* ("holy, bringing health"), from Proto-Germanic **hailaz* ("healthy, whole"), from Proto-Indo-European **kailo-* ("whole, uninjured").

Holy is a very interesting word that has roots in pre-Christian terminology from various Germanic languages, where it meant whole or healthy, that which is inviolate or inviolable.

It was adopted at the general conversion to Christianity as a translation of the Latin word sanctus, so this means that before that, it was a pagan word.

In Christian terminology, the word holy means something that was sanctified by God, in contrast with sacred, which means something that was sanctified by humanity. They would refer to "The Holy Bible" because the Christian scriptures were sanctified by God, but they would refer "to the sacred writings of the Hindus," so it was actually a way of talking down to other religions, by implying that their writings are merely sacred, whereas Christian writings were sanctified by God.

Pagans tend to only use the word "holy" when it would be more easily understood by a general audience, in phrases which are already in general usage like "holy book," "holy well," "holy water."

Initially, I thought that the Pagan aversion to the term "holy" was just an adverse reaction to its usage in Christian discourse, but I think the avoidance of it may be due to something deeper—the widespread Pagan view that everything is sacred in its own right, and does not depend on divinity to sanctify it. In addition to this, the connotations of "holy" in Christian discourse often include abstinence from sex, whereas "sacred" can include sexuality.

In Pagan usage, the sacredness of a thing or place can be either an inherent quality, or something conferred on it by using it in a ritual, or consecrating it. If something was directly affected by, or associated with, a deity, you could use the term "holy." The phrase "Holy Names" appears in a Gardnerian Book of Shadows dating from 1957.[173]

I feel that Pagans should reclaim the word holy for more general use, because we're quite comfortable with using the terms hallowed, hale and hearty, healthy, and whole—all of which come from the same Proto-Indo-European root. Holy can be used as a parallel word for hallowed and whole and healthy.

The word holy was clearly in use before the mass conversion to Christianity. It has also been used extensively in magical discourse. For example, Aleister Crowley, founder of Thelema, wrote about the knowledge and conversation of the Holy Guardian Angel. Magical texts also refer to consecrating things "in the holy names of" various deities.

---

173   Gerald B Gardner and others (1957), Book of Shadows.

Hospitality

Every ancient pagan culture had strong traditions of hospitality. These were often reinforced by telling stories of gods, goddesses, and angels disguised as mortals visiting people.

The Greeks had a strong tradition of xenia, care for the stranger. This carried its own obligations and traditions. When Nausicaa found Odysseus washed up on the shore, her care for him was very much in the tradition of xenia.

The *Hávamál*, which means "the speech of the High One" (Oðinn) also contains stanzas about hospitality, and about the duties of both host and guest.

Ultimately, the words host and guest are derived from the same Indo-European root word, which implies that they were viewed as inseparable parts of the same relationship. I like to think of them as the two halves of a hinge. The relationship of guest and host is reciprocal, with sacred obligations on both sides.

The concept and practice of hospitality are important in India, too, which suggests that the practice is very ancient indeed. Both Pakistan and Germany (and other places too) have the tradition of the guest gift, where a guest will give you a gift the first time they visit your home. People from Latvia have a tradition of giving bread and salt as a gift when you have a new house. The sharing of bread and salt are considered sacred in many cultures. Once they have been shared, the relationship of guest and host is established and sacred.

When small villages were scattered among great forests, the arrival of a stranger with news from other places, new stories, new songs, and new jokes—maybe even new farming or weaving or metalworking techniques—must have been very welcome.

There were also great movements of people in ancient times: Goths, Visigoths, Vandals, and Alans; settlers from the rest of Europe and North Africa who came with the Romans; Angles, Saxons, and Jutes who fled the rising waters of the North Sea and settled in Britain.

More recent arrivals in England include silver miners from Germany who settled in the Mendip Hills; many African and Middle Eastern people; the Huguenots fleeing persecution in France; Sephardic Jews from Amsterdam, Ashkenazi Jews from Eastern Europe, who began to arrive in England after the interdict against Jews was lifted in 1654 (it was put in place by King Edward I in 1290).[174]

Everyone in Britain probably has a refugee or an economic migrant in their ancestry, if you go back far enough. For example, Kate Middleton, the current Princess of Wales, is related to the Martineaus, a prominent Huguenot family who became Unitarians.[175] And both refugees and economic migrants have contributed hugely to the UK by creating jobs and boosting the economy with their spending power and tax contributions (and if they are not from the EU, they have "no recourse to public funds" stamped in their visa—so they receive no benefits and no free health care from the NHS).

And in the US and Canada of course, unless you are 100 percent Indigenous, you are an immigrant, or descended from

---

174   National Archives, "Jews in England, 1290."
175   Stuart Hobday (2010), 'Kate Middleton's ties to radical Norwich family.' Norwich Evening News.

immigrants, or descended from people who were enslaved and brought to North America.

I feel instinctively that openness to other cultures and welcoming the stranger and the refugee are good things. What kind of civilization would we be if we were not open and hospitable? One that was both ethically and culturally impoverished, would be my answer.

But I think that the gods and goddesses of Paganism—who frequently come to Earth to test the hospitality of mortals, reward those who are hospitable, and punish those who are not—would agree that hospitality is a sacred practice and should be held in high honor.

In the case of migration to other lands, there is the point of transition from guest to resident. Here again, you can see the process of reciprocity at work. The migrant has paid their tax, contributed work and money to the system, and in many cases their food style and folk customs to the culture. So after a time they become a member of the community. Immigration is not the same as colonialism, however. Immigrants expect to conform to the mores of the society they are moving to, or to exist as a small enclave within it. Colonialists expect to replace or dominate the culture of the place they are moving to, and to take over the governance of the place and control of the land.

Hospitality and reciprocity have been Pagan virtues since ancient times. Honor is also important in many Pagan traditions, and I think the honorable thing to do is to welcome the stranger. Hoarding wealth was frowned upon in ancient societies; wealth was displayed by the generosity of the loaf-giver who fed her people (*hlafdiga*, the origin of the word lady) and of the "ring-giving lord" who gave gold arm rings to his thegns. The social fabric was woven through the sacred practices of hospitality, fosterage, gift exchange, and reciprocity. People in "Western" countries would do well to cultivate these virtues instead of xenophobia and suspicion. So I would definitely say that Pagan religions definitely encourage us to show hospitality toward migrants and compassion for refugees.

Perfect

Perfect means complete, flawless, excellent, accomplished, exquisite. It is rare to find anything that is flawless, which is the way people most commonly use the word perfect.

"Perfect love and perfect trust" is a maxim that is often quoted. It is often misused to mean that no one should question the person who drops it into the conversation—trying to imply that you should love and trust them so completely that you do not question their ideas or actions. In reality, our love and trust of other people is only as solid as their most recent action.

In "The Charge of the Goddess", Doreen Valiente wrote, "Keep pure your highest ideal; strive ever towards it; let naught stop you or turn you aside." I strive for perfect love and perfect trust, but I do not expect to reach it. When I mention perfect love and perfect trust, I am expressing an aspiration, not stating that it has been achieved.

The ideal situation in any group of people is that everyone feels safe and welcome, but there are always times when it is necessary to question people's actions or intentions. People have a tendency to put leaders on a pedestal and trust them too much; there needs to be a system of accountability and mentoring for leaders too. No one is perfect.

Pilgrimage

In ancient times, people made pilgrimages to ancient pagan shrines and sacred sites such as Delphi, Eleusis, Dodona, Thebes, Andania, Samothrace, the temple of Sequana (goddess of the River Seine), dream incubation temples at Lydney on the River Severn and the Asklepion on Kos, and many more.[176]

According to the *Encyclopedia Britannica*, the practice of pilgrimage is part of all world religions—including the pagan religions of ancient Greece and Rome.

It has been demonstrated that the Camino to Santiago de Compostela (the name means "Saint James of the Field of Stars") has its origins in ancient pagan pilgrimages. There was a pre-Christian necropolis on the site, and the route of the Camino existed long before Saint James' remains were found in the ninth century.[177] The ancient pagan name of the route was the Via Finisterre (Latin for "the Way to Land's End"), and archaeological sites found along the route demonstrate that Celtic and other ancient peoples traveled along it from 1000 bce toward Land's End and the Sun's resting place, on a path following the Milky Way. Some say that the Via Finisterre was in honor of the Roman god Janus, as it proceeds from the Temple of Venus Pyrinea (where the Pyrenees mountain range meets the Mediterranean) to Ara Solis or Finisterre.

Some archaeologists define pilgrimage as "a journey made with the purpose of reaching a sacred destination" (which would mean there is no requirement to see the travel itself as sacred for it to be understood as a pilgrimage).[178]

---

176   Troels Myrup Kristensen, Wiebke Friese, eds. (2017), Excavating Pilgrimage: Archaeological Approaches to Sacred Travel and Movement in the Ancient World. London: Routledge.
177   Iberian Adventures (2014), 'A Pagan History of the Camino.' Iberian Adventures.
178   Martin Grünewald (2017), 'Roman healing pilgrimage north of the Alps.' In: Excavating Pilgrimage. London: Routledge.

I would define pilgrimage as travel to a sacred destination where the travel itself is part of the ritual, and that seems to be the generally accepted definition.

Travel along the Sacred Way to Eleusis symbolized the journey of Demeter and Persephone. It was therefore part of the ritual associated with Eleusis, so it definitely qualifies as a pilgrimage.[179]

Although the words pilgrim and pilgrimage have medieval origins, it is clear that ancient pagans did make pilgrimages to the sacred sites of antiquity. Pilgrimage is widely practiced in other religions, so it stands to reason that it was also widespread among ancient pagans.

The practice of pilgrimage also occurs in Hinduism:

> The Sanskrit and Hindi word for pilgrimage center is tirtha, literally a river ford or crossing place. The concept of a ford is associated with pilgrimage centers not simply because many are on riverbanks but because they are metaphorically places for transition, either to the other side of particular worldly troubles or beyond the endless cycle of birth and death.[180]

In Islam, the two main pilgrimages are the Hajj (a visit to Mecca undertaken from the seventh to the twelfth day of Dhū al-Hijjah), which is considered to be one of the five pillars of Islam; and the Umrah, which is a journey to Mecca undertaken at any other time. All Muslims also make pilgrimages to other mosques, and Sufi and Shi'ite Muslims visit the tombs of Sufi and Shia saints.

---

179 Monique Skidmore (2023), 'Secrets of Eleusis: Eleusinian Mysteries.' Trip Anthropologist.
180 'Hinduism—Pilgrimage, Rituals, Beliefs.' Encyclopedia Britannica.

In Buddhism, the sites associated with the Buddha's life are destinations for pilgrimage,[181] along with "active temples, archaeological sites and ruins, stupas marking the passing of Buddhist saints, and natural wonders, often sacred groves in India or heavenly mountains in East Asia." [182]

Although pilgrimage is not compulsory for Sikhs (and many of them prefer to give the money to charity instead), many Sikhs go on pilgrimage to the Harmandir Sahib (also known as the Golden Temple) in Amritsar, North India. Harmandir means "The Temple of God" and referring to it as Sahib is a sign of respect.[183]

Contemporary Pagans also practice pilgrimage, and this can be a transformative experience. Anthropologist Kathryn Rountree explains:

> In the course of Pagans' bodily performances at sites, inner and outer landscapes co-create and flow into one another: the lived body becomes a fundamental text and starting point for knowledge. Through somatic modes of attention—by attending to and with their bodies in surroundings that frequently include the embodied presence of others—Neo-pagan pilgrims experience themselves not as isolated subjectivities but as sharing an intersubjective milieu with other pilgrims and with the Earth itself.[184]

---

181   'Pilgrims' Guide to Buddhist India: Buddhist Sites.' BuddhaNet. https://www.buddhanet.net/e-learning/pilgrim/places.htm
182   Pico Iyer, 'What Are the Different Kinds of Buddhist Practice?' Tricycle: Buddhism for Beginners. https://tricycle.org/beginners/buddhism/buddhist-pilgrimage/
183   'Pilgrimage—Ways of Sikh living.' BBC Bitesize. https://www.bbc.co.uk/bitesize/guides/zhp26yc/revision/10
184   Rountree, K. (2006). 'Performing the Divine: Neo-Pagan Pilgrimages and Embodiment at Sacred Sites.' Body & Society, 12(4), 95-115.

In Ireland, contemporary Pagan pilgrimages bear some resemblance to Catholic styles of pilgrimage, but the sacredness of the land is very important to contemporary Pagan pilgrims.[185]

Pilgrimage for contemporary Pagans can be about connecting to the land, the flora and fauna, ancestors, deities, and sacred sites. It can also be undertaken at one of the festivals of the wheel of the year.[186]

For me, the differences between a pilgrimage and a walk are in the intention of the journey, the focus on the sacred destination, and the ritual aspects of the walk. There are many ways that you can deepen the experience of visiting a sacred site, such as circumambulating it (walking around it in a sacred manner), asking permission of the spirits of place before entering the sanctuary, visiting the site with other Pagans, performing a small discreet ritual at the site itself, making drawings of the site, journaling about it, and collecting a feather, a twig, or a small stone (without disturbing any archaeological remains) while you are there. It is best not to leave tangible offerings at sacred sites unless they are biodegradable and harmless to wildlife. Instead, you might like to offer something intangible such as clearing litter from the site (including non-biodegradable offerings left by other people) or reading a poem or playing some music for the spirits of the place.

---

185   Jenny Butler (2020), 'Contemporary Pagan Pilgrimage: Ritual and Re-Storying in the Irish Landscape.' Numen.
186   Nimue Brown (2017), 'Pilgrimage to the flowers.' Druid Life.

Recommended Reading

- Phil Cousineau (2012), The Art of Pilgrimage: The Seeker's Guide to Making Travel Sacred. Conari Press.

- Alain de Botton (2014), The Art of Travel. Hamish Hamilton UK.

- Troels Myrup Kristensen, Wiebke Friese, eds. (2017), Excavating Pilgrimage: Archaeological Approaches to Sacred Travel and Movement in the Ancient World. London: Routledge.

- Nimue Brown (forthcoming), Pagan Pilgrimage. https://druidlife.wordpress.com/2023/10/16/spirits-of-place-2/

- Cleaner Clootie Campaign. https://www.instagram.com/cleanerclootiecampaign/

Prayer

The modern word prayer dates from the thirteenth century, but it is almost certain that ancient pagans would have prayed to their gods. There's no reason why contemporary Pagans can't do that too.

A lot of contemporary Pagans—especially on the occult end of the pagan spectrum—tend to see prayer as a weak form of magic. However, they are thinking of what is known as "results magic" (magic geared toward a specific goal).

Prayer has many purposes, and it is not just about asking the gods or the Divine to do things for you (although that may have been its original purpose). In essence, prayer is a Western form of meditation, an opportunity to introspect, commune with the Divine, go within yourself and reflect on your day, express gratitude for the good things in life, and examine your innermost thoughts.

Prayer can be spontaneous and from the heart, or it can be a pre-written prayer, or you can practice *lectio divina* (one of my favorite spiritual practices, where you read a poem or a section of scripture, meditate on it, wordlessly commune with the divine, then pick a phrase from the poem or scripture, and write a poem inspired by it).

There are many types of prayer, including adoration, devotion, prayer of approach, invocation (asking the Divine to be present), bidding prayer, confession and penitence, words of reassurance, thanksgiving, intercession (asking for help for someone else), petition (asking for help for yourself), healing prayer, expressing aspiration, and reflection.

There are also many modes and techniques of prayer: centering prayer, contemplative prayer, and body prayer (using dance or other special movements in prayer). Contemplative prayer is similar to meditation and is very transformative. Contemplative prayer is not "asking for stuff" or "results magic." It involves resting in the presence of your chosen deity (or deities). It is also an embodied practice, in that the body must be in a comfortable and relaxed state for the practice to succeed.

In the Wiccan text "The Charge of the Goddess", Doreen Valiente wrote,

> Arise and come unto me. For I am the soul of
> Nature, who gives life to the Universe. From me,
> all things proceed and unto me all things must
> return; and before my face, beloved of Gods and
> men, let thine innermost divine self be enfolded
> in the rapture of the infinite.

To "be enfolded in the rapture of the infinite" expresses very well for me what contemplative prayer feels like.

Writer and teacher Ceisiwr Serith produced *A Book of Pagan Prayer* (2002), which is an excellent starting point if you are new to this practice. The book suggests a lot of different types of prayer to many different deities.

As a polytheist, my contemplative prayer practice is focused on specific deities with whom I feel a connection.

Charles Williams, a Christian mystic who was also a member of the Hermetic Order of the Golden Dawn, believed that the Divine is in everything and everything is in the Divine, and that we are all part of each other. If this is true, then it has profound consequences for prayer, because when you pray, you are connecting with the entire cosmos and all beings within it, and so the healing of your own soul is also the healing of all other souls.

Mother Teresa was once asked about her prayer life, and she said that she didn't talk to God, she just listened. The interviewer asked her what God did, and she replied "He just listens too." Silent prayer and contemplation is probably the most powerful form of communication with the Divine, because many people spend so much time focused on words that they lose touch with the more instinctual side of their nature.

Contemplative prayer is an age-old tradition of mystics. It is quite similar to centering prayer, but it doesn't involve a specific concept; it's more of a wordless communion with the Divine. It is usually preceded by more verbal forms of prayer, which lead into contemplation or meditation.

In Kabbalah, the mystical tradition of Judaism, there are four worlds or stages of creation, and when people pray, they ascend through these worlds to come closer to the Divine Source. They also correspond to psychological states. The closest world to the Divine Source is Emanation (Proximity in Hebrew); the next is Creation, then Formation, then Action. The soul in prayer ascends through the worlds of action (the body), formation (the ego), creation (the soul) and emanation (the Divine presence).

In Eastern Orthodox Christianity, there is a tradition called hesychasm. Hagia Hesychia or Holy Silence is an aspect of Christ, and hesychasm is the practice of silent prayer. In some ways it is similar to Quaker practice (which is interesting when you consider that there is no historical connection between them). Holy Silence is traditionally represented as a woman, and there is a lovely icon of her by William Hart McNicholls.

Centering prayer was developed by an interfaith dialogue group of Christians and Buddhists. These Christians admired the technique of Buddhist meditation but didn't want to cultivate the awareness of the Void recommended by Buddhist tradition; so instead they choose a single concept and focus on it during the meditation, which they call "centering prayer." So for instance you might choose the word "Love" or "Peace" or "Joy" to focus on during the prayer. The technique is similar to that of meditation, in that you relax your breathing and focus on the body, but you hold the concept you wish to focus on in your heart for the duration of the prayer, perhaps repeating the chosen word.

Body prayer is where you involve your whole body in the act of prayer. This might be gardening and praying, or dancing and praying, or walking and praying. Walking a labyrinth can be a prayerful act, as you deliberately focus on the spiritual journey. Another example of body prayer is the Dances of Universal Peace, a dance tradition in their own right, designed to engender peace and love in the participants. Yet another is the Salute to the Sun found in Yoga (which is a sacred Hindu practice designed to stimulate spiritual growth). One more example is the Muslim style of prayer, which was also used by many Christians in the Middle East (indeed in some places, Christians and Muslims used to pray side by side). Similarly, Taizé prayer is an ecstatic form of Christian prayer and singing and chanting that involves the whole body. It uses whole body movements and simple songs with lilting melodies.

So prayer can begin with words, and end with silent contemplation. There are many kinds of prayer, using words, gestures, dance, and silence. All are beneficial to the spiritual practitioner, and to those around them, as they cultivate peace.

Prayer and other contemplative practices are helpful for the development of self-awareness and compassion. It is difficult to practice compassion unless you are also at peace with yourself; and it is hard to be at peace with yourself unless you practice compassion. You cannot separate the inner work from the outer work, because your inner state and the outer world are intimately connected. Zen meditation teacher Shunryu Suzuki describes the ego as just a swinging door between our outer and inner world.[187] And, I would add, it is prayer that opens the door between the two worlds.

---

187   Shunryu Suzuki (1970), Zen Mind, Beginner's Mind. John Weatherhill, Inc. New York and Tokyo.

Priesthood

My working definition of priesthood is being able to facilitate contact between the other-than-human and the human, being able to create meaning, community, and a sense of connectedness for others (note that this definition includes atheists and animists). If you feel a calling toward priesthood, then you probably are a priestix or priest or priestess, at least potentially.

Traditionally priesthood involves making contact between the divine realm and the human. The divine realm can include deities, spirits, and the numinous in general. From an animist perspective, deities and spirits include spirits of place, tree spirits, rock spirits, water spirits, and so on. The priestix is a specialist in communication between the human and the other-than-human, using trance, spirit travel, invocation, evocation, and other techniques. They create a sense of connectedness for others.

One of my tests of who is a priestix is whether they can produce an atmosphere of calm and safety in a room full of distraught or agitated people. If you can, you're a priestix. Another such test is whether they can switch into priestly mode even when they feel tired, ill, agitated, or not in the mood for ritual.

A priestix builds community, creates safe spaces, resolves conflicts. They serve the community, and in exchange, the community values their efforts.

The priestix is also a storyteller for the community. They keep track of traditions, rituals, lore, and the history of the community, lineage, or tradition. They interpret the cosmology and symbolism of the tradition for others. In short, they help to create meaning. Of course, meaning is co-created by the whole community, but the priestix keeps track of the changing lore and rituals, and offers expert input.

Probably the most important aspect of the making of a priestix is the person experiencing a vocation or call to be a priestix. Without that call, you wouldn't set foot on the path toward priesthood.

A formal initiation can be valuable for the creation or formation of a priestix, but it is neither necessary nor sufficient. The inner transformation has to occur, and that's an alchemical mystery. An initiation can trigger that transformation, but the trigger can also be an encounter with a deity or with the numinous, or a sense of the awesomeness of Nature.

In Wicca, there are three levels of initiation. The first degree initiation is generally held to make you a priestix unto yourself. The second degree makes you a priestix to others in your coven. The third makes you a priestix for the wider community. I regard the Wiccan degree system as being like the apprenticeship system in medieval guilds (apprenticeship, journeyman, master).

The first degree is like exploring a garden. I like to compare it to the first year after you move into a new house, when you are getting used to the earth and the climatic conditions in your new garden. You wait to see what flowers come up before you plant anything new. In terms of the guild system, it's the equivalent of the apprentice role: You watch and learn from others, and also learn by doing. It's okay to make mistakes. You are a member of the priesthood of Wicca, but as yet, you are a priest unto yourself only.

The second degree enables the person to initiate others. It also means that the person can visit other covens to see how they do things, and in some lines it means they can hive off. It is like the journeyman role in the guild system, and now the person can train others and is more confident in ritual. They may also have developed a specialism such as healing or divination or herbs. In terms of the garden metaphor, the person is ready to start moving plants around and digging deeper.

The third degree is the equivalent of the role of master in the guild system. At this point, the person has achieved a level of maturity where they are able to teach others and run a coven—and possibly serve the wider community in some way. In terms of the garden metaphor, the garden is now at a new level of maturity—an understanding has been achieved with it, and the gardener is in harmony with the garden.

Other roles within the coven include the High Priestix, High Priest, and High Priestess. Most covens have two leaders (usually a high priestess and a high priest, but they could be two people of any combination of genders). The leader of the coven is first among equals. They are there to ensure that everything runs smoothly, facilitate the ritual, and run the training, and they may delegate these tasks to others.

Another role is the coven Fetch (also known as the Summoner or the Man in Black). It is generally their role to summon everyone to the ritual. These days that involves managing the coven social media group, website, and Google calendar. The Fetch can be of any gender.

The Freemasons have a role called a Tyler, who guards the door to prevent non-initiates gaining entry. The word is probably derived from the French word *tailleur*, one who cuts out. Some Wiccan covens have borrowed this role from Freemasonry.

Another very important role is that of the Maiden, who sets up the temple and passes things to the High Priestess during cakes and wine. The Maiden can also be a person of any gender.

Other coven roles have been suggested by Thista Minai in their book *Casting a Queer Circle: Nonbinary Witchcraft* (2017), such as the Guardian (rather like the Tyler) and the Greeter (a bit like the Fetch or Summoner).

Druidry also has a system of three levels: Bard, Ovate, and Druid. The Bard creates meaning by creating stories and songs. The Ovate communicates with spirits and deities. The Druid is more community-based. The Ovate incorporates the functions of the Bard. The Druid incorporates the functions of the other two.

Each of these levels is conferred by your ability and calling. The initiation may just be a recognition that you have already achieved that level.

Obviously real priesthood exists outside of formal systems of recognition and training, but within those systems, you're not going to be recognized as a priestix of that system without going through the required training and initiations. That is not a comment on your general competence or priestly status, only about your validity within that specific system.

Words for Priests

The most common words currently in use for Pagan priests are Priestex or Priestix, Priestess, and Priest.

The word "priest" comes from Latin *presbyter* (elder), of which the feminine form is *presbyterissa*. The root of *presbyter* is from Greek and means "old man."

The grammatical problem with priestix is that "-ix" is a feminine suffix; and the problem with priestex is that it sounds to me like an ex-priest. However, these seem to have caught on as the accepted gender-neutral terms, and I use them for people who wish to be known by these titles. (People's lived experience of gender is more important than being a grammar nerd.)

In modern English, the unmarked default (meaning an unmodified root word) is masculine. Examples include actor, director, and pretty much any word ending in -or. That's because these words were imported from Latin, where -or is a masculine suffix, and the corresponding feminine suffix is -rix.

In Old English (presumably an amalgam of several different Germanic dialects with an occasional Welsh-derived word such as combe), the unmarked default was gender-neutral, and gender was added with a prefix or suffix—at least, in two examples that I'm aware of. The word god was originally gender neutral, and the word man was originally gender neutral. So a male human was a weap-man (a man who carries weapons) and a female human was a weave-man (a man who weaves).

In some Middle English words that survive as surnames, the feminine form was created by adding -st- in the middle of the word, so a male weaver was a webber, and a female weaver was a webster; a male spinner was a spinner, and a female one was a spinster; a male brewer was a brewer, and female one was a brewster. (Brewster and Webster survive as last names; and spinster as the term for a single woman.)

The word priest was imported from Latin sometime in the Middle Ages. By this time the masculine form of a word tended to be the unmarked default; the root word had to be modified to produce the feminine form.

So the logical thing would be to make the male form of priest "priester," the female form "priestess," and priest ought to be the gender neutral form of the word. Unfortunately, because of when the word priest entered the English language, modern English adds a suffix to the word to make it gender neutral.

The word priestess entered the English language in about 1690, when antiquarians started writing about female pagan religious functionaries in late classical antiquity. So the word has always been used to refer to Pagan officiants, whereas priest has been used to refer to Christian officiants. That's why I choose the word priestess to refer to myself, even though I am nonbinary.

I have absolutely no objection to other people referring to themselves as a priestex or a priestix. I will refer to them as their chosen title, and 100 percent support them using the word. A gender-neutral version of the word would be very useful, and I doubt that there would be enough traction to make priester the male form (or perhaps prester, as in Prester John) and priest the gender neutral form (although the Anglican Church refers to all genders as priests, for what it's worth).

I gather that the Reclaiming Tradition uses the title priestess for everyone, regardless of gender. I was very pleased when the Assembly of the Sacred Wheel announced that they were officially embracing the title priestex for use in their organization.

Another possibility for a gender-neutral term would be *sacerdos* (pronounced /sa`ker.do:s/), one who makes things sacred (which is essentially the role of a priest or priestess). This term referred to a pagan priestly role in Ancient Greece.

I toyed with creating a hybrid of *gothi* and *gythja* (the Norse words for priest and priestess respectively), such as *gotha* or *gythi*. I think I prefer *gythi*. Another alternative would be to use the plural form, by analogy with using 'they' as a gender neutral pronoun. The plural is *gothar*.

Another alternative is *flamen* and *flaminia*, which were ancient Roman priestly roles. The plural is *flamines*, so the gender neutral word could be *flamine*. Unfortunately the title sounds to most people like a burger-related advertising slogan.

So, whatever titles you use in your traditions, I hope it is possible to agree on some gender-neutral options for people who want them.

Pure

> Keep pure your highest ideal; strive ever towards
> it; let naught stop you or turn you aside.
>
> — Doreen Valiente,
> "The Charge of the Goddess"

Many people, when they hear the words pure or purity, tend to think of puritanical attitudes, chastity, and an excessive attention to whether or not a person has engaged in sexual intimacy.

I would like to suggest that a better way to think about the word pure is in terms of metals or substances: pure and unalloyed. In the thirteenth century, pure meant unalloyed, possibly because of the rise of alchemy. The alchemical quest for gold was an allegory of the quest for spiritual enlightenment. The association of the word pure with alchemy always makes me think of the Blackadder episode where Lord Percy succeeds in making a nugget (well, more of a splat) of the purest green.[188]

A pure substance is one that is not mixed with any other substance. You can be purely assertive, or purely artistic, or purely witchy, or purely poetic. So purity (and ritual purification) is about focusing on one thing at a time, not about purging away sin. Pagans do not use the word sin. Ritual purification helps to focus the magical or spiritual practitioner on the ritual at hand, sifting out distracting thoughts such as what shows you watched last night.

Similarly, the concept of chastity as abstinence from sexual intimacy does not exist in Pagan religions. Chastity comes from a root word meaning to cut off or to separate. However, there is one connotation of the word chastity that I think is useful. It is

---

188   Blackadder, S2 E4, 'Money.'

the concept of "having the body in the soul's keeping" suggested by the novelist Robertson Davies.[189] This does not mean that one refrains from sexual intimacy; it means that one only engages in sexual intimacy when one's soul approves of it. One person's soul might approve of polyamory; while another's may be drawn to monogamy.

The word pure is also related to the Old High German verb *fowen*, to sift. So it could also be about clarifying or discerning what is worthwhile, as one does when panning for gold—sifting out the sand and retaining the valuable gold.

The development of the self through spiritual practice is an alchemical process of purification or refinement where you are becoming the most authentic version of yourself—unalloyed by accretions from practices that do not serve you, and I am comfortable using the word 'pure' to refer to the result of this process.

---

189   Robertson Davies (1958), A Mixture of Frailties. Macmillan.

Religion

A religion is a set of shared practices, values, and narratives that make the world meaningful for its adherents. Religions usually have a set of practices that are designed to facilitate a sense of connection with the numinous (the mysterious other that some call the divine) and with fellow adherents of the religion. Most of the world's religions are not focused on shared beliefs in the same way as Christianity, but on a shared set of practices and, in the case of more esoteric religions, around a shared experience of the numinous or of mystery. Even those religions that have a foundational text are in dialogue around their traditions and beliefs. A religion is also the community of people who adhere to it, however tenuously. Some writers have asserted that since it is hard to define religion in such a way as to include all the different versions of it, the word is essentially meaningless. But since people know what they mean when they say the word, even if they do not all agree on which traditions count as a religion and which do not, it is possible to say with some certainty that if it looks like a religion, smells like a religion, and sounds like a religion, it probably is a religion.

For a lot of people, the word religion conjures up repressive practices, boring rituals, and people with rigid moral codes.

Religions do not have to be rigidly orthodox or orthopraxic. A religion can include a wide variety of viewpoints and rituals. Religion can mean a variety of things to different people; it can mean orthodoxy and excessive adherence to a rigid moral code, or it can mean joyous connection to Nature and the wild, and other exhilarating activities.

The word religion may be derived from the Latin word *religare*, to reconnect, or to bind. Or it may be derived from *relego*, to re-read. I like the connotations of reconnection, as it implies compassion and connection, to other people and to the divine. Binding can be seen as a negative connotation, but it can also be seen as providing security and safety (as in a safety harness). It can also be compared with the word ligature, which means a connection (usually referring to a muscle of the body).

What are you reconnecting with? You could be reconnecting with nature, the old gods, your true self. Reconnecting is a good thing; no-one wants to feel lost, detached, disconnected and disassociated from everything around them. Most people want to feel compassionate and caring.

The connotation of re-reading implies living an examined life, interpreting experience, and pursuing knowledge. It also relates to one particular person's conversion experience: He saw a Bible and heard the words, "Tolle et lego" (Take it and read). This implies that revelation can only happen through reading, and not from experience. The experience of reading can be powerful and revelatory, but people often respond to the contents of a book because it resonates with their experience of the world. Many people like to contrast religion with spirituality, implying that spirituality is freer and easier, but there are many issues with spirituality, and many opportunities for spiritual abuse occur in spiritual settings—so let the buyer beware.

Even in traditions that have codified beliefs that their adherents are supposed to subscribe to, individuals' interpretations of their creeds vary considerably. If you start an interfaith dialogue with a Catholic or any other type of Christian, you are likely to encounter many interpretations of their tradition—even within the same denomination. For example, there are seventeen versions of the doctrine of atonement, and many other variations on other doctrines. The notion of a single unified truth that all Christians adhere to starts to look pretty shaky once you look at the history of theological disputes within Christianity. In practice, individual believers do not all believe the same things, even if they pay lip service to the idea that they should do. Even in evangelical Christianity, there are a variety of opinions about being gay, for example.

The traditions of Jewish interpretation and exegesis (whether Orthodox, Liberal, or Reform) say that there are many interpretations of the Torah, and they really enjoy debating them.

Even though Islam is often thought of as having a fixed set of beliefs, there is still room for interpretation of the Quran, and a tradition of interpreting it in the light of the hadith (sayings of the Prophet) and Islamic tradition. The word fatwa means an interpretation or an opinion. So if you are unsure about what to do about a particular thing, you go and ask a mullah or a qadi for an interpretation of the Quran. So it is not assumed by most Muslims (except Wahhabis) that there is only one possible interpretation of the Quran.

There is religion as it is officially supposed to be according to the doctrine of the tradition in question; and then there is the reassuringly messy, fuzzy, and human way that people actually do it.

In religions where the divine is usually viewed as immanent in the world, or as so diffuse that it is not a person, the source of authority is viewed as the self (as in one's conscience) and not a "higher power." Fundamentalists usually believe that God is the source of moral commandments. An excellent book by

Richard Holloway called *Godless Morality: Keeping Religion Out of Ethics* (2000) explains why God being the source of moral commandments cannot possibly work even if you actually believe in God (which he does not). The reason is this: Because no-one can be sure what "God" wants, or even if They exist, no one can claim in their moral pronouncements to speak for God. If two people both claim to be doing what God wants, but they are doing exactly opposite things, how do other people decide between them? By using ordinary evidence, reason, and compassion to decide.

I see religion as spirituality practiced in community. Spirituality is another concept that is difficult to define, but I regard it as a sense of mystical connection with the universe and all beings within it. In feeling this sense of connection, people experience compassion for the sufferings of other beings, and empathy with their joys. It is possible to enhance this sense of connection by finding a community where you can be yourself and practice compassion and connection. If people do not engage in spirituality in a community setting, it can become self-centered and shallow, disconnected from everyday reality. People need the experience of living and sharing with others to enable them to grow and become their authentic selves. This can be done by the creation of a community of shared values and shared experience of mystery, which models in microcosm the desired qualities of community. There will be conflicts and tensions, but it is in how these are resolved that the real values of the community will be tested and refined.

I believe that the religious life is a shared spiritual journey toward greater communion with the cosmos, where Spirit descends into matter rather than escaping from it. This communion does not involve erasing individuality; rather it is the celebration of diversity and the quest for authenticity, because the "divine" (the vision of ultimate worth) is the potentiality of all life to share in mystical communion. But humanity must expand compassion to embrace all beings, not just to those with shared beliefs, and people can do this by engaging in social action—caring for the marginalized and the oppressed, protecting the environment, standing up for human rights, and promoting freedom, peace and justice.

Sacraments

A rite of passage is a ritual designed to make sacred a particular life event or transition from one stage of life to another. These rituals can also be called "sacraments."

The Oxford English Dictionary defines a sacrament as "a thing of mysterious and sacred significance; a religious symbol." The word is used in Catholicism to refer to the seven sacraments of baptism, confirmation, the Eucharist, penance, anointing of the sick, ordination, and matrimony—which are mostly rites of passage. In Protestant traditions it refers to baptism and the Eucharist, also known as Holy Communion or "the Lord's Supper," depending on the denomination. The etymology of the word is from Latin *sacramentum* "solemn oath" (from *sacrare* "to hallow," from *sacer* "sacred").

An important element of rites of passage and sacraments is that they have a physical component, often linked to one or more of the classical four elements (earth, air, fire, water). Immersion in water is used in Judaism and Christianity to signify entering into a new phase, being consecrated (baptism) or re-consecrated (mikveh). Fire is used as a purifying medium in the Hindu ritual of aarti, which is an offering and a purificatory ritual. Water is used for the Sikh baptism ceremony called Amrit Sanskar. The ancient druids are reported to have used sensory deprivation by requiring candidates for initiation to lie in darkness for several days and then thrusting them into the light, according to OBOD.[190] All these rituals signify some sort of symbolic death and rebirth experience.

---

190   'A Brief History.' Order of Bards, Ovates, and Druids.

The Sacraments in Pagan Traditions

There is no standard list of sacraments for any contemporary Pagan tradition, but it is possible to identify sacraments for most of them.

In Wicca, the sacraments could be said to be preparing the circle, cakes and wine, naming (sometimes called "Wiccaning"), initiation, handfasting, and croning.

In Druidry, the sacraments could be said to be preparing the circle, naming, initiation, and handfasting.

In Heathenry and Ásatrú, the sacraments could be said to be the blot, the sumble (or symbel), and the handfasting.

In Religio Romana, there are many rituals designed to connect the practitioner with the deities and sacralize life. These include libations, a prayer for ablutions (a ritual formula to purify oneself before the performance of other rituals), and various daily rituals at the lararium or home shrine.

Life Rites

Most Pagans presume that everything is already sacred, because deities are immanent in the world. Therefore, rituals of consecration are about creating extra sacredness or reconnecting us with the deities, the community, or the natural world.

Birth and naming. Pagans do not perceive a need to purify either the mother or the child after birth, considering that people are born innocent. The child will typically be welcomed into the community and given a name, but they will not be committed to any particular religious tradition, as most Pagans believe that children should be able to choose their religion or belief system when they are old enough. Although the naming ceremony in

Wicca is sometimes called a Wiccaning, it does not mean that the child is considered to be a Wiccan as a result of the ceremony.

Coming of age. There is a distinct lack of coming of age rituals in Western culture generally, and this is echoed in Pagan traditions, although some groups do celebrate the onset of menstruation, as long as the young person in question actually wants this.

Initiation. Wicca and Druidry both have initiation rituals, often based on the initiation rituals of occult orders such as Freemasonry. American author and founder of Ár nDraíocht Féin, Isaac Bonewits, identified three types of initiation ritual:

- Initiation as a recognition of a status already gained
- Initiation as an ordeal of transformation
- Initiation as a method for transferring spiritual knowledge and power

I have identified six aspects of initiation, which may be present in a single ritual or may be a gradual process. There is the inner process of transformation; the initiation by the gods and goddesses (making contact with the numinous); experiencing the Mysteries (that which cannot be spoken, or Arrheton); being given the secrets of the initiating group (that which must not be spoken, or Aporrheton); joining the group mind of the initiating group; and the joining of the lineage or tradition of which the coven is part.

In Heathenry, initiation is replaced by profession, a ceremony where someone professes a desire to become part of the Asatruar (people who are true to the Aesir, the Heathen deities), and then takes an oath.

Handfasting. This is the term for a wedding, mainly in Wicca and eclectic Paganism, but it is also popular with humanists and non-religious people. The ceremony generally involves the symbolic crossing of a threshold, such as leaping over a broomstick or a small fire. The use of ribbons or cords to fasten the couple's hands together may date back to pre-Christian times. Rings and vows are usually exchanged.

In Heathenry, wedding ceremonies are usually hallowed by holding them beneath the hammer of Thor (Mjöllnir), and arm rings are exchanged. The couple may also hold an oath ring while exchanging vows.

Croning. A ceremony for a woman who has reached menopause, usually celebrated in Wicca. A croning ceremony usually takes place around the age of fifty, and it celebrates the achievement of elder status in the community and feminine wisdom.

Dying. There is no set ritual for preparing for death, but there are many excellent resources in The Pagan Book of Living and Dying (1997), by M Macha Nightmare (formerly of the Reclaiming tradition) and Starhawk.

Other Rituals

Preparing sacred space (the circle). Most Pagan traditions have a preparation for ritual, as rituals are often held in spaces that also have other uses, such as a living room, a garden, or a park. Therefore sacred spaces are temporary and have to be reconsecrated. It is also necessary for the participants in a ritual to be prepared for the ritual, in order to help us enter into the right mind-set. Preparation typically includes some form of consecration of the space and of the participants with the four elements (earth, air, fire, and water). Incense, water, salt, and other symbols of the four elements may be used to create sacred space.

Blot (Heathenry). This ritual has three parts, the hallowing or consecrating of the offering, the sharing of the offering, and the libation. The offering, shared with the deities, is typically mead, beer, or juice.

Sumble / Symbel / Sumbel (Heathenry). This is a sacred drinking ceremony. The host begins the proceedings by greeting the guests and making a short statement of intent, and then offers the first toast. People then pass the horn around the table and each person makes their toasts in turn. In the first round, people brag of prior accomplishments; in the second round, they boast of what they will do in the future; and in the third round, they toast the gods and heroes. At the end of the brag, boast, or toast, the person making it drinks from the horn, and in doing so "drinks in" what they said. An oath made over a consecrated drinking horn is sacred.[191]

Cakes and wine (Wicca). In Wicca, cakes and wine are consecrated by a priest and priestess and shared with the coven. In inclusive Wicca, cakes and wine may be consecrated by two people of any gender. This happens at every circle.

Libations. These are offerings of mead or wine poured for the deities and spirits of place. The libation is important in Religio Romana, Heathenry, and Wicca.

What Do All These Rituals Have in Common?

They all involve one or more of the four elements (earth, air, fire, and water). Earth may be represented by stone, salt, crystals, or soil. Air may be represented by blades, wands, feathers, or incense. Fire may be represented by a candle flame, a bonfire, incense, or wands. Water is represented by water, chalices, and

---

191   'The Rituals of Asatru.' Raven Kindred.

cauldrons. Each element has a sacred direction, which can vary among traditions.

Initiation ceremonies all include a section where the candidate is asked whether they wish to be there. In naming ceremonies, where the baby cannot be asked if it wishes to take part, a simple welcome to the wider community of humanity is all that takes place.

There is an assumption that things are already sacred, because deities are immanent in the world, but sometimes people forget their connection with the divine and need reconnecting.

They generally involve marking the transition from one phase to another—sometimes by actually crossing a threshold: stepping into the sacred space, or leaping across a fire or a broomstick.

They generally involve deities or spirits being asked for their blessing and/or protection.

These features suggest that a sacrament makes something sacred by transitioning it across a boundary—either between the profane and the sacred, or between two phases of life—and by bringing it into contact with other things that are already sacred, preferably in a way that provides a balance of all four elements (earth, air, fire, and water) or by bringing it into the presence of the numinous, in such a way that a sense of communion with the consecrated thing, person, or experience is established.

Theology

Theology is important because if our rituals are not underpinned by something meaningful, Pagans will just end up repeating the norms of our contemporaries.

The word theology was coined by Cicero in his book *De Natura Deorum* ("On the Nature of the Gods") in 49 ce. It was a book written in defense of paganism in the context of the rise of Christianity. This could be called defensive theology but it is usually known as apologetics.

Theology comes from the Greek theo, a god, and logos, a word, so it means "words about the gods." Some people like to rewrite the word as thealogy ("words about the goddess"), or theoilogy ("words about the gods"). I typically refer to theologies, to make it clear that multiple theological perspectives are welcomed and expected in Pagan discourse.

There are lots of other words that end in '-ology,' like psychology ("words about the psyche"), biology ("words about life"), all derived from Greek.

The other thing that people tend to say when the subject of Pagan theology (or thealogy or theoilogy) is brought up is that they fear that discussing theology will lead to entrenched dogma. Dogma, though, is a completely different concept. You have to have an organized religion in order to have dogma, along with a body that will enforce that dogma. This does not yet exist in contemporary Pagan religions, and I think most Pagans would prefer to keep it that way.

Theology is a discursive discipline, and there are many schools of thought within it—in every religion.

The situation that is more likely to lead to dogma is an unthinking approach to ritual and Pagan concepts. If people avoid discussing and thinking about the underlying theories of ritual and practice, then they will just accept the prevailing orthodoxy on whatever the topic at hand happens to be.

My favorite example of this in action is the topic of gender in ritual. It is necessary to discuss concepts like whether the gods have gender, if the gods care about gender, and whether the gods perform gender in the same way as humans do. If people do not discuss these ideas, it will be harder to resolve questions around how to address deities, whether ritual roles need to be gendered, and so on.

Clearly gods do not generally have biology, so their sexual characteristics may be fluid. There are numerous instances of deities changing gender in mythology, so deities can have multiple genders and multiple ways of performing gender. How might this be reflected in our rituals? How could the multiple genders of people be reflected in our rituals and in the imagery used to represent our deities? Your choice of pictures and statues to represent Pagan deities will be influenced by whether you see deities as purely immanent in Nature, visible as stars and trees, mountains, and landscapes, or whether you like anthropomorphic representations of deities. Many contemporary depictions of Pagan deities are hypersexualized and unrealistically exaggerated. Most Pagans, me included, value sexuality, but not every statue or picture needs to have pneumatic curves and muscles. This is one of the reasons I tend to prefer archaic and abstract representations of deities.

As a polytheist, I like depictions of specific deities with historical antecedents, but others may want a more generic depiction of deities to reflect a more pantheistic theological perspective.

Author and Gardnerian Wiccan Jack Chanek has made an excellent point about specific appearance (skin color, body shape) being applied to depictions of deities: that it might cause people to think goddesses must be a certain shape or color.[192]

Theology doesn't only relate to gods, it also relates to our relationship with the gods and our relationship with religion. If you're an atheist, it relates to your relationship to the universe or nature or whatever you work with. It is about ethics and values and how rituals are performed.

Another of my favorite examples of why theology is important is the topic of light and darkness in Pagan theology, which is completely different from how many other religions tend to view light and darkness. In other religions, people tend to talk about how the light conquers the darkness and subdues it. In Pagan theology (or at least in Wiccan theology), there's a lot of talk about the marriage of light and darkness. They are seen as complementary opposites, not adversaries in some cosmic struggle.

I think it is really important to have theological discussions among Pagans—and to articulate clearly what our theology is—so that we can have meaningful ritual and meaningful discussions about ritual. If we operate in a theological vacuum, we will end up repeating whatever the norms of the day happen to be, which is not necessarily what we want.

---

192   Jack Chanek (2024), Goddess Statues and Deity Representations.

Tradition

We should reclaim the concept of tradition from traditionalists who want to set customs in stone instead of allowing them to evolve and change.

A tradition (whether that is a single custom or a group of customs and practices) is something that evolves and grows and changes in response to its environment but is still recognizable as the same thing. It is not set in stone, but is more like a discourse; if you start with a particular set of premises, ideas and values, you will get further ideas and practices that are consistent with the initial set of ideas. Religious traditions evolve with social, cultural, and political circumstances. For example, there are Christian traditions that have evolved and changed in response to culture and environment, but they are still recognizable as Christian. A Catholic community in India had the tradition of having a procession in honor of the Virgin Mary. It was a special honor to carry a flag in the procession and to raise and lower the flag on a flagpole along the route. This meant that more people wanted to have the honor than could be accommodated by a single flag and a single raising of the flag. So more flags were added to the procession, and more occasions of raising and lowering the flag were added, and the processional route was extended. Over the years, the original custom was elaborated by considerable additional flags and flag-raising, but it was still the same procession: They were still carrying a statue of the Virgin Mary, but extra features were added.[193] It is possible to modify a traditional practice quite extensively before it becomes something completely different.

---

[193]   Matthias Frenz (2008), "Struggles and strategies in the contest for ritual space. Ritual design at a Marian sanctuary in India." Presented at the Heidelberg conference on Ritual Dynamics (SFB 619), September 29 – October 6, 2008.

Some people think that tradition is rigid and unchanging (or that it ought to be so), but this is not the case. Some people also think that saying "because it's traditional" is sufficient reason for doing a thing. But because tradition evolves in response to circumstances, and because customs can sometimes be harmful, saying "because we've always done it that way" is not a sufficient reason for doing something. Consider why it was done that way in the first place. If the reason for doing it that way is still valid, then that is not a problem. But if there is a new group of people to be taken into consideration who were not considered when the custom was first devised, then it may be necessary to adapt or drop the custom to include them. Traditions evolve all the time in response to the changing needs of the community. This applies to religious traditions as a whole and to traditional practices within them.

Folklorists pay attention to the transmission and context of a tradition, as well as to its content. The means of transmission is also important in Pagan traditions. In Wicca, the validity of an initiation is important (it has to be done by someone who is already initiated, and it must be done according to certain criteria). In reconstructionist and polytheist traditions, some think it is important to have a cultural or ethnic connection to the religion being reconstructed; others derive the legitimacy of their practice from ancient texts about their religion, mythology, and deities. Before a new insight (an unverified personal gnosis) can be more widely adopted by practitioners, it needs to be compared to textual evidence and/or substantiated by comparison with insights from other contemporary practitioners. It then becomes a substantiated personal gnosis.

If a traditional practice that you have received is actively harmful, then it is legitimate to change it. An obvious example is the tradition of marriage. In the past, the definition of marriage included polygamy. Some people regarded this as injurious to the individuality of the additional wives, and so polygamy became widely frowned-upon. It also included a woman being required to marry a man who raped her; this was obviously harmful, so the practice has been discontinued in most cultures. Until the early twentieth century, it was extremely difficult to obtain a divorce, which meant that many people were trapped within failed marriages; again, this was regarded as harmful, so marriage was redefined as something that could be terminated. Many same-sex couples were harmed by their exclusion from the possibility of being married, so the law was changed so they can get married. Some have argued that this is a redefinition of marriage; maybe it is, but marriage has been redefined many times, and it is still popular. The evolution of marriage shows that it is possible to modify a custom to include more people, or to reduce the harm that it may cause, without changing the basic features of the tradition.

The same applies to Pagan customs and traditional practices. They can and should be expanded or modified to make them work for more people.

If a traditional practice excludes a whole category of people because of their core identity, then I would argue that it needs to be expanded to include them. There is no need to abolish the practice for the people for whom it works. The obvious example here is Wiccan initiation. For the vast majority of people, cross-gender initiation works just fine. If you are cisgender and heterosexual, there is no reason to change how you will be initiated. But what if a person is transgender? Should they be initiated by someone of a different gender identity to themselves, or someone of a different physical sex? Or should they be allowed to choose? What about nonbinary, genderfluid, and genderqueer people? What about those who are exclusively attracted to members of the same sex? This depends on whether you think initiation depends on polarity, what you think polarity is, and how you think it is created. Is it created by erotic attraction, biological characteristics, or other differences?

If a traditional practice is either physically or psychologically harmful to a large group of people (examples include child marriage, genital mutilation, and foot-binding), then it needs to be modified or abolished.

If a traditional practice excludes a category of people because of their innate characteristics (e.g., not allowing same-sex couples to get married, or refusing Wiccan initiation to people with a disability), then it needs to be expanded to include that category, provided that it does not harm anyone else.

If a traditional practice affirms the identity of your group by making derogatory claims about other groups, then it needs to be changed so that it is not derogatory toward the identity of another group. An example might be a Christian affirmation that they are "not like the heathen," or that they renounce "wicked idolatry." The Vatican officially dropped a part of the Catholic liturgy that said something rude about Jews, for example.

If it is claimed that a traditional practice excludes a category of people because of an acquired characteristic that is not part of their core identity, then it may be necessary to think a bit harder about modifying it. For example, I would argue that the Wiccan practice of working skyclad is empowering and life-affirming and enhances group trust, but some people claim that it is harmful for people who have been raped or molested. I would certainly not want to add to their trauma by insisting that they work skyclad, but I would want to encourage them to work toward a state of trust and self-confidence where they felt able to work skyclad, because it may provide healing for their trauma. This is obviously a difficult area because it is still asking people to work on themselves to fit into something they may not be comfortable with, but if you are approaching a group that works skyclad, and working skyclad is something you are not prepared to explore, you may need to look for a different group.

Conversely, a traditional practice does not need modifying if it is life-affirming. Does everyone in your group or religious tradition feel included in it? Does it affirm the core identity of everyone in your group? Does it express and affirm the core values of your group or religious tradition? Does it help to transmit your values, beliefs, stories, and identity to new members of the group? Does it accurately describe a key magical or cosmological concept or experience? Does it help rather than harm? If the answer to all or most of these questions is yes, then congratulations, you have a worthwhile traditional practice.

Transcendence

Many people think of transcendence as a concept that is alien to Pagan theologies, but there are two kinds of transcendence.

Ontological transcendence is the idea (quite rare among Pagans) that the divine (whether viewed as a single deity or as multiple deities) is outside Nature, that spirit and matter are separate realms. It is often found in dualist traditions—that is, religions with a strong separation between spirit and matter.

Epistemological transcendence is the idea that people can participate in collective forms of knowing, such as the collective unconscious, group mind phenomena, and shared consciousness with a deity. This idea is quite common among Pagans, although we do not tend to refer to it as transcendence. Epistemological transcendence is best understood by thinking about having a transcendent experience, for example when you are in a crowd of other people and you feel carried away by emotion because you are all having a wonderful experience such as listening to a beautiful piece of music.

A position halfway between ontological transcendence and immanence is Panentheism. The easiest way to understand Panentheism is to contrast it with Pantheism.

Pantheism is the idea that the Divine and Nature are one and the same. If a pantheist made a Venn diagram of the universe and the Divine it would be a circle, because in pantheism they are the same thing. There is nothing outside the universe. This is quite an old idea and it appears in a number of religious traditions. One of the earliest expressions of it in modern times was philosopher Benedictus de Spinoza's idea of the Divine as Nature (*Deus sive Natura*). Similarly, much later, the architect Frank Lloyd Wright said, "I believe in God, only I spell it Nature." Some people confuse pantheism with polytheism, but polytheism is a belief in many gods (who can be immanent in Nature), and pantheism is the idea of a single divine being immanent in the universe. Typically in pantheism, there is no sense of a personal deity; instead, everything in Nature is divine. Although that feels like a very Pagan idea, it appears in a variety of religious traditions. It might not be inherently Pagan, but it is certainly compatible with Pagan thought.

Panentheism is the idea that the divine exists, all-pervading through the universe and also existing beyond it, so it involves immanence and ontological transcendence. The Divine is seen as encompassing the universe and transcending it. This idea also appears in a variety of religious traditions, including Hinduism. It is not incompatible with Pagan thought, but Pagans are rarely panentheists.

Virtue

Virtue ethics were first described by ancient pagan writers such as Socrates, Aristotle and the Stoics. The term virtue is from Latin and the root word 'vir-,' a man, and originally meant "valor, merit, moral perfection."

A virtue is an internal quality or moral reflex that an individual possesses or cultivates.

Ancient pagan virtues were ones that would characterize a pagan household or pagan person, such as hospitality, honor, fortitude, and the four cardinal virtues enumerated by Aristotle (prudence, justice, temperance, and courage) which were in balance with each other and led to *eudaimonia* (happiness and flourishing).[194] Prudence is necessary because it helps people to determine the right course of action. People can gain prudence by learning from others with more experience, and by gaining experience themselves. Justice involves dealing with others in a fair and decent manner, ensuring that everyone is treated fairly and given their due. Temperance does not mean abstinence, but rather enjoying pleasures in a healthy and balanced way. Courage is a balance of fear and bravery (not the absence of fear); it is doing what is right even in the face of danger and death.

Another useful virtue is wisdom: "the ability to use your knowledge and experience to make good decisions and judgments,"[195] which could be seen as a combination of justice and prudence.

Many people think of virtue as a Christian concept, possibly because it has been associated with qualities that are not

---

194   'What Were Aristotle's Four Cardinal Virtues?' The Collector.
195   'WISDOM | English meaning.' Cambridge Dictionary.

virtues, such as obedience. Obedience is not a virtue because if somebody gives you an order to do something that goes against your conscience, then obeying that order is not virtuous. In the nineteenth century, Felicia Hemans wrote the dreadful poem *Casabianca* (1826), about the boy who stood on the burning deck, from whence all but he had fled.[196] It was based on a real incident in the Battle of the Nile in 1798. The poem is about a boy who was on a boat that was burning, and he ended up dying because he was obeying the order to stay on deck given to him by his father. For decades afterwards, the boy in the poem was held up as a virtuous example to British children, and they were made to learn the poem as a performance piece, which is doubtless why there are numerous parodies of the first verse.[197] I think this is a good illustration of the idea that obedience is not a virtue. Another example is from the Nuremberg Trials, where "I was only obeying orders" was not accepted as a defense. In a way, obedience should be seen as a vice. It is necessary in dangerous situations where someone more experienced needs to give orders quickly; but if it is obvious that the order is invalid or immoral, then the person should take the initiative to act.

These examples are an illustration of why it is necessary to reclaim the concept of virtue from people who have co-opted it for nefarious purposes—like persuading others to obey them without question.

Ancient and modern virtue ethics talk about the cultivation of virtues to lead to *eudaimonia*, which literally means blessedness or harmony or human flourishing. The cultivation of virtue is part of the inner work. How does one cultivate virtue? I would say, mainly

---

196   Felicia Hemans (1826), 'Casabianca.' Poetry By Heart. https://www.poetrybyheart.org.uk/poems/casabianca
197   Catherine Robson (2005), 'Standing on the Burning Deck: Poetry, Performance, History.' PMLA. https://www.sas.upenn.edu/~cavitch/pdf-library/Robson_Standing.pdf

by performing actions that express that virtue. Practice being kind and you will become kind. Practice not offering sharp and bitter criticism, and it will become natural to you. Holding others in your thoughts can help with developing your compassionate side. Finding out why people are homeless, or refugees, or oppressed, can also increase your compassion.

Heathens and Religio Romana practitioners have lists of virtues. There are the Nine Noble Virtues of Heathenry, and there is a very long list of Roman virtues on various Religio Romana websites. So virtue is very definitely a Pagan and polytheist concept.

The Nine Noble Virtues of Heathenry are courage (standing up for what you know to be right and just), truth (speaking the truth), honor (having a moral compass), fidelity (keeping your word), discipline (using your personal will to uphold the other virtues), hospitality (the reciprocal respect between guest and host), self-reliance (taking care of yourself), industriousness (work), and perseverance (carrying on even when life is difficult).[198]

I have been writing about the eight Wiccan Virtues for some years.[199] These were first enumerated by Doreen Valiente in "The Charge of the Goddess" and are beauty and strength, power and compassion, honor and humility, mirth and reverence. My high priestess referred to them as virtues, and I started referring to them as the eight Wiccan Virtues (to distinguish them from lists of virtues in other religions). Not all Wiccans refer to them in their rituals, but many of us like them as an alternative or a supplement to the Wiccan Rede.

---

198   Patti Wigington (2018), 'The Nine Noble Virtues of Asatru.' Learn Religions. https://www.learnreligions.com/noble-virtues-of-asatru-2561539
199   Yvonne Aburrow (2020), Dark Mirror: the inner work of witchcraft (2nd edition).

Yvonne Aburrow (2020), The night journey: witchcraft as transformation (2nd edition).

Yvonne Aburrow (2014), All acts of love and pleasure: inclusive Wicca.

Each of the pairs of virtues is carefully balanced. Too much honor can mean excessive touchiness on every potential ethical dilemma, perhaps even pomposity. Too much humility could make you a doormat, or a Uriah Heep figure. Taken together and balanced, honor and humility make for dignity and integrity. The word humility derives from *humus*, earth, and so implies closeness to the earth. This is not false humility or self-deprecation, but rather an accurate assessment of one's powers. This is especially important in magic, where it can be disastrous to overreach one's capabilities. Ideally, leaders in Wicca are not primarily motivated by the aggrandizement of their ego, and they are aware of the needs of their coveners as they seek to develop them as priests and priestesses in their own right. We do not lord it over the initiate, but receive them with humility, aware of the talents and insights they bring to the circle. Behaving honorably is also important—keeping one's word and behaving with a high standard of integrity.

Too much mirth can lead to cynicism, and too much reverence can lead to boredom—but balanced, these virtues can lead to good companionship. Mirth is a wonderful thing, especially for pricking the pomposity of the powerful, but you have probably met people who can never take anything seriously. After a while, it would be good if they would take off the mask of comedy and show their real face. But those who always insist on reverence are rather puritanical, and one wishes that they would lighten up. Hence a balance between mirth and reverence is vital, especially the ability to laugh at ourselves.

Beauty and strength also need to be balanced—a graceful person is often also a strong person, because they are in control of their body and their mind. Beauty alone can be fragile and vulnerable, and strength alone can be brutal; but together, they create balance.

Too much power can lead to cruelty, and so can too much compassion. Some Buddhists call compassion without wisdom "silly compassion"—the compassion that gives money or time or effort while having no insight into the situation of the recipient can do more harm than good. Too much power can be corrupting, especially if it is not tempered with compassion. When people wield the power of magic, they had better be sure they do so wisely and compassionately.

The balance of these opposites recalls the twin pillars of the Kabbalistic Tree of Life, which are reconciled in the central pillar. Together, Wisdom and Understanding create Gnosis or Knowledge; Strength combined with Mercy creates Beauty; and Power and Glory create the Kingdom. All the Sephiroth (Spheres) of the Tree of Life proceed from the Divine Source.

People talk about the virtues of an herb as the properties of an herb—or what makes it efficacious. A virtue is something that can also be understood as efficacy or effectiveness. In alchemy, people talk about the virtues of a metal, so virtue is also a magical concept.

The interesting thing about virtue ethics is that they are not a series of commandments or prohibitions, but rather a list of qualities that are good to cultivate.

The Wiccan Rede is all very well and very useful, but all that it tells us is "an it harm none do what thou wilt" (if it harms no one, do what you want). This is more usefully rephrased as "do what thou wilt, an it harm none." In other words, think about what you are going to do before you do it. This is useful, but it does not tell us what qualities people should be cultivating in themselves to get to a state of human flourishing.

One virtue that would be useful to the planet is living in harmony with the Earth, so it is interesting that two of the virtues that are mentioned in "The Charge of the Goddess" are honor and humility. Humility literally means "close to the earth," and if you put honor and humility together, they make integrity.

A couple of other traditional Pagan virtues are reciprocity and hospitality, which were also very important to ancient pagans. This can be seen from the Greek story of Odysseus and Nausicaa and the Roman story of Philemon and Baucis.

Virtue has been a Pagan concept for longer than it was ever a Christian concept. It can be seen as a secular concept, if you prefer.

Worship

Worship did not mean "honoring a deity" until around 1300. Before that it just meant the qualities of being worthy, full of dignity, and honorable. People still use it in that sense when they address a dignitary as "your worship."

Worship was reclaimed by the Unitarian Universalist Order of Abraxas to mean "honoring that which is of highest worth" which is much closer to the original meaning.[200]

Worship is the combination of the word "worth" with the suffix "-ship" which is a quality or a state (like marksmanship, the quality of being a good marksman).

People used to think of worship as getting down on your knees and abasing yourself, but that is not what worship means—despite some religious traditions practicing their worship in that style.

It is a little bit difficult to reclaim the word worship to refer to the honoring of Pagan deities because it was never used in that sense in relation to Pagan deities. The Latin word used in ancient Roman religion was *cultus*, meaning the cultivation of a relationship with a deity.[201] The Romans considered *pietas* (meaning piety, dutifulness, affection, love, loyalty, gratitude) to be an important civic and personal virtue.[202] Without the maintenance of the *cultus* and the practice of *pietas*, the *pax deorum* (the peace of the gods) could not be maintained.

Religious practices among ancient heathens varied, but could include bowing the head, prostrating oneself, or bowing deeply before a deity. It was also customary to uncover the head while worshiping a deity. Other important practices included making

---

200   Von Ogden Vogt (1976), 'Abraxan Essay on Worship.'
201   NovaRoma, Cultus deorum Romanorum.
202   Open University, 'Introducing Virgil's Aeneid: 3.1 What is pietas?' OpenLearn.

offerings (*blóta*) and prayer (*biðja*). The word "bid" for prayer is related to the German word *beten*, to ask, and is still used in the expression "bidding prayer."

I think that all liberal religions can and should reclaim the word worship to mean honoring that which is of highest worth and I think that we should give the credit for that reclaiming and reinterpretation to the Order of Abraxas.

What do you regard as being of highest worth? Is it Nature, the gods, community, your innermost divine self, or something else? How does it feel to focus on that and honor it? That is worship.

Sometimes an ecstatic connection with a deity is so powerful that people lose the sense of themselves and merge with the deity in loving bliss. That too is worship.

Conclusion

> We open our mouths and out flow words whose
> ancestries we do not even know. We are walking
> lexicons. In a single sentence of idle chatter
> we preserve Latin, Anglo-Saxon, Norse; we
> carry a museum inside our heads, each day we
> commemorate peoples of whom we have never
> heard.
>
> —Penelope Lively, *Moon Tiger* (1987)

Every spiritual tradition uses words in a specific way in line with its particular theology, mythology, vision, culture, and worldview, and Pagan communities are no exception. Pagans have a unique perspective on how the world works, as well as shared values with other religious and spiritual traditions. Pagan traditions value darkness, the feminine, the Earth, and our ancestral roots. We are people of the earth, and we are earthy. Yet, like other spiritual traditions, we value mystery and the experience of the numinous, and we wonder what lies beyond the world we can perceive.

Tolkien famously had the insight that every language must have its own mythology, and his legendarium was both an underpinning mythology for his invented languages, and an attempt to provide a mythology for the English people. Pagan religions have a lot of mythology and folklore to draw upon that can give meaning and context to the words we use.

Pagan traditions and groups can give specific meanings to words, weaving them into a web of their stories and worldview, but Pagans should avoid creating a discourse that is so incomprehensible to outsiders that it is difficult to enter the Pagan community (because the inhabitants speak their own dialect) or to leave it (because there is no longer any common ground with non-Pagans).

I hope that the unpacking and exploration of concepts in this book can provide a guide to deeper understanding of the Pagan worldview, for those within the Pagan community, for those outside it, and for those embarking on a Pagan journey. I hope that this book inspires you to explore the deep histories of the words you encounter in conversations and books, or that it encourages you to do that more if it's something you already enjoy. I hope it will encourage you to explore the true meanings, or find alternative meanings, of words that have been used to hurt you. The best way to heal psychological wounds inflicted by others is to reclaim the words they used and give them your own meanings. This is why "witch" is such a powerful word: It was once used in a hurtful way, and now people have reclaimed it to mean something beautiful and powerful.

I love words. I love to explore the twists and turns of etymology, and the endlessly creative way that people use words in poetry, prose, and everyday conversation. I love the worlds that open and unfold when we explore the connotations and stories embedded in words and how they have been used in different times and places. I love the roots of words, reaching down into the depths of ancient languages that have ceased to exist except as faint echoes in the words that are still used. I read recently that the shorter a word is, the more basic and ancient the concept it represents. Some words (such as mother) have such ancient roots that widely different language families have versions of them with related meanings.

The word "pagan" was originally meant to be a slur meaning rustic and backward, derived from *pagus*, a unit of land. But contemporary Pagans have reclaimed the word to mean a lover of

Nature, a person who is close to their roots, their ancestors, and the land: someone who cares about the Earth.

But while Pagans have our roots in the earth, we also have our branches among the stars, and we commune with the sky and the sea and the mysteries of life. Therefore we need to reclaim the words that deal with these aspects of the world and imbue them with our own meanings and stories.

Thanks

Thanks to Victoria Raschke, who suggested that the series of videos I posted on YouTube about reclaiming Pagan words could form the basis of a book.

Thanks to Lydia Knox for the beautiful cover painting, which she created especially for this book.

Thanks to Jennifer G. Stevens for her excellent editing, keifel agostini for formatting and design, and Dodie Graham McKay, Sue Woolley, and Jarred the Wyrd-worker for reading the manuscript and providing feedback.

Thanks to members of my coven past and present for support and encouragement, and for putting up with my extended excursions into etymology.

Thanks to the readers of my work and viewers of my YouTube channel—especially the people who leave comments.

Yvonne Aburrow

www.yvonneaburrow.com

Bibliography and Further Reading

Yvonne Aburrow (2020). 'The tree.' *Dowsing for Divinity*. https://dowsingfordivinity.com/2020/05/21/the-tree/

Yvonne Aburrow (2021), 'Gender and the English language.' *Dowsing for Divinity.* https://dowsingfordivinity.com/2021/12/12/gender-and-the-english-language/

Yvonne Aburrow (2021), 'Pantheism and Panentheism: A Pagan Perspective.' https://www.youtube.com/watch?v=HIlpM1fTHog

Yvonne Aburrow (2021), 'Crow: Queer Magic Interview.' https://www.youtube.com/watch?v=KKQh62D4_6k

Yvonne Aburrow (2021), 'Walking meditation.' https://www.youtube.com/watch?v=hi4QW-t-WS0

Yvonne Aburrow (2022), 'Anarchic Yule.' *Dowsing for Divinity*. https://dowsingfordivinity.com/2022/12/03/anarchic-yule/

Yvonne Aburrow (2022), 'Coven structure & roles.' *Dowsing for Divinity*. https://dowsingfordivinity.com/2022/04/23/coven-structure-roles/

Yvonne Aburrow (2022), 'Mōdraniht.' *The Moon Path*. https://yvonneaburrow.substack.com/p/modraniht

Yvonne Aburrow (2022), 'New Year Customs.' *The Moon Path*. https://yvonneaburrow.substack.com/p/new-year-customs

Yvonne Aburrow (2022), 'Reclaiming Pagan Words: Belief.' https://youtu.be/AxtBwbZsrRM

Yvonne Aburrow (2022), 'Reclaiming Pagan Words: Faith.' https://youtu.be/fWzpD-gpALw

Yvonne Aburrow (2022). 'Reclaiming Pagan Words: Fertility.' https://youtu.be/TxkX_D_Zbx8

Yvonne Aburrow (2022), 'Reclaiming Pagan Words: Grace.' https://youtu.be/divs4fpKwAU

Yvonne Aburrow (2022), 'Reclaiming Pagan Words: Heresy.' https://youtu.be/b7x4vupJjVQ

Yvonne Aburrow (2022), 'Reclaiming Pagan Words: Polarity.' https://youtu.be/E3TlOmGzuuA

Yvonne Aburrow (2022), 'Reclaiming Pagan Words: Prayer.' https://youtu.be/RSLcAy6k_TY

Yvonne Aburrow (2022), 'Reclaiming Pagan Words: Religion.' https://youtu.be/oK_HspSDTe4

Yvonne Aburrow (2022). 'Reclaiming Pagan Words: Sovereignty.' https://youtu.be/-0530ahxpx4

Yvonne Aburrow (2022), 'Reclaiming Pagan Words: Theology.' https://youtu.be/JGFA4YN-hXo

Yvonne Aburrow (2022), 'Reclaiming Pagan Words: Tradition.' https://youtu.be/9Y_1wh0XgUo

Yvonne Aburrow (2022), 'Reclaiming Pagan words: Virtue.' https://youtu.be/CXbKRMGc84M

Yvonne Aburrow (2022), 'Reclaiming Pagan Words: Worship.' https://youtu.be/jYPd-VkVyVg

Yvonne Aburrow (2022), 'Reflections on Yule.' *The Moon Path*. https://yvonneaburrow.substack.com/p/reflections-on-yule

Yvonne Aburrow (2023), 'A Caricature of Paganisms.' *Dowsing for Divinity*. https://dowsingfordivinity.com/2023/12/27/a-caricature-of-paganisms/

Yvonne Aburrow (2023), *Changing Paths*. 1000Volt Press.

Yvonne Aburrow and Adrian Bott (2015),'Move over Easter Bunny, here comes the Easter Fox.' *Dowsing for Divinity*. https://dowsingfordivinity.com/2015/03/20/move-over-easter-bunny/

Yvonne Aburrow, 'Cultural appropriation.' *inclusive Wicca*. http://www.inclusivewicca.org/p/blog-page_27.html

Madeleine Aggeler (2023), 'Divorce doulas: "like having that best friend you've always wanted, but you're paying for."' *The Guardian*. https://www.theguardian.com/wellness/2023/nov/28/divorce-coach-doulas

Karen Armstrong (2009), 'Metaphysical mistake: Confusion by Christians between belief and reason has created bad science and inept religion.' *The Guardian*. http://www.theguardian.com/commentisfree/belief/2009/jul/12/religion-christianity-belief-science

Brian Bates (2005), *The Way of Wyrd: Tales Of An Anglo-Saxon Sorcerer*. (Revised Edition) Hay House.

Jenya T Beachy (2015), 'Danger and Delight in the Season of Sex.' *Dirt Heart Witch*. https://www.patheos.com/blogs/dirtheartwitch/2015/04/danger-and-delight-in-the-season-of-sex/

Mary Beard, J.A. North, and S.R.F. Price (1998), *Religions of Rome: A History*. Cambridge University Press, p. 50.

John Beckett (2023), 'The Future of Paganism.' *Under the Ancient Oaks*. https://www.patheos.com/blogs/johnbeckett/2023/12/the-future-of-paganism.html

Henry A. Bellows' translation of *The Hávamál*. http://oaks.nvg.org/havamal-bellows.html

Susa Morgan Black (undated), 'Samhain—Rituals and Traditions.' *Order of Bards, Ovates, and Druids*. https://druidry.org/druid-way/teaching-and-practice/druid-festivals/samhain-festival

Jenny Blain (2001), N*ine Worlds of Seid-Magic: Ecstasy and Neo-Shamanism in North European Paganism*, Routledge.

Sasha Blakeley (2023), 'Wyrd: Overview, Definition & Significance.' *Study.com*. https://study.com/academy/lesson/wyrd-in-beowulf.html

Alex Boyd (2022), 'What is the Doctrine of Discovery? And why do people want the Pope to denounce it?' *Toronto Star*. https://www. thestar.com/news/canada/what-is-the-doctrine-of-discovery-and-why-do-people-want-the-pope-to-denounce/article_eb9198f7-8063-57f9-83c3-89201e27ac07.html

Cristina Florentina Braia (2020), 'The history of cake: Has it lost its meaning?' *Canadian Military Family Magazine*. https://www. cmfmag.ca/the-story-behind-cake-bringing-back-the-ancient-dessert/

Michael P. Branch (2004). *Reading the Roots: American Nature Writing Before Walden*. University of Georgia Press. p. 63. ISBN 9780820325484.

Lucy Bregman (2006), 'Spirituality: A Glowing and Useful Term in Search of a Meaning.' *OMEGA-Journal of Death and Dying*, 53(1). DOI:10.2190/40NU-Q4BX-9E9K-R52A. https://www. researchgate.net/publication/228379187_Spirituality_A_Glowing_and_Useful_Term_in_Search_of_a_Meaning

'Tiamat: Goddess, Dragon, Mythology, & Popular Culture.' *Britannica*. https://www.britannica.com/topic/Tiamat

Josho Brouwers (2018), 'Arion and the dolphin.' *Ancient World Magazine*. https://www.ancientworldmagazine.com/articles/arion-dolphin/

Maressa Brown (2021), 'What Your Solar Return Means — and How to Make the Most of It.' *Shape*. https://www.shape.com/lifestyle/mind-and-body/astrology/solar-return-chart-meaning-astrology

Nimue Brown (2017), 'Pilgrimage to the flowers.' *Druid Life*. https://druidlife.wordpress.com/2017/04/12/pilgrimage-to-the-flowers/

'Corn Rigs—Robert Burns.' *BBC*. https://www.bbc.co.uk/arts/robertburns/works/corn_rigs/

Robert Burns, 'The Rigs O' Barley.' https://www.robertburns.org/works/30.shtml

Jenny Butler (2020), 'Contemporary Pagan Pilgrimage: Ritual and Re-Storying in the Irish Landscape.' *Numen*. https://brill.com/view/journals/nu/67/5-6/article-p613_8.xml?language=en

Stephanie Butler (2012, 2020), 'Hoppin' John: A New Year's Tradition.' *HISTORY*. https://www.history.com/news/hoppin-john-a-new-years-tradition

Joseph Campbell (1988), 'Indra's Lesson,' from *The Power of Myths*. Edited by Peter Y. Chou. *WisdomPortal.com*. http://www.wisdomportal.com/Enlightenment/IndraUniverses.html

Denise Canning (2013), *The Wife of Bath's True Quest for Sovereignty*. Thesis submitted to the Department English at California State University, Bakersfield. https://scholarworks.calstate.edu/downloads/b8515s85g

Edward Carpenter (1889), *Civilisation: its cause and cure*, quoted in Ronald Hutton (1999), The Triumph of the Moon: A History of Modern Pagan Witchcraft, Oxford: Oxford University Press.

Mark Cartwright (2018), 'Northern Crusades.' *World History Encyclopedia*. https://www.worldhistory.org/Northern_Crusades/

Jack Chanek (2023), *Queen of All Witcheries: A Biography of the Goddess*. Llewellyn Publications.

Jack Chanek (2024), *Goddess Statues and Deity Representations*. https://www.youtube.com/watch?v=DHPRS-ZDXxY

Chas Clifton (2006), *Her Hidden Children: The Rise of Wicca and Paganism in America*. Altamira Press. Page 42 ff.

Coifi (undated), 'Autumn Equinox—Alban Elfed.' *Order of Bards, Ovates, and Druids*. https://druidry.org/druid-way/teaching-and-practice/druid-festivals/autumn-equinox-alban-elfed

Conner, R.P., Sparks, D.H., and Sparks, M. (1997) *Cassell's Encyclopedia of Queer Myth, Symbol and Spirit*. London and New York: Cassell. p. 173

Linda Crampton (2023), 'Soul Cakes and Souling: A Musical Tradition From the Past.' *Spinditty*. https://spinditty.com/genres/Soul-Cakes-and-Souling-A-Musical-Tradition-From-the-Past

Vivianne Crowley (1989), *Wicca: The Old Religion in the New Age*. (revised and updated in 1996 as Wicca: The Old Religion in the New Millennium) Element Books Ltd. ISBN 0-7225-3271-7, ISBN 978-0-7225-3271-3

Robertson Davies (1958), *A Mixture of Frailties*. Macmillan.

Robbie E. Davis-Floyd (2003), *Birth as an American Rite of Passage*. Second Edition. University of California Press. https://www.jstor.org/stable/10.1525/j.ctt1pndwn

Christian de la Huerta (1999), *Coming Out Spiritually: The Next Step*. TarcherPerigee.

Kimberley Debus (2017), 'STLT#311, Let It Be a Dance.' *NOTES FROM THE FAR FRINGE: Hymns, Sermons, and Other Reflections*. https://farfringe.com/2017/08/07/stlt311-let-it-be-a-dance/

Ethan Doyle White, 'Paganism.' *Encyclopedia Britannica*, October 10, 2023. https://www.britannica.com/topic/paganism

Frédéric Ducarme, Denis Couvet (2020), 'What does "nature" mean?' *Nature*. 6 (14). Palgrave Communications. Springer doi:10.1057/s41599-020-0390-y

Georges Dumézil (1996), *Archaic Roman Religion: With an Appendix on the Religion of the Etruscans*. Baltimore, MD: Johns Hopkins University Press. p. 366.

Alan Dundes (1997), 'The Motif-Index and the Tale Type Index: A Critique.' *Journal of Folklore Research*. 34 (3): 195–202. https://www.jstor.org/stable/3814885

Eilthireach (undated), 'Lughnasadh—Harvest Festival.' *Order of Bards, Ovates, and Druids.* https://druidry.org/druid-way/teaching-and-practice/druid-festivals/lughnasadh

Ralph Waldo Emerson (1841), *Compensation.* https://archive.vcu.edu/english/engweb/transcendentalism/authors/emerson/essays/compensation.html

Derrick Everett (1996), *The Question, the Fisher King and the Amfortas Wound.* https://www.monsalvat.no/question.htm

Tina Fields, 'Bioregional Awareness Quiz.' *Department of Bioregion.* https://deptofbioregion.org/resources/bioregional-quiz/

Martini Fisher (2023), 'Baubo, the Great and Forgotten.' *History Made Beautiful.* https://martinifisher.com/2023/02/01/baubo-the-forgotten-great-goddess/

Dion Fortune (1938), *The Sea Priestess.* Weiser Books.

Foster, N. (undated) 'A Prayer in the Dark.' *Lesbian and Gay Christian Movement.* http://www.lgcm.org.uk/archive/archive4a.html [no longer available]

Selena Fox, 'I Am Pagan.' *Circle Sanctuary.* https://www.circlesanctuary.org/index.php/about-paganism/i-am-pagan

Mara Freeman (undated), 'Summer Solstice—Alban Hefin.' *Order of Bards, Ovates, and Druids.* https://druidry.org/druid-way/teaching-and-practice/druid-festivals/summer-solstice-alban-hefin

Matthias Frenz (2008), "Struggles and strategies in the contest for ritual space. Ritual design at a Marian sanctuary in India." Presented at the Heidelberg conference on Ritual Dynamics (SFB 619), September 29–October 6, 2008. https://web.archive.org/web/20080919065059/http://www.rituals-2008.com/p_5.php

Gerald B. Gardner and others (1957), *Book of Shadows.* http://www.sacred-texts.com/pag/gbos/gbos37.htm

Ben Gazur (2022), 'The weird folklore of British cakes.'
Wellcome Collection. https://wellcomecollection.org/articles/
Yfe1NxAAACUADUKQ

Adèle Geras (2005), 'Piskies and puritans.' *The Guardian*. https://
www.theguardian.com/books/2005/feb/12/featuresreviews.
guardianreview29

Kenneth Grahame (1908), *The Wind in the Willows*, https://www.
britannica.com/topic/The-Wind-in-the-Willows

Kenneth Grahame (1893), *Pagan Papers*. https://www.britannica.
com/biography/Kenneth-Grahame

Richard Grant (2021), 'The Lost History of Yellowstone.'
Smithsonian Magazine. https://www.smithsonianmag.com/history/
lost-history-yellowstone-180976518/

Martin Grünewald (2017), 'Roman healing pilgrimage north of
the Alps.' In: *Excavating Pilgrimage*. London: Routledge.

Lihua Gui (1998), 'Robertson Davies' Innovative Use of the
Trilogy Form in his Fiction.' Ph.D. thesis, p. 263. https://tspace.
library.utoronto.ca/bitstream/1807/12282/1/NQ35168.pdf

Adrian Harris (2011, 2018), 'The sit spot.' *Body Mind Place*. https://
adrianharris.org/blog/2018/08/16/the-sit-spot/

Jessica B. Harris (2012), *High on the Hog: A Culinary Journey from
Africa to America*. Bloomsbury USA.

Lou Hart (2005), *Magic is a many-gendered thing*, https://www.
academia.edu/31935408/Magic_is_a_many_gendered_thing

Lou Hart (undated), "Profile," *Queer Spirit*. https://queerspirit.net/
festival/whatson/facilitators/lou-hart

Robin Hawley-Gorsline (2003), 'James Baldwin and Audre Lorde
as Theological Resources for the Celebration of Darkness.'
Theology and Sexuality, 10(1) pp 58–72.

Lydia Helasdottir, 'Utiseta, Breath, and Mound-Sitting.' *Northern Tradition Shamanism*. https://www.northernshamanism.org/utiseta-breath-and-mound-sitting.html

Felicia Hemans (1826), 'Casabianca.' *Poetry By Heart*. https://www.poetrybyheart.org.uk/poems/casabianca

Philip Heselton (2003), *Gerald Gardner and the Cauldron of Inspiration: An Investigation into the Sources of Gardnerian Witchcraft*, Capall Bann Publishing.

Stuart Hobday (2010), 'Kate Middleton's ties to radical Norwich family.' *Norwich Evening News*. https://www.eveningnews24.co.uk/news/22386935.kate-middletons-ties-radical-norwich-family/

A E Housman (1896), A Shropshire Lad: XXXII. Quoted in Ursula K. Le Guin (2018), 'Ursula K. Le Guin on Housman's Classic Poem "From Far."' *Lion's Roar: Buddhist Wisdom for Our Time*. https://www.lionsroar.com/ursula-k-le-guin-on-from-far/

Rosalind Hursthouse and Glen Pettigrove, 'Virtue Ethics.' *The Stanford Encyclopedia of Philosophy* (Fall 2023 Edition), Edward N. Zalta & Uri Nodelman (eds.). https://plato.stanford.edu/entries/ethics-virtue/

Ronald Hutton (2001), *Stations of the Sun: A History of the Ritual Year in Britain*. Oxford Paperbacks.

Ronald Hutton (1999), *The Triumph of the Moon: a history of modern Pagan witchcraft*. Oxford: Oxford University Press, p. 27.

Ronald Hutton (1994), *The Rise and Fall of Merrie England: The Ritual Year, 1400–1700*. Oxford University Press.

Ronald Hutton (2022), Queens of the Wild: Pagan Goddesses In Christian Europe: An Investigation. Yale. Reviewed in: Francis Young (2022), 'The Real History of Paganism.' *First Things*. https://www.firstthings.com/web-exclusives/2022/06/the-real-history-of-paganism

Pico Iyer, 'What Are the Different Kinds of Buddhist Practice?' *Tricycle: Buddhism for Beginners.* https://tricycle.org/beginners/ buddhism/buddhist-pilgrimage/

George Jacinto, Julia W Buckey (2013), 'Birth: A Rite of Passage.' *The International journal of childbirth education: the official publication of the International Childbirth Education Association* 28(1):38–42. https://www.researchgate.net/ publication/270571428_Birth_A_Rite_of_Passage

Derek Jarman (1992), *At Your Own Risk: A Saint's Testament.* London: Hutchinson.

Scott Jeffrey (undated), *A Closer Look at Carl Jung's Individuation Process: A Map for Psychic Wholeness.* https://scottjeffrey.com/ individuation-process/

Scott Jeffrey (undated), *A Definitive Guide to Jungian Shadow Work: How to Get to Know and Integrate Your Dark Side.* https:// scottjeffrey.com/shadow-work/

Lisa Joyner (2020), '8 Unusual New Year's Eve Traditions From Around The World.' *Country Living.* https://www.countryliving. com/uk/homes-interiors/interiors/a35094774/new-years-eve-traditions/

Carl Gustav Jung (1960), *The structure and dynamics of the psyche.* Collected Works of C. G. Jung, Volume 8. Princeton University Press.

Carl Gustav Jung (1916), *Seven Sermons to the Dead.* http://gnosis. org/library/7Sermons.htm

Carl Gustav Jung (1944, 2015), *Psychology and Alchemy.* Routledge.

A Jyotsna (2020), 'Indra: the King of Gods.' *Temple Purohit.* www.templepurohit.com/indra-king-gods/

Aidan Kelly (2017), 'About Naming Ostara, Litha, and Mabon.' *Including Paganism.* www.patheos.com/blogs/aidankelly/2017/05/ naming-ostara-litha-mabon

Molly Khan (2015), 'Beltane for Kids.' *The Pagan Families Blog.*
www.patheos.com/blogs/paganfamilies/2015/04/beltane-for-kids/

Thomas King (2012), *The Inconvenient Indian: A Curious Account of Native People in North America.* Doubleday Canada.

Rudyard Kipling (1906), *Puck of Pook's Hill.* www.britannica.com/
biography/Rudyard-Kipling

Rudyard Kipling (1910), *Rewards and Fairies.* www.britannica.com/
biography/Rudyard-Kipling

A.S. Kline (2004), 'Homer: The Odyssey. Book VI.' *Poetry in Translation.* www.poetryintranslation.com/PITBR/Greek/
Odyssey6.php

A.S. Kline (2000), 'Ovid: The Metamorphoses. Book VIII.' *Poetry in Translation.* www.poetryintranslation.com/PITBR/Latin/
Metamorph8.php

Robert B. Klymasz (2006, 2015), 'Folklore.' *The Canadian Encyclopedia.* www.thecanadianencyclopedia.ca/en/article/
folklore

Troels Myrup Kristensen, Wiebke Friese, eds. (2017), *Excavating Pilgrimage: Archaeological Approaches to Sacred Travel and Movement in the Ancient World.* London: Routledge. https://doi.
org/10.4324/9781315228488

Dale M. Kushner (2022), 'Dream Incubation: Solving Problems in Your Sleep.' *Psychology Today Canada.* www.psychologytoday.
com/ca/blog/transcending-the-past/202208/dream-incubation-
solving-problems-in-your-sleep

Tommy Kuusela (2016), '"He met his own funeral procession": The Year walk-ritual in Swedish folk tradition.' *Academia.edu.* Chapter in: *Folk Belief and Traditions of the Supernatural.* Edited by Tommy Kuusela & Giuseppe Maiello. Beewolf Press 2016, pp. 58–91.
https://www.academia.edu/9403910/He_met_his_own_funeral_
procession_The_Year_walk_ritual_in_Swedish_folk_tradition

Lao Tsu, *Tao Te Ching*, stanza 28. https://www.wussu.com/laotzu/laotzu28.html

Andy Letcher (2009), *Paganism and the British Folk Revival*. https://www.academia.edu/16443118/Paganism_and_the_British_Folk_Revival

Dennis Lewis, *The Elephant & The Student*. https://www.dennislewis.org/articles-other-writings/parables/the-elephant-the-student/

Penelope Lively (1987), *Moon Tiger*. Grove Press.

Emily Lou (2023), '99 divorce cake ideas you have to see to believe!' *Divorce Club*. https://www.divorceclub.com/support/99_divorce_cake_ideas/

Victoria Loutas (2020), 'All you need to know about Greek New Year's Eve customs and traditions.' *Greek Herald*. https://greekherald.com.au/culture/all-you-need-know-about-greek-new-years-eve-customs-tradition/

Edward Verrall Lucas (1906), *The Open Road: A little book for wayfarers* (1906). https://books.google.ca/books?id=upQ9AAAAYAAJ&source=gbs_book_other_versions

Tanya Luhrmann (1989/1991), *Persuasions of the Witch's Craft: Ritual Magic in Contemporary England*. Harvard University Press.

Robert Macfarlane (2015), *Landmarks*. Penguin.

Sabina Magliocco (2019), 'Aradia in Sardinia: the Archaeology of a Legend.' *Academia.edu*. www.academia.edu/584599/Aradia_in_Sardinia_the_Archaeology_of_a_Legend

Marc (2017), 'Mōdru and Mōdraniht.' *Of Axe and Plough*. https://axeandplough.com/2017/12/17/modru-and-modraniht/

Edwin Markham (1913), *The Shoes of Happiness, and Other Poems*.

Ric Masten (1972), 'Let It Be a Dance' in *Singing the Living Tradition* (UU hymnal). https://mluuc.org/ML2/hymnal/hymns/311.php

C.M. McDonough (1997), 'Carna, Proca, and the Strix on the Kalends of June.' *Transactions of the American Philological Association*, 127. https://www.jstor.org/stable/284396

Brian McGrath Davis (2009), 'Religion is not about belief: Karen Armstrong's The Case for God.' *Religion Dispatches*. https://religiondispatches.org/religion-is-not-about-belief-karen-armstrongs-ithe-case-for-godi/

F. Marian McNeill (1959), *The Silver Bough, Vol.2: A Calendar of Scottish National Festivals, Candlemas to Harvest Home*. William MacLellan, pp. 20–21.

The Dream Song of Olaf Åsteson. Translated by Eleanor C Merry. Rudolf Steiner Press.

Brian Mertins (undated), 'How To Connect With Nature.' *Nature Mentor*. https://nature-mentor.com/how-to-connect-with-nature/

Thomas Moore (2015), 'A Dark Night of the Soul and the Discovery of Meaning.' *Kosmos Journal*. https://www.kosmosjournal.org/article/a-dark-night-of-the-soul-and-the-discovery-of-meaning/

NASA (2021), 'What Causes the Seasons?' https://spaceplace.nasa.gov/seasons/en/

Nathan (2013), 'Laughing All the Way to Olympus.' *VoVatia*. https://vovatia.wordpress.com/2013/10/28/laughing-all-the-way-to-olympus/

National Archives, "Jews in England, 1290." www.nationalarchives.gov.uk/education/resources/jews-in-england-1290/

Conor Neill (2018), *Understanding Personality: The 12 Jungian Archetypes*. https://conorneill.com/2018/04/21/understanding-personality-the-12-jungian-archetypes/

Chani Nicholas (2022), 'What is your Jupiter Return, and how can you work with it?' *Chani*. https://chaninicholas.com/your-jupiter-return-explained-2022/

Chani Nicholas (undated), 'How to Explore Your Saturn Return.' *Chani*. https://chaninicholas.com/saturn-return/

National Institute of General Medical Sciences (undated), Circadian Rhythms. https://nigms.nih.gov/education/fact-sheets/Pages/circadian-rhythms.aspx

Michelle Nijhuis (2021), 'Don't cancel John Muir. But don't excuse him either.' *The Atlantic*. https://www.theatlantic.com/ideas/archive/2021/04/conservation-movements-complicated-history/618556/

Steve Nitah (2021), 'Indigenous peoples proven to sustain biodiversity and address climate change: Now it's time to recognize and support this leadership.' *One Earth*, Volume 4, Issue 7, 23 July 2021, pp. 907–909. ScienceDirect. https://www.sciencedirect.com/science/article/pii/S2590332221003572

Dana O'Driscoll (2013), 'The Wheel of the Year in the Druid Tradition—Description of Druidic Holidays.' *The Druid's Garden*. https://thedruidsgarden.com/2013/04/06/the-wheel-of-the-year-in-the-druid-tradition-description-of-druidic-holidays/

Garson O'Toole (2012), 'St Paul's Cathedral Is Amusing, Awful, and Artificial.' *Quote Investigator*. https://quoteinvestigator.com/2012/10/31/st-pauls-cathedral/

Patrick Olivelle, 'Karma.' *Encyclopedia Britannica*. https://www.britannica.com/topic/karma

Mary Oliver (1986), 'Wild Geese.' In: *Poetry Chaikhana*. https://www.poetry-chaikhana.com/Poets/O/OliverMary/WildGeese/index.html

Mary Oliver, '*The Summer Day*.' http://www.phys.unm.edu/~tw/fas/yits/archive/oliver_thesummerday.html

Ovid, *Fasti*, 2.534–539.

Alex Owen (2004), *The Place of Enchantment: British Occultism and the Culture of the Modern*, Chicago: University of Chicago Press.

Jude Paler (2023), 'Shadow work: 7 steps to heal the wounded self.' *Hack Spirit*. https://hackspirit.com/7-shadow-work-techniques-to-heal-the-wounded-self/

Will-Erich Peuckert (1993), *Schlesische Sagen*. Munich, p. 263.

Pindar, *The Ode*s. https://archive.org/stream/odesofpindar035276mbp/odesofpindar035276mbp_djvu.txt

Clarissa Pinkola Estés (1992), *Women Who Run with the Wolves: Myths and Stories of the Wild Woman Archetype*. Ballantine Books.

Ian Pittaway (2016), 'The Lyke-Wake Dirge: the revival of an Elizabethan song of the afterlife.' *Early Music Muse*. https://earlymusicmuse.com/lyke-wake-dirge/

Terry Pratchett (1996, 2006), *Hogfather*. Corgi.

Eugenia Recio, Dina Hestad (2022), 'Indigenous Peoples: Defending an Environment for All.' *The International Institute for Sustainable Development (IISD)*. https://www.iisd.org/articles/deep-dive/indigenous-peoples-defending-environment-all

Kathrin Reikowski and Veronika Baum (2023), 'Zwischen Weihnachten und dem 6. Januar: Rauhnächte—Eine wilde Zeit "zwischen den Jahren."' *BR Kinder*. https://www.br.de/kinder/rauhnaechte-raunaechte-brauchtum-weihnachten-kinder-lexikon-100.html

Catherine Robson (2005), 'Standing on the Burning Deck: Poetry, Performance, History.' *PMLA*. https://www.sas.upenn.edu/~cavitch/pdf-library/Robson_Standing.pdf

K. Rountree (2006), 'Performing the Divine: Neo-Pagan Pilgrimages and Embodiment at Sacred Sites.' *Body & Society*, pp. 12(4), 95–115. https://doi.org/10.1177/1357034X06070886

Saadaya (undated) *Coming Out as a Rite of Passage*. http://www.angelfire.com/journal/saadaya/ComingOut.html [no longer available]

Ceisiwr Serith (2002), *A Book of Pagan Prayer*. http://books.google.co.uk/books/about/A_Book_of_Pagan_Prayer.html?id=tquqpfeL7BsC

Shunryu Suzuki (1970), *Zen Mind, Beginner's Mind*. John Weatherhill, Inc. New York and Tokyo.

Ed Simon (2023), 'A new paganism.' *Aeon*. https://aeon.co/essays/why-we-need-a-new-expression-of-the-sacred-a-pagan-theology

Jacqueline Simpson and Steve Roud (2000), 'New Year.' *A Dictionary of English Folklore*. Oxford University Press. ISBN 0-19-210019-X.

Michael John Simpson, Michelle Filice (2016), 'History of Powwows.' *Canadian Encyclopedia*. www.thecanadianencyclopedia.ca/en/article/history-of-powwows

Monique Skidmore (2023), 'Secrets of Eleusis: Eleusinian Mysteries.' *Trip Anthropologist*. https://tripanthropologist.com/eleusis-and-eleusinian-mysteries/

Charmaine Sonnex, Chris A. Roe, and Elizabeth C. Roxburgh (2020) 'Flow, Liminality, and Eudaimonia: Pagan Ritual Practice as a Gateway to a Life With Meaning.' *Journal of Humanistic Psychology*, Vol 62, issue 2. https://doi.org/10.1177/0022167820927577

Starhawk (1989), *Truth or Dare: Encounters with Power, Authority, and Mystery*. HarperCollins.

Starhawk (1999), *The Spiral Dance: A Rebirth of the Ancient Religions of the Great Goddess*. HarperOne.

Laura Strong (2023), 'What is a Psychopomp?' *Psychopomps*. https://www.psychopomps.org/what-is-a-psychopomp.html

Quintus Aurelius Symmachus (384), *The Memorial of Symmachus, Prefect of the City*, 415:10. https://sourcebooks.fordham.edu/source/ambrose-sym.asp

Jhenah Telyndru (2021), *Blodeuwedd: Welsh Goddess of Seasonal Sovereignty*. Pagan Portals series. Moon Books.

Three Initiates (1912), *The Kybalion*. https://sacred-texts.com/eso/kyb/kyb12.htm

Amy Tikkanen, 'Grace.' *Encyclopedia Britannica*. https://www.britannica.com/topic/Grace-Greek-mythology

JRR Tolkien, *Mythopoeia*. https://www.tolkien.ro/text/JRR%20Tolkien%20-%20Mythopoeia.pdf

Victor Turner (1974), 'Liminal to Liminoid, in Play, Flow, and Ritual: An Essay in Comparative Symbology.' *Rice Institute Pamphlet–Rice University Studies*. 60 (3). hdl:1911/63159

Doreen Valiente (c.1954), *The Charge of the Goddess*. https://www.doreenvaliente.com/doreen-valiente-Doreen_Valiente_Poetry-11.php

Joanna van der Hoeven (2020), 'Mothers' Night/Mōdraniht.' (*Heathen on the Heath Series*). https://www.youtube.com/watch?v=qZgPP8Kx6HI

Joanna van der Hoeven (2020), 'Paganism, Anthropomorphisation and Gender.' *Order of Bards, Ovates & Druids*. https://druidry.org/resources/paganism-anthropomorphisation-and-gender

Laurens van der Post (1974), *A Far-Off Place*, p.304. Harcourt Brace Jovanovich, 1978.

Arnold van Gennep (1977). *The rites of passage*. Routledge & Kegan Paul. p. 21.

Robert van Ness (2014), 'The Prussian Crusades—The fascinating story.' *History is Now Magazine*. https://www.historyisnowmagazine.com/blog/2014/8/11/the-prussian-crusades-the-fascinating-story

Linda Vance (1997), 'Ecofeminism and Wilderness.' *NWSA Journal*, Vol. 9, No. 3, Women, Ecology, and the Environment (Autumn, 1997), pp. 60–76. The Johns Hopkins University Press. https://www.jstor.org/stable/4316530

Von Ogden Vogt (1976), 'Abraxan Essay on Worship.' https://www.cres.org/pubs/abraxas.htm

Tracey Wallace (undated), 'Death Rituals, Ceremonies & Traditions Around the World.' *Eterneva*. https://www.eterneva.com/resources/death-rituals

Anne Warner (2008), 'The construction of "wilderness": an historical perspective.' Contributed paper for the *Canadian Parks for Tomorrow: 40th Anniversary Conference,* May 8–11, 2008, University of Calgary, Calgary, AB. PRISM Repository, University of Calgary. https://prism.ucalgary.ca/server/api/core/bitstreams/6a17bb0f-292c-4e9a-b7b3-33a8c42fc825/content

Sam Webster (2015), 'Genus before species: What are the Gods?' *At the Herm*. http://www.patheos.com/blogs/paganrestoration/2015/08/genus-before-species-what-are-the-gods/

Stefan Weinstock (1946), 'Martianus Capella and the Cosmic System of the Etruscans.' *Journal of Roman Studies*. Vol. 36, p. 106. https://www.jstor.org/stable/i213258

Patti Wigington (2018), 'The Nine Noble Virtues of Asatru.' *Learn Religions*. https://www.learnreligions.com/noble-virtues-of-asatru-2561539

Oscar Wilde (1996 [1905]: 90), *De Profundis*. New York: Dover Publications, Inc.

William Butler Yeats (1903), *'Ideas of Good and Evil,'* in *The Celtic Element in Literature*. https://en.wikisource.org/wiki/Ideas_of_Good_and_Evil_(Yeats)/The_Celtic_Element_in_Literature

YinYoga (undated), 'Yin and Yang.' https://yinyoga.com/yinsights/yin-and-yang/

Michael York (2009), 'A Pagan Defence of Theism.' Theologies of Immanence Wiki. http://pagantheologies.pbworks.com/w/page/13621955/A%20Pagan%20defence%20of%20theism

Elizabeth Yuko (2021), "How Ghost Stories Became a Christmas Tradition in Victorian England." *History Channel.* www.history.com/news/christmas-tradition-ghost-stories

Oberon Zell (undated), 'The Legacy of Oberon Zell.' https://oberonzell.com/the-legacy-of-oberon-zell/

'12 Grapes For 12 Months: An Unusual New Year's Tradition.' *Advantage Air Tech blog.* www.advantageairtech.com/blog/12-grapes-for-12-months-an-unusual-new-years-tradition

'A Brief History.' *Order of Bards, Ovates & Druids.* www.druidry.org/druid-way/what-druidry/brief-history-druidry

'A Pagan History of the Camino.' *Iberian Adventures.* www.iberianadventures.com/a-pagan-history-of-the-camino/

'Eat, Drink And Be Merry: Meaning & Context Of Phrase.' *No Sweat Shakespeare.* https://nosweatshakespeare.com/quotes/famous/eat-drink-and-be-merry/

'Hajj: Definition, Importance, & Facts.' *Encyclopedia Britannica.* www.britannica.com/topic/hajj

'Hinduism: Pilgrimage, Rituals, Beliefs.' *Encyclopedia Britannica.* www.britannica.com/topic/Hinduism/Pilgrimage

'John Barleycorn (Roud 164; G/D 3:559).' *Mainly Norfolk: English Folk and Other Good Music.* https://mainlynorfolk.info/lloyd/songs/johnbarleycorn.html

'Pilgrimage—Ways of Sikh living.' *BBC Bitesize.* www.bbc.co.uk/bitesize/guides/zhp26yc/revision/10

'Pilgrimage: Spiritual Journey, Rituals & Traditions.' *Encyclopedia Britannica.* www.britannica.com/topic/pilgrimage-religion

'Pilgrims' Guide to Buddhist India: Buddhist Sites.' *BuddhaNet*. www.buddhanet.net/e-learning/pilgrim/places.htm

'Revels at Merrymount Today.' *Ancient Lights*. http://ancientlights. org/revels.html

'Roman Virtues.' *Roman Republic | Res publica Romana*. https:// romanrepublic.org/roma/bibliotheca/roman-virtues/

'Sir Gawain and the Green Knight.' *Oxford Reference*. www.oxfordreference.com/display/10.1093/oi/ authority.20110803095845144

'The History of Christmas Carols.' *WhyChristmas.com*. www. whychristmas.com/customs/carols-history

'The Lyke Wake Dirge (Roud 8194; TYG 85).' *Mainly Norfolk: English Folk and Other Good Music*. https://mainlynorfolk.info/ peter.bellamy/songs/thelykewakedirge.html

'The Origins of Midwifery.' *The International Confederation of Midwives*. www.internationalmidwives.org/icm-news/the-origins-of-midwifery.html

'The Rituals of Asatru.' *Raven Kindred*. http://www.ravenkindred. com/RBRituals.html

'The Three Ravens (English Folk Ballad).' *Poem Analysis*. https:// poemanalysis.com/thomas-ravenscroft/the-three-ravens/

'Wassail Song / Gower Wassail' (Roud 209). *Mainly Norfolk: English Folk and Other Good Music*. https://mainlynorfolk.info/watersons/ songs/gowerwassail.html

'What are the Mirrie Dancers?' *Shetland.org*. 2021. https://www. shetland.org/blog/what-are-the-mirrie-dancers

'What Were Aristotle's Four Cardinal Virtues?' *The Collector*. https://www.thecollector.com/aristotle-four-cardinal-virtues/

'Wisdom: English meaning.' *Cambridge Dictionary*. https:// dictionary.cambridge.org/dictionary/english/wisdom

'World Book Night: Ten writers' reasons for reading.' *The Guardian*. 2013. https://www.theguardian.com/books/2013/apr/23/world-book-night-10-reasons-reading

'Wyrd & Orlog.' Skald's Keep. https://skaldskeep.com/norse/wyrd/

'Wyrd and Orlog.' *The Modern Heathen*. https://themodernheathen.home.blog/wyrd-and-orlog/

'Merry man, n.' *Oxford English Dictionary*. 2001. http://www.oed.com/view/Entry/116877

'Merryman Definition & Meaning.' *Merriam-Webster*. https://www.merriam-webster.com/dictionary/merryman

'Well, we'll fight you for it.' *Imgur*. https://imgur.com/yJ4bDHn

'When Does a Baby Bird Need Help?' *Ottawa Valley Wild Bird Care Centre*. https://www.wildbirdcarecentre.org/bird-emergency

1 Corinthians 13:1, *New International Version*.

'The Three Ravens (or Twa Corbies).' *Bluegrass Messengers*. http://www.bluegrassmessengers.com/26-the-three-ravens-or-twa-corbies.aspx

'About The Druid Network.' https://druidnetwork.org/about-the-druid-network/

Alliance for Inclusive Heathenry. https://www.facebook.com/inclusive.heathenry/

Anonymous, 'The Twa Corbies.' *Scottish Poetry Library*. https://www.scottishpoetrylibrary.org.uk/poem/the-twa-corbies/

Ár nDraíocht Féin: A Druid Fellowship (ADF). https://ng.adf.org/

Assembly of First Nations (2018), 'Dismantling the Doctrine of Discovery.' https://www.afn.ca/wp-content/uploads/2018/02/18-01-22-Dismantling-the-Doctrine-of-Discovery-EN.pdf

'Basics of Gaulish Polytheism.' *Touta Galation*. https://toutagalation.org/basics-of-gaulish-polytheism/

Blackadder, S2 E4, 'Money.' https://blackadderquotes.com/blackadder-series-2-episode-4-money-full-script

Cleveland Clinic (2023), 'What an End-of-Life Doula Can Do for You.' https://health.clevelandclinic.org/death-doula

Covenant of the Goddess. http://www.cog.org/

Covenant of Unitarian Universalist Pagans. https://www.cuups.org/

Death Cafe (undated), 'What is Death Cafe?' https://deathcafe.com/what/

Druidry.org (undated), 'Spring Equinox—Alban Eilir.' *Order of Bards, Ovates, and Druids.* https://druidry.org/druid-way/teaching-and-practice/druid-festivals/spring-equinox-alban-eilir

Druidry.org (undated), 'Winter Solstice—Alban Arthan.' *Order of Bards, Ovates, and Druids.* https://druidry.org/druid-way/teaching-and-practice/druid-festivals/winter-solstice-alban-arthan

'Etymology of apotheosis by etymonline.' https://www.etymonline.com/word/apotheosis

'Etymology of belief by etymonline.' https://www.etymonline.com/word/belief

'Etymology of faith by etymonline.' https://www.etymonline.com/word/faith

'Etymology of fertility by etymonline.' https://www.etymonline.com/word/fertility

'Etymology of god by etymonline.' https://www.etymonline.com/word/god

'Etymology of grace by etymonline.' https://www.etymonline.com/word/grace

'Etymology of heresy by etymonline.' https://www.etymonline.com/word/heresy

'Etymology of holy by etymonline.' https://www.etymonline.com/word/holy

'Etymology of immanence by etymonline.' https://www.etymonline.com/word/immanence

'Etymology of merry by etymonline.' https://www.etymonline.com/word/merry

'Etymology of priestess by etymonline.' https://www.etymonline.com/word/priestess

'Etymology of pure by etymonline.' https://www.etymonline.com/word/pure

'Etymology of sacred by etymonline.' https://www.etymonline.com/word/sacred

'Etymology of virtue by etymonline.' https://www.etymonline.com/word/virtue

'Etymology of wild by etymonline.' https://www.etymonline.com/word/wild

Fair Folk Podcast (2022), 'The Twelve Days: December Almanac.' https://podcasts.apple.com/ca/podcast/the-twelve-days-december-almanac/id1177770160?i=1000590343233

Havamal English Text—*The Hávamál*. http://www.ragweedforge.com/havamal.html

Heathens Against Hate. https://www.heathensagainst.org/

Heathens United Against Racism. https://www.facebook.com/HeathensUnited/

http://1734-witchcraft.org/

http://faerytradition.org/

http://inclusivewicca.org/

http://www.1734.com/

http://www.clanoftubalcain.com/

http://www.feritradition.org/

http://www.reclaiming.org/

https://andersonfaery.org/

https://clantubalcain.com/

Keening Tradition. http://www.keeningwake.com/keening-tradition/

Native Land Digital. https://native-land.ca/

NovaRoma, 'Cultus deorum Romanorum.' http://www.novaroma. org/nr/Cultus_deorum_Romanorum

'Numen.' https://brill.com/view/journals/nu/67/5-6/article-p613_8. xml?language=en

OBOD: About us. https://druidry.org/about-us

Open University, 'Introducing Virgil's Aeneid: 3.1 What is pietas?' *OpenLearn.* https://www.open.edu/openlearn/history-the-arts/ introducing-virgils-aeneid/content-section-3.1

'Pagan: English meaning.' *Cambridge Dictionary.* https://dictionary. cambridge.org/dictionary/english/pagan

'Pagan: Definition & Meaning.' *Merriam-Webster.* https://www. merriam-webster.com/dictionary/pagan

The British Druid Order. https://www.druidry.co.uk/

The Society of Obstetricians and Gynaecologists of Canada. 'Doulas—Pregnancy Info.' https://www.pregnancyinfo.ca/your- pregnancy/preparing-for-birth/doulas/

The Welsh Fairy Book: The Lady of the Lake. https://www.sacred-texts. com/neu/celt/wfb/wfb03.htm

United Nations Permanent Forum on Indigenous Issues, 'Who are indigenous peoples?' https://www.un.org/esa/socdev/unpfii/ documents/5session_factsheet1.pdf

Weston Area Health NHS Trust (2020), *Paganism.* https://www. waht.nhs.uk/en-GB/Our-Services1/Non-Clinical-Services1/ Chapel/Faith-and-Culture/Paganism/

Yvonne Aburrow